基于合作学习理论的英语
专业教学实践研究

张丽丽 著

Research on the Teaching of English-majors' Courses Based on Cooperative Learning Theory

中国纺织出版社有限公司

内 容 提 要

我国高等院校英语专业的听力、阅读、写作及翻译课程作为英语专业学生的必修课程，在整个学习阶段非常重要。应用合作学习的教学理论，快速定位教学思路与内容，解决教学过程中的实际问题，会推动英语专业教学工作的更快更好发展。本书是作者在多年的高校英语教学工作基础上，结合近年来自身的科研经历编著而成。在编著过程中，结合国内外研究的成果与进展，在保证科学性、先进性的基础上，更注重专业针对性、适应性和实用性，力求内容丰富，条理清晰，特色突出。本书适宜作为高等院校英语专业科技工作者、教师、博士、硕士等有关人员的参考书。

图书在版编目（CIP）数据

基于合作学习理论的英语专业教学实践研究：英文／张丽丽著. -- 北京：中国纺织出版社有限公司，2021. 7
ISBN 978-7-5180-8668-9

Ⅰ.①基… Ⅱ.①张… Ⅲ.①英语—教学研究—高等学校—英文 Ⅳ.①H319.3

中国版本图书馆 CIP 数据核字（2021）第 126429 号

责任编辑：潘博闻 国 帅 责任校对：王花妮
责任印制：王艳丽

中国纺织出版社有限公司出版发行
地址：北京市朝阳区百子湾东里 A407 号楼 邮政编码：100124
销售电话：010 — 67004422 传真：010 — 87155801
http://www.c-textilep.com
中国纺织出版社天猫旗舰店
官方微博 http://weibo.com/2119887771
三河市宏盛印务有限公司印刷 各地新华书店经销
2021 年 7 月第 1 版第 1 次印刷
开本：710×1000 1/16 印张：15.5
字数：252 千字 定价：88.00 元

前　言

　　合作学习理论在 20 世纪 70 年代兴起于美国，并在 20 世纪 70 年代中期至 80 年代中期取得了实质性的进展，进入 21 世纪后已发展为成熟的教学理论，被广泛运用于教学之中。在应用过程中，合作学习注重以学生为中心，强调教学动态因素间的互动，给语言习得的发生创造有利的条件。我国高等院校英语专业的听力、阅读、写作及翻译课程作为英语专业学生的必修课程，在整个学习阶段非常重要。把合作学习理论应用于英语专业的课程教学是有益的尝试并具有积极的意义，对于改变传统教学模式、提高英语专业学生的英语综合能力有着重要的作用。

　　本书作者是吉林农业科技学院外国语学院专职教师。本书是其在多年的高校英语教学工作基础上，依托《合作学习在英语泛读课中的应用研究》《农业院校特色英语教学理论与实践的研究》《普通高校学生英语自主学习能力问题分析及对策研究》等科研课题成果，结合近年来自身的教科研经历独立撰写而成。全书共分为十一章。第一章是引言部分，介绍了写作背景，提出了研究问题，分析了现阶段英语专业一些主干课程的教学现状，论述了将合作学习应用于这些课程教学的重要意义；第二章是合作学习理论系统概述；第三章是合作学习理论应用于高等教育的理论研究与进展；第四到第七章，分别是英语专业的听力课程、阅读课程、写作课程和翻译课程的理论研究与进展；第八章是合作学习理论应用于阅读教学实践的理论研究与进展；第九章是合作学习理论应用于高校英语教学的实践部分，作者在自己所教授的班级进行了合作学习实证研究，研究其对于英语专业学生的学习效果和学习兴趣的影响；第十章是对实践研究进行分析与讨论；第十一章是基于实践研究得出的结论及展望。

　　作者在研究中肯定了合作学习理论的应用对英语专业阅读课程的积极作用，也对今后基于合作学习理论的英语专业其他课程教学提出针对性的建议。作者编著此书，期待英语专业的课程教学能够应用合作学习的教学理论，不断积累新的经验，快速定位教学思路与内容，解决教学过程中的实际问题，推动英语教学工作的更快更好发展。在编著过程中，本书参考了国内外许多作者的著作和文章，在此表示衷心的感谢。限于作者的水平和经验，本书中难免有种种缺陷甚至错误，恳请同行、专家和广大读者指正。

目　录

Chapter One Introduction

1.1　Writing Background

As an international language, English has played an increasingly important role in China than ever before with the development of economy and China's entry into WTO. An increasing number of people begin to learn English with great enthusiasm, so not surprisingly, a new boom of English learning arises. English–majors' courses are very important for English-majors. But in the teaching and learning of them, there exist many problems. In 1991, Johnson D once pointed out the flaws of traditional teaching: "The information is transferred from teachers' teaching notes to students' notes, escaping from their brains". Courses teaching in China also have this flaw. For years the traditional teaching method is called "feeding ducks", that is, the class is teacher-centered and teachers just "feed" information to students who receive passively. In class, teachers often translate the passage and pass the information to students who have little chance to participate in the construction of information. Teachers unconsciously turn classes of language skill training into classes of knowledge or grammar explanation. As a result, on the one hand, the integrity and artistry of the passage is damaged and the nature of reading is lost; on the other hand, students form the habit of dependence of study. Students' reading ability is limited and their reading interest can not be arisen.

In recent years, many researchers have been exploring the method of courses teaching. They find some reading skills and strategies can help students improve their reading ability. At the same time some educators put forward that in reading class, emphasis should be laid on the process of reading. Teachers should instruct students to read, analyze and reflect different types of passages on the basis of the principle that the class is student-centered. Students can improve their reading ability through their thoughts and reflection. At the same time their reading interest can be reinforced. CL is a teaching theory and strategy with group activities being the main form. With CL students can participate the activities actively and achieve learning aims. The application of CL is a breakthrough and supplement to traditional teaching. It might improve the teaching atmosphere and stir students' learning motivation.

1.2 Purpose of the Research

The purpose of this research is to explore the effectiveness of applying CL theory on English-majors' reading ability and interest. Most of the previous CL research has been done in elementary school and middle school. The author wonders whether it fits for college, esp. for English-majors in the teaching and learning of courses.

Traditional teaching method focuses on language point, grammar rules rather than cultivating communicative ability. Therefore, although undergoing several years of studying English, students can express a little, hardly communicate fluently in English. So do English-majors. The state of the affairs dampens extremely learners' confidence and the enthusiasm of participating in class activity, block the effectiveness of teaching. Class teaching effectiveness is closely connected with the degree of students' participating in class activity as well as the quality of class communication; therefore, it is a core for raising teaching quality to arouse students' enthusiasm for involving in class action as well as raising the quality of class communication, which remain to be solved before every language teacher.

In this study, the author tries to apply CL theory to courses teaching for English-majors. Through the result analysis of the pretest, posttest, questionnaires and interviews, the author makes an initial exploration about the operation and effect of CL in courses teaching and learning for English-majors. This study might contribute to the language teaching reform and provide language teachers with some experience for reference.

1.3　Present Situation of the Teaching of English-majors'　Courses(TEMC) in China

At present in China, foreign language (generally English) is taught to both English majors and non-English majors.

TEMC (the teaching of English-majors' courses) classroom is a unique social, educational, and communicative environment. For such a long time, the foreign language teacher (generally English teacher) has a strong concern with the mastery of language knowledge. In the traditional TEMC classroom, the teacher controls the class and pours out what he knows about the language, i. e., specifying the new words, explaining grammar regulations, analyzing complicated sentence structures, and finishing some preparatory exercises for all kinds of examinations. However, the outcome of present TEMC is far from satisfactory and has not reached the goal for syllabus.

Oriented towards exam preparations, TEMC compels both teachers and students involving in College English Test Papers for Band 4 and 6. It is ignored to carrying out the Quality Oriented Education with the popularity of Test-oriented Education. This results in that many students of excellent scores are unable to talk with foreigners freely in English, unable to read an English newspaper, even unable to write an application letter. The unsatisfactory situation is associated not only with the isolation of English teaching from the teaching of other subjects at various stages, and unqualified teachers, but also with the traditional "teacher-centered" model popularly adopted in TEMC. Practice has demonstrated that the "teacher-centered" model, which corresponds to the Test-oriented Education, can not meet the requirements for implementing Quality-oriented Education. This phenomenon indicates that the TEMC is of high investment but of low proficiency.

It is usually pointed out that Chinese students are good at grammar, but are at a loss during practical communication, which is mainly because in the language classroom learners hardly have any opportunities to communicate with the teachers and his classmates. These set us in deep thinking about the current methods dominating TEMC. The above discussion proves that the current teaching methods, which concentrate on the usage of the language but neglect its use, have legged behind. To gear to the world advanced science and technology, it is necessary to seek an appropriate approach to suit the need of TEMC.

1.4　Significance of Implementing CL for TEMC

Due to its scientific rationale and obvious effectiveness, Cooperative Learning (CL) which is advocated by educationists Slavin R E, Johnson D W, Johnson R T, Mevarech R, and etc., originally proposed for large class teaching, has gained great attention in the world these years. For one reason or the other, CL has had a pervasive influence on foreign language teaching today. Unfortunately, the situation in China differs from that in world.

According to Johnson D W and Johnson R T, who are well known for their studies of second and foreign language education, teachers have three main ways to structure in-class interaction pattern. The first way is individual working pattern, within which teacher becomes the only language input and output sources available and students learn and are evaluated in isolation from one another. The second way is competitive working pattern, Johnson and Johnson claims that students engage in a win-lose struggle in an effort to determine who is best in a competitively structured classroom. The third way, the cooperative model, which this thesis deals with, encourages the student-to-student interaction.

CL takes heterogeneous groups as the basic form of classroom structure, requiring social interaction and negotiation of meaning among group members engaged in tasks in which there is a genuine information gap. CL, which is based on students' psychological needs, combining cognitive, affective and psychomotor objectives into one, has been proved to be a most creative and practical approach and strategy in classroom. Many countries have employed this approach to teach various subjects, including the foreign and second language. In China, some efforts have been taken and the effect of CL on the educational outcomes has been noted. However, most of the research is done in subjects other than foreign language, and furthermore, in primary schools and middle schools. Implementing CL in foreign language teaching, particularly in foreign language teaching in colleges and universities is still a new attempt.

This research combines CL and TEMC, making a theoretical effort to explore the actual effects of implementing CL in TEMC in China from the perspective of communication. The cultivating a sense of cooperation in the form of groups which is the requirement proposed by our society through establishing teacher-learner and learner-learner interaction, developing students' interpersonal intelligence.

This is why the author of the dissertation thinks it is of urgent necessity to conduct CL in TEMC and to explore an efficient way of implementing CL in TEMC in present China.

Since its birth, Cooperative Learning theory (CL) gradually becomes a world-wide, creative, and actual effective teaching theory and strategic learning method, which is widely used in Foreign Language Teaching. However, the reform on College English Teaching is still in their infancy. The present research, therefore, intends to apply CL to this field, aiming at investigating and guiding the Teaching of English-majors' Courses (TEMC).

Chapter Two Review of CL Theory

2. 1   Definition of CL

It's really difficult to give a definite definition of CL. Many researchers at home and abroad have defined CL with different focus or at different angles, as a result, diverse definitions exist although they are very similar. So, it's important to mention some definitions given by the representatives of CL experts in order to better understand what CL is.

According to Johnson R et al. , "CL is the instructional use of small groups so that students work together to maximize their own and each other's learning". According to their theory, five essential components must be included: (a) active interdependence; (b) face-to-face interaction; (c) interpersonal accountability; (d) interpersonal skills; (e) group processing. Bother Johnson place their focus on combining social skills with student academic tasks by working together in small groups. Much of their research is based on social interdependence theory.

Spencer Kagan, another specialist, contributes over 200 CL structures which can be used with almost any academic content. He maintained that four factors must be combined with each of the structures: (a) positive interdependence; (b) interpersonal accountability; (c) equal participation; (d) simultaneous interaction. In kagan's definition, the importance of the equal chance for every student to practice in simultaneous communication is noticed. Slvain, professor of Johns Hopkins University, promotes CL by combining concepts of Johnson and Kagan. CL is a kind of class teaching techniques. Students are encouraged to perform varieties of learning activities in small teams and they are rewarded for achievements or performance of the entire group, so that teacher-student and student-student interactions are enhanced and students are promoted to carry out CL efficiently. Slavin recognized the teacher's role and guidance in CL and mentioned the unique rewarding system containing two levels, i. e. , the individual level and the group level.

There are some other CL experts defining CL from their own point of view, which can't be all listed here. However, in spite of the diversity in definition, all cooperative theorists and practitioners agree that real CL must incorporate the concept of positive interdependence and individual accountability which distinguishes CL from any other small group learning.

Students' learning goals may be structured to promote cooperative, competitive, or individualistic efforts. In every classroom, instructional activities are aimed at accomplishing goals and are conducted under a goal structure. A learning goal is a desired future state of demonstrating competence or mastery in the subject area being studied. The goal structure specifies the ways in which students will interact with each other and the teacher during the instructional session. Each goal structure has its place. In the ideal classroom, all students would learn how to work cooperatively with others, compete for fun and enjoyment, and work autonomously on their own. The teacher decides which goal structure to implement within each lesson. The most important goal structure, and the one that should be used the majority of the time in learning situations, is cooperation.

Cooperation is working together to accomplish shared goals. Within cooperative situations, individuals seek outcomes that are beneficial to themselves and beneficial to all other group members. Cooperative learning is the instructional use of small groups so that students work together to maximize their own and each other's learning. It may be contrasted with competitive (students work against each other to achieve an academic goal such as a grade of "A" that only one or a few students can attain) and individualistic (students work by themselves to accomplish learning goals unrelated to those of the other students) learning. In cooperative and individualistic learning, you evaluate student efforts on a criteria-referenced basis while in competitive learning you grade students on a norm-referenced basis. While there are limitations on when and where you may use competitive and individualistic learning appropriately, you may structure any learning task in any subject area with any curriculum cooperatively.

The concept of cooperative learning was put forward in the mid-1960s in the United States because of two reasons: to change the situations of traditional education and to eliminate the discrimination and segregations between racial and ethnic relationships. Slavin defines cooperative learning as a set of instructional methods in which students are encouraged or required to work together on academic tasks. The definition stresses the form of cooperation to deal with academic tasks. Murray F B asserts that the term, cooperative learning, refers to a family of instructional practice in which the teacher gives various directions to groups of pupils about how to work together. It describes the cooperative learning from the perspective of the teachers. P. Abrami summarizes cooperative learning as "an instructional strategy in which students work together in groups that are carefully designed to promote positive interdependence". The scholar stresses the whole process of the cooperative learning method. Panitz T believed that cooperative learning is defined by a set of process which help people interact together in order to accomplish a specific goal or develop an end product which is usually content specific. It stresses the importance of the effect and advantage of cooperative learning. Jacob asserts that "cooperative learning is a diverse group of instructional methods in which small groups of students work together and aid each other in completing academic tasks". It can be seen that Jacob also stresses the form of cooperative model. Students from different groups work together and help each other to achieve the goal set by the teacher.

In Akan, a cooperative classroom team is a relatively permanent, heterogeneously mixed, small group of students who have been assembled to complete an activity, to produce a series of projects or products, and/or who have been asked to individually master a body of knowledge. This version explains the specific elements, the process and aims of implementation of CL which is widely used by most researchers. Wang defined cooperative learning as a kind of activity guided by aims. He also believed that cooperative learning is a pedagogy system which aims at promoting the study for heterogeneous students, utilizing systematically teaching elements and evaluating common achievement, then attaining mutual purposes.

From the above discussions, the researcher concludes the CL definition as follows: CL is more than just asking students to form groups and cooperate with each other to do tasks, it is a formal instructional approach and strategy that students actively work together to complete the task after whole instruction from their teachers.

Although the researchers give the definition of cooperative learning from different perspectives, they share one common point that the importance of cooperation and collaboration are stressed. Scholars regard cooperative learning as a positive relationship between group members. Besides, within a group, cooperative learning facilitates students in achieving academic goals. All of the students are not only responsible for themselves but also for assisting others to learn well. In order to accelerate students' cooperation, elements and techniques of cooperative learning should be taken into consideration.

The teams are small but heterogeneous. The activities and tasks are actively structured to include the key elements of CL so that students can work through the tasks cooperatively until each one understands and all group members perceive that they share a common goal and they gain from each other's efforts. Furthermore, each member should be responsible for helping other members as well as his or her own learning. So in CL, students care about each other, help and support each other so that all of them learn.

2. 2　Elements of CL

Not all groups are cooperative. Placing people in the same room, seating them together, telling them they are a group, does not mean they will cooperate effectively. To be cooperative, to reach the full potential of the group, five essential elements need to be carefully structured into the situation: positive interdependence, individual and group accountability, promotive interaction, appropriate use of social skills, and group processing. Mastering the basic elements of cooperation allows teachers to: take existing lessons, curricula, and courses and structure them cooperatively; tailor cooperative learning lessons to unique instructional needs, circumstances, curricula, subject areas, and students; and diagnose the problems some students may have in working together and intervene to increase the effectiveness of the student learning groups. Brown and Ciuffetelli Parker discuss the 5 basic and essential elements to cooperative learning.

2. 2. 1　Positive Interdependence

Students must fully participate and put forth effort within their group. Each group member has a task/role/responsibility therefore must believe that they are responsible for their learning and that of their group.

The first and most important element is positive interdependence. Teachers must give a clear task and a group goal so students believe they "sink or swim together." Positive interdependence exists when group members perceive that they are linked with each other in a way that one cannot succeed unless everyone succeeds. If one fails, all fail. Group members realize, therefore, that each person's efforts benefit not only him- or herself, but all other group members as well. Positive interdependence creates a commitment to other people's success as well as one's own and is the heart of cooperative learning. If there is no positive interdependence, there is no cooperation.

2.2.2　Face-to-Face Promotive Interaction

Members promote each others success. Students explain to one another what they have or are learning and assist one another with understanding and completion of assignments.

The second essential element of cooperative learning is individual and group accountability. The group must be accountable for achieving its goals. Each member must be accountable for contributing his or her share of the work (which ensures that no one "hitch-hikes" on the work of others). The group has to be clear about its goals and be able to measure (a) its progress in achieving them and (b) the individual efforts of each of its members. Individual accountability exists when the performance of each individual student is assessed and the results are given back to the group and the individual in order to ascertain who needs more assistance, support, and encouragement in completing the assignment. The purpose of cooperative learning groups is to make each member a stronger individual in his or her right. Students learn together so that they can subsequently perform higher as individuals.

2.2.3　Individual Accountability

Each student must demonstrate master of the content being studied. Each student is accountable for their learning and work, therefore eliminating "social loafing".

The third essential component of cooperative learning is positive interaction, preferably face-to-face. Positive interaction occurs when members share resources and help, support, encourage and praise each other's efforts to learn. Cooperative learning groups are both an academic support system (every student has someone who is committed to helping him or her learn) and a personal support system (every student has someone who is committed to him or her as a person). There are important cognitive activities and interpersonal dynamics that can only occur when students promote each other's learning. This includes orally explaining how to solve problems, discussing the nature of the concepts being learned, teaching one's knowledge to classmates, and connecting present with past learning. It is through promoting each other's learning face-to-face that members become personally committed to each other as well as to their mutual goals.

2.2.4 Social Skills

Social skills that must be taught in order for successful cooperative learning to occur. Skills include effective communication, interpersonal and group skills: (a)Leadership; (b)Decision-making; (c) Trust-building; (d) Communication; (e)Conflict-management skills.

The fourth essential element of cooperative learning is teaching students the required interpersonal and small group skills. In cooperative learning groups students are required to learn academic subject matter (task-work) and also to learn the interpersonal and small group skills required to function as part of a group (teamwork). Cooperative learning is inherently more complex than competitive or individualistic learning because students have to engage simultaneously in task-work and teamwork. Group members must know how to provide effective leadership, decision-making, trust-building, communication, and conflict-management, and be motivated to use the prerequisite skills. Teachers have to teach teamwork skills just as purposefully and precisely as teachers do academic skills. Since cooperation and conflict are inherently related, the procedures and skills for managing conflicts constructively are especially important for the long-term success of learning groups. Procedures and strategies for teaching students social skills may be found in Johnson and F. Johnson.

2.2.5 Group Processing

Every so often groups must assess their effectiveness and decide how it can be improved. In order for student achievement to improve considerably, two characteristics must be present (a) Students are working towards a group goal or recognition and (b) success is reliant on each individual's learning.

(1) When designing cooperative learning tasks and reward structures, individual responsibility and accountability must be identified. Individuals must know exactly what their responsibilities are and that they are accountable to the group in order to reach their goal.

(2) Positive Interdependence among students in the task. All group members must be involved in order for the group to complete the task. In order for this to occur each member must have a task that they are responsible for which cannot be completed by any other group member. The fifth essential component of cooperative learning is group processing. Group processing exists when group members discuss how well they are achieving their goals and maintaining effective working relationships. Groups need to describe what member actions are helpful and unhelpful and make decisions about what behaviors to continue or change. Continuous improvement of the process of learning results from the careful analysis of how members are working together.

These five elements are essential to all cooperative systems, no matter what their size. When international agreements are made and when international efforts to achieve mutual goals (such as environmental protection) occur, these five elements must be carefully implemented and maintained.

From the above elaboration of CL, we can see that CL does not mean having students sit side-by-side at the same table to talk with each other. Nor does it mean having the students who finish first help the slower ones, nor assigning a report to a group of students wherein one student does all the work and the others put their names on the product. CL means much more than these. Some scholars pointed out, although everyone of the five elements does not have to be used every time the teacher assigns students to work in groups, teachers who fail to include these requirements encounter more difficulties with their students' and their groups' activities, and students' academic achievements are less. In addition, teachers should not expect many positive long-term results of CL, unless these elements are used frequently and correctly.

2.3 Types of CL

Formal cooperative learning is structured, facilitated, and monitored by the educator over time and is used to achieve group goals in task work (e. g. completing a unit). Any course material or assignment can be adapted to this type of learning, and groups can vary from 2-6 people with discussions lasting from a few minutes up to a period. Types of formal cooperative learning strategies include jigsaw, assignments that involve group problem solving and decision making, laboratory or experiment assignments, and peer review work (e. g. editing writing assignments). Having experience and developing skill with this type of learning often facilitates informal and base learning.

Informal cooperative learning incorporates group learning with passive teaching by drawing attention to material through small groups throughout the lesson or by discussion at the end of a lesson, and typically involves groups of two (e. g. turn-to-your-partner discussions). These groups are often temporary and can change from lesson to lesson (very much unlike formal learning where 2 students may be lab partners throughout the entire semester contributing to one another's knowledge of science). Discussions typically have four components that include formulating a response to questions asked by the educator, sharing responses to the questions asked with a partner, listening to a partner's responses to the same question, and creating a new well-developed answer. This type of learning enables the student to process, consolidate, and retain more information learned.

In group-based cooperative learning, these peer groups gather together over the long term (e. g. over the course of a year, or several years such as in high school or post-secondary studies) to develop and contribute to one another's knowledge mastery on a topic by regularly discussing material, encouraging one another, and supporting the academic and personal success of group members. Base group learning is effective for learning complex subject matter over the course or semester and establishes caring, supportive peer relationships, which in turn motivates and strengthens the student's commitment to the group's education while increasing self-esteem and self worth. Base group approaches also make the students accountable to educating their peer group in the event that a member was absent for a lesson. This is effective both for individual learning, as well as social support.

2.4   Techniques of CL

According to Johnson, five essential techniques are consisted in cooperative learning: positive interdependence; face-to-face promotional interaction; individual accountability; social skills and group processing.

Positive interdependence makes cooperative learning possible. Teachers assign tasks to every student who has the thought that only with joint efforts can they succeed under the given situation. Students who can gain equal encourage and reward will strengthen such value in learning. Face-to-face means students can transfer what they have learnt to others in various ways, such as to give an account of what the students have learnt in the speech. Individual accountability ensures that CL can carry out smoothly under the principle of fairness. Social skill provides CL the validity because CL could not go on without students' social ability; teachers improve and perfect it during the learning process.

Group processing is developed by Johnson and Johnson in 1975, which are also named as Johnsons' methods. In such a kind of cooperative method, students work in a heterogeneous group of five or six members to complete one mutual task and all members in a group would receive help from others in order to get a reward as a whole. The group members can receive good marks only if everyone in this group is involved and understand. This method laid its emphasis on the building of teams. The difference between learning together and other methods is that this model is more concrete and more descriptive. Group processing model provides a conceptual framework for teachers to plan and cooperative learning instruction according to their circumstances, student needs, and school contexts.

Kagan identifies four basic principles in Structural Approach: simultaneous interaction, equal participation, positive interdependence and individual accountability. It has the same meaning with different forms of expression compared with the claim of

Johnson. Many cooperative learning methods are being used and developed in those years. Each of them should be paid attention because of its feasibility. In order to make CL methods clear and definite for English teachers who are the freshman to CL. The author intends to introduce some of the techniques that are widely used and popularized in classroom. Besides, English teachers should make it clear that in what kind of situation cooperative techniques can be adopted. The main techniques of cooperative learning are listed as follows.

2.5   Activities of CL

2.5.1   Jigsaw

It's developed by Aronsen and his associate. When using Jigsaw, the teacher divides the task into several parts and assigns one part to each member in a team which is essential for the completion and understanding of the final product. After getting familiar with and making research on his part, students who are assigned the identical part from each group meet first as an expert group to discuss and exchange information. Then, students go back to their groups and teach the other members about their specialty and answer questions for clarification. Finally, a quiz on all aspects of the task is given to each student. Jigsaw is a remarkably effective way to learn the material. It encourages students in listening, speaking and critical-thinking. Since every part is essential, every member is essential in the learning process. The only access for each student to the other parts is listening and thinking carefully to the explanation of their peers. Or, there's a slim chance for him or her to do well on the quiz. It's appropriate to be used for reading comprehension and conversational activities.

Elliot Aronson and his colleagues designed original Jigsaw method which aimed at reducing social conflicts among schoolchildren. In Aaronson's Jigsaw structure, students are divided into six-member groups to work on the small portions of a chapter of a test. Each group member works on their own part of the task. Then the students of different groups who have the same assigned part meet in the "expert groups" to exchange information on the same part they have completed. Next, the students return to their original groups and take turns to teach the parts to their partners. jigsaw Ⅰ provides students with the opportunities in listening to others and positively depending on partners' information. But there are no quizzes and evaluations to students. Students' performance in class is individually accountable and their academic achievements are based on individual exam grades. Slavin modified Aronson's method in 1995 by improving it, then Jigsaw Ⅱ was emerged. Students are divided into four or five-member groups. All students complete a common material, such as a whole text. Each one is assigned a topic on the task to become an expert. Next, the students with same topic meet in "expert groups" and after that the students return to original groups to teach their partners. Instead of being tested individually, students take their individual quizzes and one point is given if they present the right answer Groups that meet standards may get certificates. Jigsaw Ⅱ earns a great reputation for it's multifunctional structure in implementing CL and issued widely in English reading classroom.

In Jigsaw, students are assigned to small heterogeneous teams, as in TGT and STAD. Academic material is broken into as many sections as there are team members. For example, a biography might be broken into "early years," "schooling," "first accomplishments," and so forth. The students study their sections with members of other teams who have the same sections. Then they return to their teams and teach their sections to the other team members. Finally, all team members are quizzed on the entire unit. The quiz scores contribute to individual grades, not to a team score as in TGT and STAD. In this sense, the Jigsaw technique may be seen as high in task interdependence but low in reward interdependence, as individual performances do not contribute directly to a group goal. In the Jigsaw technique, individual performances contribute to others' individual goals only; since the group is not rewarded as a group, there is no formal group goal. However, because the positive behavior of each team member (learning the sections) helps the other group members to be rewarded (because they need each other's information), the essential dynamics of the cooperative reward structure are present.

Slavin constructed a modification of Jigsaw called Jigsaw Ⅱ. In Jigsaw Ⅱ, students all read the same material but focus on separate topics. The students from different teams who have the same topics meet to discuss their topics, and then return to teach them to their teammates. The team members then take a quiz, and the quiz competition at each table will be fair-the highest three students in past performance scores are used to form team scores as in STAD. Thus, Jigsaw II involves less task interdependence and more reward interdependence than Jigsaw.

2.5.2 STAD-Student Team Achievement Division

Developed by Slavin, STAD (student team achievement division) can be easily integrated into the traditional instruction, so it becomes the optimal choice for teachers who start to use cooperative learning. STAD begins with the teacher's whole instruction to teach basic knowledge and background information which is closely related to the tasks and questions. After receiving the task and questions, students meet in their groups to help each other fully understand the learning material and master skills required to promote their performances. Then students take individual quiz and they are graded by individual quiz scores plus team scores. Team scores are average scores of all members' individual increasing scores over the previous quiz. That is to say, students' improvement on his or her own right is emphasized. Anyone can make contribution to his team scores as long as he makes efforts. Either the top students or the poor students have the same opportunity to earn increasing points, which is of significance to motive students to make progress on their own right.

David De Viries and Keith Edwards put forward Teams Games Tournaments in Johns Hopkins University. The essential component of TGT is that each of team members competes as a representative of their group with those from other groups who are on similar English level. The score of individual is the team's score. As for EFL purposes, STAD is an effective method that can be used for teaching and learning basic skills such as grammatical rules, vocabularies, etc.

Student Teams-Achievement Divisions (STAD) uses the same 4- to 5-member heterogeneous teams used in TGT, but replaces the games and tournaments with simple, 15-minute quizzes, which students take after studying in their teams. The quiz scores are translated into team scores using a system called "achievement divisions." The quiz scores of the highest six students in past performance are compared, and the top scorer in this group (the achievement division) earns eight points for his or her team, the second scorer earns six points, and so forth. Then the quiz scores of the next highest six students in past performance are compared, and so on. In this way, student scores are compared only with those of an ability-homogeneous reference group instead of the entire class. A "bumping" procedure changes division assignments from week to week to maintain equality. Students know only their own division assignments; they do not interact in any way with the other members of their division. The achievement division feature maintains the equality of opportunity for contributions to the team score as in TGT. A complete description of STAD appears in Slavin.

2.5.3　TGT-Team Game Tournament

It's developed by Slavin. TGT (team game tournament) is quite similar to STAD except the way of testing and scoring. After the whole instruction, students study the common worksheet together in their groups. Then the teams compete against each other on tournament instead of quit. Each student acts as the representative of his team and competes against those of other teams to earn points for the team. Each student competes against others at the similar academic level. Then each student's points of a team add up to form the team scores which decides the rank of the team. Teams are ranked at three levels: Super team, excellent team and good team according to the given criteria.

TGT method is a process of continuity to adjust competitors of different level SO as to ensure the fairness and validity ofactivities. Students Team Achievement Division is developed by Robert Slavin. He extended TGT method by Devries and Edwards and developed STAD. This method can be carried out like this: at first, teacher should give out the tasks to each group. Each of students is required to learn an assigned task together within their teams. Then everyone will get the examination without any help from others. The scores they get would be the final achievement of this team. STAD is a kind of cooperative method in which the competition is among teams. These two similar methods contribute to students' sense of responsibility, because individuals' performance has close relationship with the group achievement and reward. Students try their best to help each other to master the assigned knowledge or ability. However, it is obvious that it costs much time in calculating group final score. TGT is a good way to teach and analyze the text content and to check students' comprehension of the text content.

The bulk of the research on practical cooperative learning techniques has focused on four major models: Teams-Games-Tournament; Student Teams-Achievement Divisions; Jigsaw; and Small-Group Teaching. These techniques are emphasized in this review both because they have been well researched in field settings and because they are well-defined teaching strategies that are in use in many classrooms. All four have books or manuals written about them so that teachers can easily implement them. Other classroom research involving less widely used cooperative techniques is also reviewed. Teams-Games-Tournament (TGT) is built around two major components: 4- to 5-member student teams, and instructional tournaments. The teams are the cooperativeelements of TGT. Students are assigned to teams according to a procedure that maximizes heterogeneity of ability levels, sex and race. The primary function of the team is to prepare its members to do well in the tournament. Following an initial class presentation by the teacher, the teams are given worksheets covering academic material similar to that to be included in the tournament. Teammates study together and quiz each other to be sure that all team members are prepared. After the team practice session, team members must demonstrate their learning in the tournament, which is usually held once each week. For the tournament, students are assigned to three person "tournament tables. " The assignment is done so that three students are assigned to Table 1, the next three to Table 2, and so on. At the tables, the students compete at simple academic games covering content that has been presented in class by the teacher and on the worksheets. Students at the tournament tables are competing as representatives of their teams, and the score each student earns at his or her tournament table is added into an overall team score. Because students are assigned to ability-homogeneous tournament tables, each student has an equal chance of contributing a maximum score to his or her team, as the first place scorer at every table brings the same number of points to his or her team. Following the tournament, the teacher prepares a newsletter which recognizes successful teams and first place scorers. While team assignments always remain the same, tournament table assignments are changed for every tournament according to a system that maintains equality of past performance at each table.

2.5.4 GI-Group Investigation

It is the most successful CL method for specialized tasks. According to the complexity of the task, GI (group investigation) may last from one week to months. The teacher proposes a general problem after introducing the background information and asks student to raise questions around the problem. Each group is assigned the same general problem but each member of a team takes a different question around the general one. Then, students begin to search and organize relevant information and share their ideas with the group mates. Next, students work independently to make a report that reflects their group view. After that, students present their individual reports alternately to each other allowing other members in the group to ask for clarification. At last, the group makes a group-presentation. Certainly, the final product of the group investigation isn't necessarily in a form of a report. It can be a role-play, essay or even drama. Each team competes against each other to gain points by its performance which will be evaluated by both the teacher and other teams.

Group Investigation method is developed by Yael S and Shlomo S of Tel Aviv University Israel. In Group Investigation students decide what they will learn and how. The team is build up on the basis of common interest. They exchange views exactly what they want to focus on. It conducts in a 2-6 students group which responsible for a part of the task that is assigned to the whole class. Then they divide the work among themselves, and each group members carries out his or her part of the investigation. Finally, the group synthesizes and summarizes its work and presents these findings to the class. The reward would be given according to the random sample score from every group if it meets the criteria.

GI is suitable for writing exercises. It involves students in a variety of socio-affective, cognitive and meta-cognitive strategies.

Small-Group Teaching is a general classroom organizational plan in which learning takes place through cooperative group inquiry, discussion, and data gathering by students. Students select subtopics within a general area selected by the teacher, and then organize themselves into small groups of two to six members. These groups further subdivide their topic into individual tasks to be performed by group members in preparation for a group presentation to the total class. This group presentation is then evaluated by the other students and by the teacher. Thus, Small-Group Teaching is very high in student autonomy and involves a high degree of task interdependence because of the assignment of students to special tasks within the group, but it is relatively low in group reward interdependence (group rewards are not well-defined) and individual accountability.

2.5.5 Team Assisted Individualization (TAI) and Cooperative Integrated Reading and Composition (CIRC)

Slavin and Karweit developed TAI in a randomized controlled experiment for a year. TAI is a highly structured cooperative learning strategy. Students are divided into 4 or 5 member learning group according to their initial test. The grouping of students depends on participants' different levels in English and each student complete individualized materials with assistance from partners as well as their teacher's instruction. Students take responsibility for each other in a team for both individual score and group reward. This sort of learning method is adapted to the certain curriculum such as mathematics more often.

Cooperative Integrated Reading and Composition is conducted by Bob Slavin and Nancy Madden in 1983 for reading and composition course. It is a success and independent model. Students of mixed abilities would be placed in a group. They work together in reading, discuss and revise partner's vocabulary, pronunciation, understanding of the main idea, language skills in writing and edit each others work.

CIRC gives students related reading and writing skills during the learning of traditional syllabus, then those knowledge skills would be used in expanding drills.

For example, in order to finish an assigned reading task, students are acquired to learn vocabulary, pronunciations, sentences, meaning and discuss the questions in the text.

CIRC motivates students to try their best for the team performance which is depending on the sum of individual score. Besides, it is used in 90 minute lessons to get a comprehensive achievement in one specific topic on reading and writing. Direct instruction is the most remarkable points compared with other methods.

2.5.6 Kagan's Cooprative Learning Structures

In 1989, Kagan have identified approximately 200 CL (cooperative learning) structures which can be described as steps of CL classroom activities and can be applied to any course and any level. The following are selected ones which were used in this research.

2.5.6.1 Paraphrase Passport

In this structure, students are required to paraphrase what others have said when they're engaging in a group discussion. Only when the former speaker is satisfied with his paraphrase, can one give his own comments. The practice that all the students take turns to speak and listen ensures that every student gets a chance to be heard and understood.

This structure is a good devise for increasing comprehensible input and checking comprehension.

2.5.6.2 Brain Storming

It's a simple structure. Students encourage each other to contribute ideas of a given topic and then they generate a view representing the team.

2.5.6.3 Numbered Heads together

In this structure, students in a team put their heads together to discuss the answer after the teacher puts forward a question. They must make sure that everyone knows the answer in order to gain points for the team because the teacher randomly signals one of them to answer. It's quite effective to be used in the following aspects:

(1) Giving definitions of words and making sentences with given words.

(2) Discussing setting, plot, theme and character traits of an article and appreciating the writing styles and devices, etc.

(3) Revising and editing essays.

(4) Discussing and analyzing grammatical structures.

2. 6　Features of CL

2. 6. 1　Heterogeneous Groups

Composing heterogeneous groups is the first step to implement CL. CL groups must be formed by teachers intentionally with respect to student's differences in sex, academic ability, learning style, talent and personality. The heterogeneity and diversity provide an environment where individual strong points are recognized and individual needs are addressed among positive peer relationship. Each member acts as the information source or small-teacher from certain aspects. Students provide their own ideas from different perspectives, which help all members to think about a large number of alternatives of ideas. That helps to avoid the limitation of one's unitary perspective. What's more, challenges and negotiations are increased because of different thinkers are present. In the process, students learn to accept and appreciate individual differences and view situations from a variety of angles. In the meantime, student's ability in critical-thinking can be enhanced.

Of course, taking diversities into consideration in group formation consumes much more time than simply asking students to choose their group mates or randomly forming groups by the teacher, but it is of great significance to maximize students' learning and social competence development.

2. 6. 2　Equal Participation of All Students

In CL, various ways are designed to avoid student unequal participation and the emergence of free-riders. By dividing labor and materials, students are clear of the fact that everyone is needed to contribute his own part to do the task which can't be done by only one or a few members so that students view each other as an unique role in the completion of the task. Individual accountability also helps to ensure equal participation.

2. 6. 3　Unique Rewarding System

CL is characterized by its unique rewarding system which combines two levels,

i. e. , the individual test scores and the group scores. Students learn together cooperatively but they need to demonstrate what they've learned alone in tests without any group mate's help. The group scores are bonus points added up in the CL activities if the group goal is achieved and each member performs well enough. Certainly, if each member of a team exceeds a certain criterion in individual tests, extra bonus points will be given to all members. In this rewarding system, students' progress is recognized so each student can get bonus points on his or her own right as long as he or she makes efforts. Since students' scores in tests take a large proportion in their final scores, the top students won't be pulled down while the average-level and low-level students are greatly stimulated to make progress.

2.7　Theoretical Approach of CL

Researchers have shifted their focus to being more interested in identifying the mediating factors and the inter-psychological mechanisms involved in the effectiveness of cooperative learning.

There is little knowledge on this specific topic when applied to virtual education; however, contrastive information from face-to-face education on the effectiveness of cooperative learning techniques and the required specific processes, can prove useful in furthering understanding of their internal dynamics in virtual contexts.

Beyond the discussion about the cooperation and collaboration concepts, in the practice, both processes are referred to active and interactive learning. In fact, cooperative learning groups rely on positive interdependence among the constituents of the group. The students feel they can reach their learning goals only if the rest of the group also achieve them. But not all groupings are cooperative, since the latter form can only be accomplished by observing certain basic elements. Rusbult and Van Lange point out that it is necessary to gain further understanding of interdependence so as to appreciate how these processes are transformed in communication, how motivational factors and the concern for the welfare of another member of the group intervene during the interaction, and their effects on goal accomplishment.

The effectiveness of cooperative learning depends upon multiple conditions such as the group composition (size, age, gender, heterogeneity…), the task features and the communication media. However, these conditions are multiple and interact with each other in such a complex way that is not possible to guarantee learning effects.

According with socio-cultural theories, verbal interaction is particularly essential in cognitive development and learning the teaching-learning process is viewed as a socially organized activity in which speech processes take place among people of different levels of command whether more or less competent. In other words and more specifically, in cooperative learning tasks, language is the basic tool to collectively understand, co-regulate, make proposals, negotiate and construct meaning.

Of great value is also the research carried out on the characteristics of virtual asynchronous communication and its differences in relation to the communication established in other educational contexts, as well as the studies performed on virtual communities, especially those analyzing the process of interaction through discourse, which contribute relevant theoretical and methodological elements that can be applied in a deeper study of the virtual cooperative learning process.

In the virtual learning environment, the majority of educational interaction relies on the use of discourse-in many in stances in a written format—as a mediating instrument to conceptualize reality, discuss and negotiate. In this sense, the students' discursive activity is partly responsible for their ability to achieve higher levels of inter-subjectivity and, therefore, advance towards shared and ever more complex representations of the contents and tasks of the joint activity.

From a cultural constructivist point of view, learning processes in an online learning environment are described as the construction of shared meanings, and the importance of discourse as a basic mediating tool for this construction is under-lined. In this sense, the participants' discursive activity is set within the larger context of the activity.

Likewise, cooperative knowledge construction in virtual environments requires high levels of continuous interaction and reciprocal communication between the participants, allowing argumentation, negotiation, discussion and the joint construction of meanings. Within this kind of interaction, different inter-psychological mechanisms that favor the constructive potential of the interaction between the students may occur. Therefore, a crucial element for understanding how knowledge is constructed has to do with what is being done and said by all the participants.

Along these lines, Mercer distinguishes the types of talk taking place in the classroom: disputative, cumulative or exploratory. Disputative or discussion talk is characterized by disagreement, making decisions individually, brief exchanges consisting of statements and discussions of doubtful points or refutations. Cumulative talk is characterized by repetitions and confirmations, speakers build on what others have said in a positive way, but not critically; they construct "shared knowledge" by means of accumulation. With exploratory talk, however, knowledge is more openly justified and reasoning is apparent in the conversation. Other students' ideas are discussed in a critical and constructive manner. Statements and suggestions are offered for joint consideration, they must be questioned and defended, but discussion on doubtful points must be justified and alternative hypotheses offered.

According to Mercer, the cultural analysis of classroom discourse is basically geared to understanding how language is used to think collectively and it focuses on the importance of dialogue quality in educative processes. Taking into account this point of view, we believe the following inter-psychological mechanisms, related with the cooperative learning are essential in order to analysis how knowledge is constructed also in an online environment:

(1) Positive interdependence among the group members in the execution of the learning activity. Most researchers, both in face-to-face and in virtual environments, focus on achieving a common goal, which involves performing a joint task or piece of work, requiring commitment and accountability from the constituents of the group.

(2) Psychosocial relations. Many authors stress the importance of interpersonal relations and the social skills of group members in ensuring cooperation and achieve positive effects in learning. They posit that the degree of emotive bonding and social support among students has an impact on the quality of their joint work.

(3) Joint construction of meaning through language. This involves the joint construction of knowledge, ideas and concepts; demanding and offering explanations and arguments; mutually negotiating and regulating the contributions and viewpoints in the interaction. The students' different uses of language are given in sequence, which produce expositive, descriptive and argumentative texts, as well as conclusions and summaries.

Additionally, we take into account that written language is the base of the communication and interaction in Computer Supported Collaborative Learning (CSCL) situations where communication is asynchronous. Much of cited researches have focused on content analysis of the transcriptions of the online conversation in order to investigate the quality of the interaction process in which the students engage.

Finally, as a result of the consideration of the discourse as the basic mediator of cooperative learning processes, we considered the possibility of explore the link between language and the mechanisms involved in cooperative learning. In summary, from this theoretical framework we hope to identify the forms adopted by virtual cooperative language in relation to their essential mechanisms.

2.8　History of CL

Prior to World War Ⅱ, social theorists such as Allport, Watson, Shaw, and Mead began establishing cooperative learning theory after finding that group work was more effective and efficient in quantity, quality, and overall productivity when compared to working alone. However, it wasn't until 1937 when researchers May and Doob found that people who cooperate and work together to achieve shared goals, were more successful in attaining outcomes, than those who strived independently to complete the same goals. Furthermore, they found that independent achievers had a greater likelihood of displaying competitive behaviors. Philosophers and psychologists in the 1930s and 40s such as John Dewey, Kurt Lewin and Morton Deutsh also influenced the cooperative learning theory practiced today. Dewey believed it was important that students develop knowledge and social skills that could be used outside of the classroom, and in the democratic society. This theory portrayed students as active recipients of knowledge by discussing information and answers in groups, engaging in the learning process together rather than being passive receivers of information (e. g. teacher talking, students listening). Lewin's contributions to cooperative learning were based on the ideas of establishing relationships between group members in order to successfully carry out and achieve the learning goal. Deutsh's contribution to cooperative learning was positive social interdependence, the idea that the student is responsible for contributing to group knowledge. Since then, David and Roger Johnson have been actively contributing to the cooperative learning theory. In 1975, they identified that cooperative learning promoted mutual liking, better communication, high acceptance and support, as well as demonstrated an increase in a variety of thinking strategies among individuals in the group. Students who showed to be more competitive lacked in their interaction and trust with others, as well as in their emotional involvement with other students. In 1994 Johnson and Johnson published the 5 elements (positive interdependence, individual accountability, face-to-face interaction, social skills, and processing) essential for effective group learning, achievement, and higher-order social, personal and cognitive skills (e. g. , problem solving, reasoning, decision-making, planning, organizing, and reflecting).

Theorizing on social interdependence began in the early 1900s, when one of the founders of the Gestalt School of Psychology, Kurt Koffka, proposed that groups were dynamic wholes in which the interdependence among members could vary. One of his colleagues, Kurt Lewin refined Koffka's notions in the 1920s and 1930s while stating that (a) the essence of a group is the interdependence among members (created by common goals) which results in the group being a "dynamic whole" so that a change in the state of any member or subgroup changes the state of any other member or subgroup, and (b) an intrinsic state of tension within group members motivates movement toward the accomplishment of the desired common goals. For interdependence to exist, there must be more than one person or entity involved, and the persons or entities must have impact on each other in that a change in the state of one causes a change in the state of the others. It may be concluded that it is the drive for goal accomplishment that motivates cooperative and competitive behavior.

In the late 1940s, one of Lewin's graduate students, Morton Deutsch, extended Lewin's reasoning about social interdependence and formulated a theory of cooperation and competition. Deutsch conceptualized three types of social interdependence-positive, negative, and none. Deutsch's basic premise was that the type of interdependence structured in a situation determines how individuals interact with each other which, in turn, largely determines outcomes. Positive interdependence tends to result in promotive interaction, negative interdependence tends to result in oppositional or interaction, and no interdependence results in an absence of interaction. Depending on whether individuals promote or obstruct each other's goal accomplishments, there is substitutability, cathexis, and inducibility. The relationships between the type of social interdependence and the interaction pattern it elicits is assumed to be bidirectional. Each may cause the other. Deutsch's theory has served as a major conceptual structure for this area of inquiry since 1949.

The history of the application of CL in classroom teaching could be divided into three stages: (a) from the late 1960s to the mid 1970s, the researchers are engaged upon theoretical researches. Thanks to their contribution, both teachers and students can benefit much from cooperative learning. (b) The second stage started from the mid 1970s to the mid 1980s at which some influential instructional techniques and strategies are formed. Large numbers of experiments are carried out in various levels of schools and subjects. (c) The third stage is from the mid 1980s to the present. At this stage, cooperative learning is advocated and applied in education. Besides, scholars and educators attach importance to experiments of integrating CL model with other teaching theories.

There are many researches in cooperative learning over past thirty years by researchers abroad. The studies on the definition of cooperative learning, elements, techniques and evaluation standard are systematically explored. For instance, the Jigsaw Classroom, it mainly describes the elements in applying Jigsaw method to classroom and how to use this method in reasonable way. Here are much more monographs on the research of CL: the theory, research and practice, the motivation and benefits of Cooperative Learning. All of these works gives teachers and students clearly guidance in perfecting ability of teaching and learning.

Most of the researches have shown the positive effects on instructional aspects in the following aspects: students' motivation in learning, academic achievement, interpersonal relationship, self-esteem, psychological status, learning atmosphere etc. However, most of the researches are carried out in primary schools and middle schools. The studies of cooperative learning in college level are limited.

2.9 Theoretical Foundation of CL

CL is an old educational view and practice. In China, it began as early as 2000 years ago when the famous educational masterpiece Xueji says: "Studying alone leads to ignorance and being ill-informed. " In the West, according to Slaving, the idea of CL can be traced back to as far as the seventeenth century, such educationists as Comenius in the seventeenth century, Rousseau in the eighteenth century, Pestalozzi in the nineteenth century and Dewey in the early twentieth century, who held some forms of cooperation among students as essential to learning. In 1994, Johnson D W et al. also stated that nearly six hundred experimental and over one hundred co-relational studies have been conducted on cooperative, competitive, and individualistic efforts to learn since 1898. CL, therefore, is not new to education. Although the term may not have been used, CL in some form has been happening for decades. Most researchers have found that CL improves academic performance in areas such as comprehension, use of critical thinking, time on task and test scores. However, there are a limited number of studies which do not find an educational advantage to using CL over individual study. Many studies have documented the social benefits of CL. Working in groups is reported to increase self-esteem, motivation, positive attitudes towards school and an internal sense of control over one's learning. Furthermore, students often prefer to work with peers than independently. Unfortunately, other researchers found evidence of group inequalities and the "free-rider" problem (lower achieving students allow, or by inaction, depend upon the more able students to complete the majority in a collaborative setting). They also discover that students begin selecting group members based upon previous, positive collaborative experiences with them. Theoretical perspectives have guided research on CL: social interdependence, cognitive developmental, cognitive elaboration and behavioral learning.

2.9.1 Social Interdependence Theory

Interaction with other people is essential for human survival. In an education setting, social interdependence refers to students' efforts to achieve and develop positive relationships, adjust psychologically and show social competence. The social interdependence theory of CL presupposes that the way of social interdependence is structured which determines the way persons interact with each other. Moreover, outcomes are the consequence of persons' interaction. Therefore one of the cooperative elements that have to be structured in the classroom is positive interdependence or cooperation. When this is done, cooperation results in promotive interaction as group members encourage and ease each other's efforts to learn.

2.9.2 Cognitive Developmental Theory

Cognitive Theory holds that interaction among students will in themselves increase students' achievements of reasoning that has to do with mental processing of information rather than with motivations. According to Slavin, there are two cognitive theories that are directly applied to CL, the development and the elaboration theories. The developmental theories assume that interaction among appropriate tasks increases their mastery of critical concepts. When students interact with other students, cognitive conflict will arise, inadequate reasoning will be exposed, and higher-quality understanding will emerge that stimulate perspective-taking ability and reasoning. From the cognitive developmental theory, the effects of CL on students' achievements would be largely or entirely due to the use of cooperative tasks. In this view, the opportunity for students to discuss, to argue, to present and hear one another's viewpoint is the critical element of CL with respect to students' achievement. For example, Damon proposes a "conceptual foundation for a peer based plan of education":

(1) Through mutual feedback and debate, peers promote one another to abandon misconceptions and search for better for solution.

(2) The experience of peer communication can help children master social processes (such as participation and argumentation) and cognitive processes (such as verification and criticism).

(3) Collaboration between peers can provide a forum for discovery learning and can encourage creative thinking.

(4) Peer interaction can introduce children to the process of generating ideas.

2.9.3 Cognitive Elaboration Theory

Research in cognitive psychology has long held that if information already in memory, the learner must engage in some sort of cognitive restructuring, or elaboration, of the material. One of the most effective means of elaboration is explaining the material to someone else. Research on peer tutoring has long found achievements benefiting for the tutor as well as the tutee.

2.9.4 Behavioral Learning Theory

The behavioral learning theory presupposes that cooperative efforts are fueled by extrinsic motivation to achieve group reward (academic and/or nonacademic). From a behaviorist's perspective, cooperative incentive structures create a situation in which the only way group members can attain their personal goals is if the group is successful. Therefore to meet their personal goal, group members must both help their group mates to do whatever helps the group to succeed, and perhaps even more importantly, to encourage their group mates to exert maximum efforts. In other words rewarding groups based on group performance (or the sum of individual performances) creates an interpersonal reward structure in which group members will give or withhold social reinforces (e. g., praise, encouragement) in response to group mates' task-related efforts.

2.10   Researches on CL

Promotive, oppositional, and no interaction have differential effects on the outcomes of the situation. The research has focused on numerous outcomes, which may be subsumed within the broad and interrelated categories of effort to achieve, quality of relationships, and psychological health.

Research on cooperative learning demonstrated "overwhelmingly positive" results and confirmed that cooperative modes are cross-curricular. Cooperative learning requires students to engage in group activities that increase learning and adds other important dimensions. The positive outcomes include: academic gains, improved race relations and increased personal and social development. Some researchers report that students who fully participated in group activities, exhibited collaborative behaviors, provided constructive feedback and cooperated with their group had a higher likelihood of receiving higher test scores and course grades at the end of the semester. Results from Brady and Tsay's study support the notion that cooperative learning is an active pedagogy that fosters higher academic achievement. Slavin states the following regarding research on cooperative learning which corresponds with Brady and Tsay's findings.

2.10.1　Researches on Cooperative Learning Abroad

The concept of cooperative method has been put forward in the first century in ancient Rome. It is not new to education. Western educationists hold that students should learn from each other and make progress. In the 1700s, Joseph Lancaster and Andraw Bell introduced cooperative groups to students in England and achieved positive results, and then American scholars, Francis Parker and John Dewey brought cooperative form into classroom. At that time, it is given great attention in American education. Morton Deutsh proposed the theory of competition and cooperation which laid foundation for the establishment of cooperative learning theory. Many practical cooperative learning methods were researched and operated for classroom application. For example, Learning Together was produced by Johnson and Johnson in 1975, Cooperative Integrated Reading and Composition was proposed by Stevens, Slavin and his associates in 1983 for reading and composition course.

In the mid of 1960s in America cooperative learning has been applied in classroom in a large scale. Through the implementation of cooperative learning, students have gained remarkable improvements in academic, affective and social aspects. Relationship between ethnic groups has been greatly alleviated. High, average and low-performing students all achieve equally from cooperative learning. Some scholars even indicate that low achievers achieve higher than high achievers, but some have found high achievers gain the most. Most scholars speak highly of it. Cooperative learning can also improve one's self-esteem, the social acceptance of mainstreamed students who are academically handicapped and the ability to work effectively with others.

2.10.2　Domestic Researches on Cooperative Learning

Cooperative learning has proven to be an effective way in teaching in America Germany, Canada, Japan, Nigeria, etc. In the late 1980s, cooperative learning was introduced to China. Researches on application of cooperative learning in various subjects have been conducted by Chinese researchers, from then on cooperative method was widely spread in China.

Cooperative learning has been carried out in all kinds of subject areas such as

Chinese, math, English, history, science course, etc. Many scholars engage in the researches of cooperative learning and focus their attention on the application of CL.

The researches conducted by the famous scholars offer much evidence to support CL theory. Wang Tan did some researches on historical development of CL, theoretical underpinnings, strategies, evaluation and empirical studies etc. Besides, large quantities of researches promote the process of application of cooperative learning. An experiment, called "Cooperative Teaching Research and Practice", was conducted by Wan Tan, a scholar in Shandong Education and Research Institute, in 1993 in 9 provinces in China. The experimental data was collected from more than one hundred schools and it lasted six years. It gained great support from most famous figures such as Slavin, Johnson and Sharan etc. This project was launched for two reasons: one was to reflect on some major problems existing in the educational and teaching areas of elementary and secondary schools at home. The other was to borrow some mature experiences from abroad. The experiment has made a significant impact nationwide.

2.11   Cooperative Learning and Classroom Technology

Classroom instructional technology can be described as a combination of three essential elements: a task structure, a reward structure, and an authority structure. The task structure is the mix of activities that make up the school day. Lecture, class discussion and seat work are different task structures in use in most classrooms.

Another dimension on which task structures may vary is the grouping system in use. Students may be working on individually prescribed tasks, in homogeneous or heterogeneous small groups in which students may or may not be permitted to help one another with their work, with or without a teacher or aide, and so on.

The reward structure of the classroom may also vary on several dimensions. Rewards for appropriate behavior vary in kind. Some possible rewards include grades, teacher approval, and tangible rewards. They may vary in frequency, in magnitude, and in sensitivity, the degree to which increases in performance are matched with increases in reward. The term interpersonal reward structure refers to the consequences for an individual of his classmates' performance. In a competitive reward structure, such as grading on the curve, one student's success necessitates another's relative failure. Michaels calls this negative reward interdependence, because students' rewards are linked to one another negatively. The opposite of competition is cooperation, such as is present in sports teams. In cooperation, or positive reward interdependence, one student's success helps another to be successful. The third interpersonal reward structure is reward independence, or individualization, where students' goal achievements are unrelated to each other. The authority structure of the classroom refers to the control that students exercise over their own activities, as opposed to that exercised by teachers and other adults.

In some classrooms students have considerable choice about what they will study, how they will learn what they need to learn, in what order they will do a prescribed set of tasks, and in some cases students have a say in how much they will do to earn a certain grade. The authority structure is relatively one-dimensional, varying from high student autonomy in any of several domains of student activities to high teacher- or school-imposed structure.

Cooperative learning may involve changes in all three of the major elements of classroom technology, but it is primarily a change in the interpersonal reward structure of the classroom, from a competitive reward structure to a cooperative one.

Of course, other changes are almost unavoidable, such as a change from a primarily individual task structure with frequent whole-class instruction to a task structure characterized by student interaction in small groups. Other changes in the reward, task and authority structures of the classroom always accompany the implementation of cooperative learning techniques, and these changes are confounded with the change in reward structure. However, cooperative learning grew out of a laboratory tradition in social psychology that was clearly focused on the changes in reward structures, and the research on cooperative learning involves task and authority structure changes as secondary in interest to the changes in the interpersonal reward structure.

2.11.1   A Brief Theory of Reward Structures

Although an elaborate theory of reward structures is beyond the scope of this review, a brief statement is necessary for understanding the research. There are two primary outcomes that are important in research on reward structures: performance and cohesiveness. Performance refers to individual and group productivity on any of a variety of tasks; cohesiveness includes such variables as liking of others, feeling of being liked, group evaluation, race relations, and so on. These major categories of outcomes have very different theoretical bases, and are thus discussed separately. A theory of the effects of different reward structures on performance is anything but straightforward. This is true because changes in reward structures often lead to mediating variables that have contradictory effects on performance. The kind of performance and its measure, the task, the particular form of the reward structure, and other factors make these mediating variables more or less important, and thus determine the net direction of the effect on performance. There are several issues that need to be considered in predicting the effects of different reward structures on performance. Some of these are listed as follows:

(1) How contingent are an individual's rewards on performance? That is, what are the chances that if an individual works hard, the extra work will be detected, recognized, and rewarded, and that if the individual does not work up to capacity that the rewards will be diminished. This is the probability of success given greater or lesser effort discussed by Slavin.

(2) How large are the potential rewards for performance? Note that with the probability of success described above, this is the familiar incentive value of success-probability of success model proposed by Atkinson and many others. This model posits a multiplicative relationship between incentive value of success and probability of success.

(3) Are others likely to help or hinder task performance? Consideration of the effects of changes in reward structures makes it clear why the answer to the question "Which reward structure has the most positive effects on performance?" must be that it depends on the task, the performance and its measure, and many other features. First, consider cooperation, or positive reward interdependence. In general, participation in a cooperative group reduces the degree to which individual performances lead to individual outcomes. A group member can have an off day and still be successful because his or her group-mates cover for the individual; a group member may work especially hard and still fail because the rest of the group does not

match his or her efforts. The larger the group, the greater the reduction in the degree to which rewards depend on an individual's performance.

On the other hand, the reward delivered to the group is not the only one present in a cooperative contingency, and it may be the least important one. When individuals in a cooperative contingency want to be rewarded, they have two primary means of increasing their chances. First, they can work hard themselves. But, second, they can try to influence or help their group mates to do their best. That is, a cooperative contingency sets up a situation in which group members administer a highly contingent reward structure with their group-mates; if they do what helps the group to be rewarded, they receive praise; if they do not, they receive blame. Even if praise and blame are not directly delivered, a cooperative reward structure can create a general group norm favoring performance. Also, group members are motivated to help one another to be successful, and will facilitate one another's performance with whatever means they have. Thus, cooperative reward structures reduce performance by reducing the connection between performance and outcome, and they increase performance by introducing interpersonal rewards for individual behavior, group norms favoring performance that helps the group to achieve its goals, and help among group members. The net outcome depends on how much each of these factors is made important. For example, on some tasks, such as solving a single problem as a group, help from group members may be very useful, so a cooperative reward structure is likely to be effective. If the task requires that each group member solve his or her own problem, group help doesn't help so much, and an individualistic or competitive reward structure might be just as good or better. On some tasks, group members can see how their group-mates are doing and can reward them effectively; on other tasks they cannot, so it may be unlikely that group member praise will work to increase individual performance.

Note that there is very little theoretical distinction between pure group cooperation and competition between groups, in most cases. Looking within the group, group competition is just another form of positive reward interdependence. All of the problems and benefits associated with cooperation as just described apply equally well to group competition; the group competition is just one way of establishing a criterion for group success. The one major distinction between group cooperation and group competition is the possibility of negative affect and hindering between groups, but the essential motivational dynamics within the team are the same in either reward structure. The few studies that have compared "pure" group cooperation to group competition have found few differences in effects.

In a competitive reward structure, the relationship between performance and outcome depends on the competitive standard, the way rewards are distributed, and the individual's ability (or perceived ability) compared to the performance level needed to be successful. For example, there is no relationship between performance and outcome, and thus very little motivation, in a competition where the competitors are so poorly matched that some cannot win and others cannot lose, or where there is such a large chance component that incremental performance does not result in an increased chance of success. On the other hand, to the degree that competitors are evenly matched and success objectively depends on effort, competition can be a highly contingent reward structure.

The size of rewards for competition also depends on the particular task. In addition to extrinsic rewards for competitive success, it is apparently satisfying to many just to "best" a competitor. The degree to which "beating" itself is valued is at least in part culturally determined; white American children, for example, will choose to sacrifice rewards for themselves if they can make their opponents lose even to a greater extent than will Mexican-American or black children. Another variable in the achievement of competitive rewards is the perceived difficulty of the task.

One set of rewards works against high performance in competitive reward structures. This is the interpersonal reward system. While peer norms and sanctions favor high performance in cooperative settings, they oppose it in competitive ones, because one person's success necessitates another person's failure. This peer opposition to performance is very important in places like schools, where standing out as an academic achiever may lead to social disapproval, and delinquent groups. Similarly, fellow competitors will be motivated to hinder one another's performances. The degree to which this interferes with performance depends on how much hindering hinders. For example, if a group of detectives are competing for a promotion, they might refuse to share clues on a common case that would help all of them solve a crime. On the other hand, if the detectives were working on different cases, it would be harder for their competitors to hinder their performance.

Individualization is the simplest reward structure. The connection between performance and outcome depends entirely on how sensitive the reward system is to individual performance variations, how attainable standards are, and so on. Of course, these considerations are also important in cooperative and competitive reward structures. Individuals in an independent reward structure are not motivated to help or hinder one another, or to praise or discourage one another's performance.

A theory of effects of different reward structures on cohesiveness related variables is easier to describe than is the theory of effects on performance, but still has its complications. Cooperation should increase group cohesiveness both because it increases contact among group members and because people tend to like those who facilitate their own rewards. Individualization should not help group cohesiveness, because it does not involve interpersonal contact or facilitation of reward among group members. The case of competition is more complicated. In face-to-face competition, interpersonal contact can be quite high and can be rewarding to the competitors, particularly if they are balanced in ability. Operating in the opposite direction, however, is the fact that competitors frustrate each others' goal achievement, and thus will not be viewed positively. While cooperation should lead to greater group cohesiveness than individualization, the relative effects of competition should depend on the particular form of the competition, including the importance of success to each competitor.

2.11.2   Other Classroom Studies

In addition to the four major techniques, there have been several studies of cooperative learning that contribute to understanding of their effects. They differ from the four techniques just described primarily in that they have been used almost exclusively in research, and are not in wide classroom use.

Three of these studies used a simple cooperative technique in which students were assigned to small groups and instructed to work together on academic tasks and hand in a single assignment as a group. The teachers praised the group as a whole, but no formal group rewards were given. These cooperative techniques resembles practical techniques presented in Johnson and Johnson's book, Learning Together and Alone, but are not similar enough for the studies of them to constitute an evaluation of the strategies outlined in the book.

Two studies used a cooperative technique like that used by the Johnsons, but considerably more structured. Students were assigned roles within cooperative groups and worked on social studies inquiry activities to produce a single workbook. The group making the best workbook received a prize. In 1975, Weigel et al. used a combination of cooperative techniques over a long period of time (in their junior high school sample an entire school year).

These techniques involved various small-group activities, with information-gathering, discussion, and interpretation conducted by the student groups. Prizes were given to winning groups based on the quality of the group product. Hamblin et al. used a group contingency for academic performance, in which students earned rewards based on (a) the lowest three quiz scores in the group, (b) the highest three scores, or (c) the average group score. Students were encouraged to work together to improve their scores.

2.11.3   A Typology of Cooperative Learning Techniques

Classroom cooperative learning techniques differ primarily along five dimensions: reward interdependence, task interdependence, individual accountability, teacher imposed structure, and use or nonuse of group competition. High reward interdependence means that there is an explicit group reward based on the group's performance. Low reward interdependence describes a situation in which students are asked to work with one another and are praised as a group, but group performance does not lead to a concrete goal in any systematic way. Jigsaw represents a special case of low reward interdependence; there is no formal group goal, but the task interdependence is so extreme that reward interdependence is indirectly created. Students cannot do well on their quizzes unless their teammates teach them well, as each group member has unique information. High task interdependence refers to a situation in which students must rely on one another to do their group tasks. In low task interdependence, individual students could opt to work alone without disrupting the group activity. Of course, "high" and "low" task interdependence are relative terms among cooperative learning techniques; even a technique very low in task interdependence would be high in comparison to a traditional, individual task structure. High individual accountability means that team members' contributions to their team scores are separately quantifiable. For example, in TGT and STAD the team scores are made up of the sum of individual, quantifiable scores. This is in contrast to the Johnson techniques, where a single paper is handed in by the group and individual contributions are impossible to quantify. Individual accountability is a particularly important feature, as without it, it is possible for group members to let others do most of the work in meeting the group goal. The opposite of individual accountability is substitutability, the condition in which all group members have the same task and can substitute for one another in performing the task. Teacher imposed structure refers to the degree to which tasks, rewards, and schedules are imposed by the teacher (or by the technique). The opposite of teacher-imposed structure is high student autonomy and student participation in classroom decision-making. The use of group competition means that a prize or recognition is given to the highest scoring groups in the class.

As is indicated, the techniques vary a great deal along the five dimensions. At present there are no data to inform a prediction about the separate effects of these dimensions on any of the dependent variables, as they have not been systematically varied. Most effects of cooperative reward structures have been attributed to reward interdependence, yet at least some degree of task interdependence is usually confounded with the reward interdependence.

The typology presented gives a rough outline of the characteristics of cooperative learning techniques that is useful in understanding the different effects that these methods have had on major student outcomes.

2. 12   Summary

The researches of cooperative, competitive, and individualistic efforts are commonly recognized as one of the oldest fields of research in social psychology. In the late 1800s Triplett in the United States, Turner in England, and Mayer in Germany conducted a series of studies on the factors associated with competitive performance. Since then over 750 studies have been conducted on the relative merits of cooperative, competitive, and individualistic efforts and the conditions under which each is appropriate. This is one of the largest bodies of research within psychology and education.

An extensive literature search was conducted aimed at identifying all the available studies from published and non-published sources. 754 studies contained enough data to compute an effect size (there are many studies from which an effect size could not be computed). The research on social interdependence, furthermore, has an external validity and a general popularity rarely found in the social sciences. The more variations in places, people, and procedures the research can withstand and still yield the same findings, the more externally valid the conclusions. The research has been conducted over twelve decades by many different researchers with markedly different theoretical and practical orientations working in different settings and countries. A wide variety of research tasks, ways of structuring social interdependence, and measures of the dependent variables have been used. Participants in the studies varied from ages three to post-college adults and have come from different economic classes and cultural backgrounds. The studies were conducted with different durations, lasting from one session to 100 sessions or more. Research on social interdependence has been conducted in numerous cultures in North America (with Caucasian, Black-American, Native-American, and Hispanic populations) and countries from North, Central, and South America, Europe, the Middle East, Asia, the Pacific Rim, and Africa. The research on social interdependence includes both theoretical and demonstration studies conducted in educational, business, and social service organizations. The diversity of these studies gives social interdependence theory wide general popularity and considerable external validity.

Cooperative learning is an old idea in education, which has experienced a substantial revival in educational research and practice in the past few years. The term refers to classroom techniques in which students work on learning activities in small groups and receive rewards or recognition based on their group's performance.

Laboratory research on the effects of cooperation on performance and other variables was already under way in the 1920s, but only recently have the principles of cooperation been made into practical programs for use in schools and evaluated as such. This paper presents a general theory and typology of cooperative learning, reviews the research on practical cooperative learning programs, and draws implications from this research for a new model of classroom instruction based on cooperation as a dominant instructional mode.

Chapter Three Cooperative Learning in Higher Education

Teaching and learning have evolved over the years. While the use of lecture is still the dominant mode of teaching in educational institutions, there has been consensus that students need to be active in learning, for which traditional styles of teaching may not be well suited. These calls for an alternative instructional mode: cooperative learning (CL) to promote active learning among students. Why is CL of such interest? In this globally and digitally interconnected world, there is a growing need to equip students with 21st century competencies such as critical thinking, interpersonal communication, collaborative skills, and global awareness in order to develop the next generation of innovators and creative thinkers. To develop those skills, educational institutions would need to consider using innovative teaching methods to ignite passion for learning and provide students with the opportunity for active learning. Previous studies have suggested that CL is one of the key teaching and learning strategies to meet the said purpose.

Although CL is especially valued in current teaching pedagogy and contemporary scholarship, far less has been written to provide a literature overview of CL in higher education. Essentially, there is a need to draw together what research has been done on CL in higher education to provide a historical overview of this particular field of research. Hence, the purpose of this article is to review prior research addressing the following questions: (a) What is CL and its importance? (b) How does CL evolve in higher education? (c) What contextual factors support or constrain the implementation of CL? The review begins with a discussion of the definition of CL as well as its theoretical underpinnings and associated elements. The paper then provides different drivers and motivations for adopting a CL approach. Additionally, this paper will review empirical research on CL in higher education and identify contextual factors strengthening or constraining CL. The review concludes with a discussion of the methodological issues in investigating CL from previous research.

3.1   Benefits of CL in Higher Education

Much has already been learned from research about the benefits of CL. In this study, the benefits of CL will be categorized and summarized into three aspects: academic, affective, and social competence. The academic benefits involve knowledge acquisitions and growth in intellectual and academic skills.

In essence, CL moves students from a passive to a more active role in the learning process. Numerous studies have shown that active learning is more effective than passive learning to encourage deep comprehension of the materials. Millis and Cottell also highlighted that CL is an approach to instruction in which students have greater use of higher-level thinking skills. This improves student attitudes toward learning and, in turn, increases retention of their subject area knowledge. It also appears that CL allows students to analyze problems via multiple perspectives, and this helps them to think in more complex ways. For students who are too shy to ask teachers questions, CL provides them a platform to seek clarification from their peers. Some studies found that students learn better through peer explanation, as they can translate teachers' language into peer conversation. During the sharing process, more competent students improve their thought articulation by making connections and synthesizing information from various sources. All these can promote their understanding through active reasoning and explanation. This helps to expand their existing ZPD to the higher potential level. Furthermore, as students mutually share their ideas, opinions, and viewpoints to each other, it pushes students to think critically in an academic context and in turn, widen their perspectives. Not surprisingly, there was a strong positive connection in the literature between CL and academic performance.

In addition to academic benefits, the affective benefits include the emotional aspects of learning, such as appreciation, enthusiasm, motivation, and values, in which one becomes more involved, committed, and self-reliant in one's own learning. When students work cooperatively in classroom activities, it helps to create a pleasant social ambience. As students interact with one another, the affinity and support they receive from peers facilitate students to feel like they are part of the group. This leads them to be committed not only to their own learning goals but to group goals as well. In the long run, students are more likely to feel empowerment and higher self-efficacy, self-esteem, and satisfaction. CL also helps to enrich autonomous learning experiences, which provides greater choice and flexibility in learning. For most students, autonomous learning can be a driving force to help them persevere in the face of challenges. Further studies have documented that students are highly motivated and will naturally enjoy learning more if they can learn autonomously. As time goes by, they prefer to learn new things and find motivation to keep learning. This may explain why students find that their personal ego-strength, self-confidence, and autonomy levels are all enhanced after they have been involved in CL.

The social competence benefits include the ability to get along with others in acceptable and appropriate ways. While learning is a complex individual process, it is also a social one. CL could also students to interact with others in a variety of ways. To complete a group task, students need to constructively navigate group interaction in order to respect each other as separate and unique individuals. These social interactions require strong interpersonal social skills and cooperative skills. With these skills, students can positively depend on each other in a team to solve problems collectively. CL could also provide the context for students to use social language, read social cues, and exchange ideas. Moreover, CL provides learners with the increased ability to view things from another's perspective. In the process of working with other members in a group, students are able to picture what others are feeling and thinking and appreciate others' views. From there, they can learn a set of interpersonal negotiation strategies for use with peers in order to resolve disagreements in constructive ways. As a result, empirical studies reported that CL is critical for students to develop social skills and competence. Eventually, students who feel good about themselves and their social skills are more likely to build a wide variety of mutually beneficial relationships.

3.2   Cooperation and Learning in Unfamiliar Situations

People often help others they do not know or will never see again, donating blood to unknown beneficiaries, tipping taxi drivers in foreign cities, and posting reviews of hotels and restaurants they attend at conferences. Such behaviors are even present in tightly controlled, anonymous laboratory experiments that strictly prevent any future interactions. What explains humans' propensity to expend resources to benefit others (to cooperate) even when they cannot expect that their kindness will be repaid? One promising explanation is that our modern day decency reflects the importance of maintaining relationships in our evolutionary past. This theory suggests that an instinct to cooperate still operates in today's interactions with strangers because it was beneficial to avoid alienating potential long-term partners in ancestral environments where people lived in small, close-knit communities. However, cooperation is not always in one's long-term self-interest. Sometimes allies prove untrustworthy, sometimes the gain from selfishness outweighs the cost of angering a social partner, and sometimes it really is unlikely that two people will ever meet again. Therefore, natural selection may have favored cognitive mechanisms that switch cooperative tendencies on or off accordingly. Because the incentives of a situation can be opaque, it is also likely that natural selection will have favored an ability to learn from experience when to modify cooperative tendencies. Here, we review an emerging literature suggesting that people can override default tendencies to cooperate, especially if they have opportunities to habituate to situations in which cooperation does not advance self-interest.

3.2.1   The Development of Social Prudence

Human development provides ample opportunities to learn the incentive structures of recurrent social situations. Young children receive commands from their parents to alter their behavior every 8 min or so. Community members pass down stories from one generation to another that communicate the virtues of cooperation and how it is enforced. Even generally law-abiding citizens occasionally commit misdeeds, and the negative consequences (or lack thereof) that they experience or observe other people experiencing affect their likelihood of behaving badly in the future. Indeed, people on average become more cooperative with age, perhaps because experience teaches them that cheating in many milieus is a losing strategy in the long run. Domain-General Process, Domain-Specific Knowledge How do people incorporate the wisdom they have accrued over development into cooperation decisions? Following other recent researchers, we propose the concept of a prediction error to explain how people learn whether to cooperate in particular situations. A prediction error represents the discrepancy between the expected outcome of a decision (e. g., "I believe that cooperating in this situation will be good for my reputation in the long term") and the actual outcome (e. g., "It turns out that cooperating had no long-term effect on my reputation"). By incorporating past prediction errors into their decisions, people can choose whether to cooperate on the basis of the presence or absence of situational factors that were correlated with desired outcomes in the past.

Prediction-error learning is involved in revising many types of beliefs in light of new evidence, not just beliefs about whether cooperation is prudent. However, learning whether to cooperate is a domain-specific task inasmuch as people bring knowledge to bear that is particularly useful for managing social relations. We theorize that people represent such knowledge in their initial belief about whether cooperation advances long-term self-interest in any particular situation. For instance, people prefer interacting with in-group members, from whom they anticipate a level of partiality that they do not expect from out-group members. As a result, prediction errors will be largest when out-group members prove benevolent and in-group members prove uncooperative. Moreover, the type of relationship that one has with an in-group member determines what constitutes acceptable behavior. For example, although reciprocation of specific deeds is expected in formal arrangements such as car pools, failing to pay back anyone favor will typically engender less opprobrium in a familial relationship.

The effect of prediction errors on subsequent cooperation decisions depends also on the certainty of initial beliefs. For example, Siegel et al. argued that it is not adaptive to reject potential social partners on the basis of a few minor infractions because even cooperative people occasion ally behave poorly. Instead, people should reserve judgment toward possibly remorseful transgressors. Consistent with such reasoning, results from Seigel et al. showed that people make weaker inferences about moral character when observing uncooperative behavior than when observing cooperative behavior. This asymmetry caused participants to more quickly change their judgment of previously selfish individuals who had begun cooperating than of previously cooperative individuals who had begun behaving selfishly. These examples demonstrate that although the flexibility of cooperation decisions depends on a domaingeneral learning process, such learning occurs in the context of beliefs and desires that are specific to cooperative interactions.

3.2.2 Learning to Cooperate (or Not)

One type of situation in which prediction errors are likely to influence future behavior are those in which it is never in one's self-interest to cooperate. For example, many experiments involving economic games require laboratory participants to decide whether to share windfalls of money with anonymous strangers in one-off interactions. Economic games present situations that differ greatly from those of everyday life, in which people typically decide whether to share resources with others they already know or might interact with again. Thus, although cooperation in economic games could reflect a desire to benefit anonymous strangers, it could also arise from participants who have yet to register the mismatch between the situations they are familiar with and the unfamiliar economic game.

To illustrate, consider the debate over the existence of so-called conditional cooperators, who choose to cooperate on the basis of whether they believe others will cooperate too. Researchers have inferred the existence of conditional cooperators from public-goods games, in which members of a group can contribute money to a common resource that benefits everyone equally. In the game, each dollar contributed benefits the group because the experimenter multiplies all contributions by a constant ($M > 1$) before doling them out equally. Thus, each dollar contributed returns M dollars to the group, and M/N dollars to each member. However, M is typicallyset to a lower value than the number of group members ($N > M > 1$), so each dollar contributed is personally costly ($N/M < 1$). The canonical result from games with several rounds of decision making is that conditional cooperators contribute much of their endowment in early rounds but contribute little by the end.

Many researchers posit that conditional cooperators want to promote the public good but eventually stop contributing out of indignation toward "free riders" who seldom contribute. In essence, the conditional-cooperation hypothesis posits that individuals perfectly understand the game but must learn whether their counterparts share their goals. This hypothesis is challenged, however, by the fact that many conditional cooperators later report that their contribution decisions were based on a desire to maximize their own income. Furthermore, the same decline in cooperation occurs when participants play with computers rather than humans. Thus, declining contributions in these cases cannot reflect a regard for other people that is eroded by exasperation toward non-cooperators. Instead, declining contributions likely reflect a mistaken belief that contributions increase personal income when other participants also contribute, a confusion that is corrected by experience.

Further support for the confusion hypothesis comes from a study in which participants played a public goods game with humans but could observe only the contributions of people in other groups, not in their own. In these cases, participants mimicked the behaviors of successful players in other groups by reducing their contributions in their own groups. These findings suggest that people were using social information to learn how to improve their payoffs, although it is also possible that they were making inferences about whether their own group members would cooperate on the basis of whether members of other groups cooperate. The experimenters confirmed the payoff-learning interpretation in a subsequent public-goods game with computers instead of humans: Participants who had observed successful players contributed less to a common resource that would "benefit" computers than those who had not observed successful human players, indicating that the former group had learned how to maximize their income better than had the latter group.

Habituation to Everyday Incentives Participants in economic games probably believe initially that cooperation promotes self-interest because they are importing the behaviors that have been rewarded in their everyday lives to novel situations. For example, participants from societies in which interactions among strangers are effectively regulated by law cooperate more ineconomic games. If people really do impose these mental models on economic games, then the same economic game may evoke different working models from real life for people from different backgrounds. An experimental demonstration of this phenomenon comes from Study 2 of Stagnaro et al., in which participants began by playing several rounds of a public-goods game. In some conditions, stingy contributions were punished, whereas in the control condition, participants could behave selfishly with impunity. Participants who had been acculturated in the punishment version of the public-goods game were later more cooperative in a second economic game that did not feature punishment.

If initial behavior inlaboratory studies is shaped by a spillover from everyday life, then behavior at the end of experiments-that is, after a period of adjustment to the local incentives-should be more reflective of participants' underlying goals. For example, although a study using samples from 16 different societies showed society-level variation in initial contributions in a repeated public-goods game, it also reported a decline in contributions across rounds in all samples. Furthermore, when participants return to the lab after having previously participated in a public-goods game, they tend to cooperate less the second time around.

In another longitudinal demonstration of spillover, McAuliffe et al. had participants play economic games with anonymous strangers and privately donate to charity on two separate occasions. People contributed less to charity and strangers on the second occasion, except in the one game in which cooperation can yield a personal profit, even when played only once with a stranger. The researchers argued that participants acted on cooperative habits from everyday life during the first session, but by the time they arrived at the second session, they had learned that nobody would thank them for behaving fairly or scold them for behaving selfishly. Consistent with this hypothesis, results showed that decisions at the first but not the second session were positively associated with peer and self-reports of cooperative traits, which do reflect how people behave in everyday social interactions.

Individual differences if registering prediction errors helps to align behaviors with incentives, then a greater ability to learn should increase the speed with which people make cooperation decisions that are congruent with their true preferences. Indeed, Burton Chellew et al. found that free riders were the only subset of participants who reliably understood that cooperation does not maximize personal income in the public-goods game. Another study revealed that Japanese adults who never shared money across multiple one-shot economic games scored higher on an intelligence test and self-reported greater skill in understanding social situations. Barreda Tarrazona et al. reported that reasoning ability is associated with less cooperation in a one-shot prisoner's dilemma game (a two-player game with the same payoff structure as the public-goods game) and with more cooperation in a repeated prisoner's dilemma with the same partner. Both patterns are optimal: In the one shot game, there is no self-interested reason to cooperate, whereas in the repeated game, inducing a long-term partner to cooperate in earlier rounds is essential to securing the benefits of cooperation in later rounds. Similarly, Burton Chellew et al. showed that participants who understood that it was pointless to contribute in a public-goods game with computer group mates were the only ones to strategically increase their initial contributions in a repeated game in which their behavior was observable to human group mates.

Although we contend that cooperation in unfamiliar situations is not evidence of unselfishness, we hasten to note that learning does not inevitably facilitate selfishness. Instead, understanding a situation's reward structure should increase alignment between people's behavior and their goals, whatever those goals happen to be. For example, Lockwood et al. had participants learn over several trials which of two choice options were associated with a monetary reward for either themselves or another person. Overall, participants minimized prediction errors more quickly when the rewards went to the self. However, the discrepancy in speed between learning on behalf of the self and another person was smaller for people higher in trait empathy, suggesting that empathic individuals are motivated to learn how to help others. Experimental economists have long emphasized the role of learning in social decision making. However, cooperation researchers have considered only recently how peoples' past social interactions shape their expectations in novel social situations. An important lesson from the research reviewed here is that people's behavior in any single situation is not necessarily a direct readout of how selfish or altruistic they are, especially if the situation's incentives differ from what they normally encounter in everyday life.

3.3　CL in Higher Education

In a higher education context, CL was examined across countries. Although there have been numerous studies demonstrating that CL is an effective learning strategy, most of the studies were conducted in Western countries, particularly the United States, Europe, and Australia. Attracted by the claimed positive outcomes from Western studies, CL was soon adopted in other parts of the world, including Asia (e.

g., Vietnam, Malaysia, Singapore, and China), the Middle East, and Africa. Tadesse and Gillies examined Ethiopian university students' and teachers' satisfaction and opinions regarding CL; Neo incorporated CL in a multimedia project to determine its impact on student learning in Malaysia; Loh and Teo investigated the effectiveness of CL to engage Singaporean students; Singh and Malatji investigated CL benefits to students' cognitive abilities in South Africa; Tombak and Altun examined Turkish university students' motivation toward CL; and Thanh et al. explored teachers' and students' perception of the use of CL in universities in Vietnam. These studies provide concrete evidence that CL is being used in higher education in other parts of the world in addition to Western countries. With more universities and colleges incorporating CL, Johnson and Johnson argued that higher education should challenge students not only in mastery of knowledge content but encourage students to analyze, accept multiple opinions shared by fellow students, and cooperate in diverse groups. This is especially important when CL implemented in higher education shows promising outcomes. Researchers have suggested that students are more mature and possess higher cognitive thinking skills; however, entrenched learning styles pose barriers for some students to respond well to CL. Perhaps there are a variety of reasons for the less promising outcomes, including teachers and students not receiving proper training in CL, varying understanding and conception of CL, barriers imposed by institutions, and even cultural differences that make teaching and learning distinct.

Based on prior studies, our paper attempts to identify five main factors that strengthen or constrain the implementation of CL in the university context: the teachers, the students, group formation, university environment and disciplines, and cultures.

3.3.1 The Teachers

In the context of CL, the role of the teacher remains that of a helper, facilitator, mentor, and guider, whereas the student's role remains central in the whole process as active participant in the learning and constructing of knowledge. The power shift from teacher to students could be a problem when students do not know how to take charge of their learning. Therefore, teachers play a key role in establishing CL experiences in classrooms. However, not all teachers are familiar with CL since didactic (teacher-focused) teaching has been the dominant teaching strategy in higher education for centuries. Some teachers may struggle to relinquish control in classes, especially when it comes to the delegation of authority to students. This explains why some researchers believe that "letting go" of power represents a key barrier to implementing CL.

Teachers' roles include designing tasks for students in groups and structuring groups and tasks so that students understand how and what to do. Moreover, teachers who facilitate students learning in CL require certain coaching skills such as encouraging students to work in small groups and assume accountability in learning, and providing constructive feedback. Johnson et al. suggested that teachers in CL should provide facilitation, behavioral modeling, and guidance. It is important for teachers to provide learners with clear directions and guidelines in order to help them in the journey of learning. They should delegate the responsibility and the role for a group so that students in groups have the chance to equally contribute to achieving mutual goals as well as constructing their own knowledge. While students are working on a task, teachers should observe and monitor their progress to evaluate their learning pace. In addition, teachers should ensure that active learning takes place by allowing closer interactions and bonding among students. Helping students to interact and work together not only enables students to learn from each other but also to nurture a sense of holding task responsibility. With encouragement and mentoring received from teachers, it creates enjoyment in their learning, and they better achieve desired objectives of learning. However, teachers need to adapt their approach to manage diverse classroom contexts and acknowledge cultural and institutional barriers.

Professional development (PD) is proposed to provide teachers with content knowledge, practical skills, and self-confidence before they adopt CL. PD is the processes and activities designed to improve teachers' knowledge, instructional approaches, and goal setting for student learning outcomes. In addition, PD also seeks to provide practical and situational wisdom to equip teachers with the necessary competency and professional capacity to deal with uncertainty since teaching and learning take place within certain contexts. Apart from considering PD as a narrow perspective to improve professionalism and expertise in teachers, it can be taken on a wider dimension that includes student development, curriculum design, or cooperation with peers that could result in transformation of educational practice that best reflects the needs of students.

In order for PD to have effective outcomes in changing teachers' practice, Opfer and Pedder suggested that three conditions need to meet. First, PD should be introduced in a setting with which teachers are familiar. When other teachers in the same work setting also receive PD and put new knowledge into practice, they will have a greater connectedness in terms of pooling their collective wisdom, sharing their experience, and psychological support. By doing so, it is much easier for teachers to seek input and improvements from their existing network systems in schools. Furthermore, collaboration with fellow teachers can change pedagogic perceptions and lead to improvement in teaching methods and improved relationships. PD can take place either in formal or informal learning contexts. In a formal learning context, activities are consciously undertaken by teachers with the intention to learn. Teachers may discuss learning goals or evaluate their own teaching practice with a peer. In the process, teachers might learn unconsciously; for example, they might unconsciously develop beliefs about collaboration with other teachers. On the other hand, for informal learning, both conscious and unconscious levels may occur. Teachers, for example, might consciously experiment with new instructional formats to change their teaching practice while unconsciously developing, through a combination of unpleasant experiences, an aversion to certain methods of instruction.

Second, PD should run progressively by focusing on a limited number of goals at a time. Some teachers might feel overwhelmed if they are exposed to too many goals in a short period of time. Since teaching is a complex activity, Ramsden suggested that it be a developmental process where one progresses from less to more sophisticated ideas. Teachers' experiential learning, knowledge, and practice all need time to develop. The idea is further supported by Chong and Kong, arguing that training needs to be sustained in order for change to be entrenched. It will also help to avoid diverting their focus and lowering their commitment levels. Hence, PD needs to go beyond supporting teachers at the initial stage of CL and be extended for a longer period.

Third, educational institutions and school administrators must support teachers in PD by allowing them to have time to meet to share and reduce structural obstacles that may impede the change processes. As teachers put their knowledge into practice, they may encounter difficulty with unpredictable outcomes. Continuous support is necessary to help teachers navigate the challenges. In addition, it facilitates teachers to internalize their knowledge into practice by having considerable time to digest what they learn, think about how it might be relevant to their teaching, and make sense of dilemmas and challenges through a process of critical appraisal. Postholm posited that critical appraisal is an important process for teachers' learning and development of good teaching practice. Opportunities can be created by schools where teachers can engage in active reflection on their teaching, either through joint work with fellow teachers or working with instructional experts to support adoption of new instructional practices.

3.3.2 The Students

The effectiveness of CL may be affected by student factors, with researchers suggesting several aspects. For instance, Prosser and Trigwell suggested that students who adopt surface learning might not find CL beneficial, as they do not actively contribute to the group learning. According to Colak , only the deep learning approach results in effective learning where students are aware of their learning experience. Likewise et al. argued that students' previous experience and prior knowledge, motivation to learn, self-confidence, learning styles, and personalities were associated with students' acceptance of CL. These could suggest that although teachers might use CL, if students do not participate with much enthusiasm, CL will not implement well. Kember and Kwan also emphasized the role of learner-learner interaction. To achieve better outcomes, learners need to engage in group or cooperative learning (e. g., sharing of materials, studying together). If they choose to remain passive in their learning, the quality of CL is deemed to be ineffective. Tadesse and Gillies further elucidated that CL takes more time compared to traditional learning methods because students need time to be familiar with CL and more time to execute. Students need time to develop, absorb, discuss, and practice new knowledge. CL activities require student initiative, so it is not surprising that CL occurs only occasionally; therefore, the benefits of CL are not maximized if students are not intrinsically motivated in CL.

3.3.3 Group Formation

Group formation can be a formidable task for teachers who implement CL in the classroom. It requires time, planning, and effort to create effective groups. There is much debate about whether homogenous or heterogeneous groupings help students learn or put them at a disadvantage. Most researchers agreed that heterogeneous grouping better supports the implementation of CL. Of these studies, students in CL groups need to be varied (heterogeneous) with different races, abilities, interests, etc. In agreement, Lou et al. suggested that heterogeneous groups have the greatest potential for success in CL, allowing more capable peer interactions and peer tutoring; they further reported that in diverse groups, low-ability students tend to benefit most. The diverse group of students allows students to actively interact with diverse individuals while at the same time learning each other's differences. Jacobs et al. argued that both higher- and lower-ability students tend to gain from CL, as high-ability students feel a sense of care for others and build autonomy while low-ability students can learn from students who understand the concepts. However, Barkley et al. disagreed with the idea and argued that high-ability students may begin to feel some resentment toward being in the heterogeneous group and low-ability students may shy away from participating with the group. Barkley et al. suggested that the efficient way is to allow students to form their own groups. This may lead students to form working groups with those who share similar backgrounds and interests. Arguments for friendship groups include: (a) students feel uncomfortable working with those they have not worked with before, and (b) it takes time to know each other or ascertain group members' abilities, unlike in friendship groups where students readily get to know each other's strengths and weaknesses. In Hofstede and Hofstede's study, affective factors exceed cognitive factors, and group harmony is a decisive factor of a successful group among Asian students. This implies that the established bonding between members in a group is much more important for Asian studentsto learn. Moreover, friendship groups may be detrimental in terms of identifying and pinpointing errors in order to maintain group harmony. Although one of the characteristics of collectivist societies is the desire to cooperate and work in groups, not all students subscribe to this behavior. The desire to stay ahead of competition limits team work.

The above discussions highlight the complexity of student group formation.

3.3.4 University Environment and Disciplines

The surrounding environment, the way that teachers manage their classrooms, and school disciplines are commonly considered central aspects in students' learning experiences. Johnson et al. concluded that whether a method is teacher-centered (transmission) or student-centered (conceptual change) depends on the type of subject. They suggested that in "hard" discipline subjects such as chemistry, medicine, and engineering, teacher-centered methods are widely used, and the student-centered approach is used for "soft" or humanities subjects such as history and social sciences. It has long been assumed that CL would be more suitable for humanities subjects and not suitable for "hard" subjects, which are seen as more academically rigorous.

Additionally, class size and level influence teaching approaches adopted by teachers. As class size and level increases, teachers tend to use a teacher-focused approach. Implementing CL with a bigger class size is not impossible, but it requires more effort since teachers need to ensure that students' behaviors are better managed. Therefore, some researchers highlighted the importance of receiving institutional support to adopt CL in higher education. One of the common obstacles teachers face during CL is a tight timeline to complete broad curriculum coverage in a semester term, as CL takes time for implementation. Consequently, some teachers may either not adopt or casually adopt CL in the classroom. This may lead some students to feel dissatisfied with CL, with the perception that CL is a waste of time. Belatedly, it may affect teachers' confidence in using CL, and they may resort to familiar instructional strategies such as traditional lectures.

3.3.5 Culture

Culture refers to "patterns of thoughts … systems of knowledge that inform us how we should interact and communicate with others as well as interpret other's behavior". Hofstede and Hofstede advocated that learning, teaching, and culture are strongly interrelated. Ignoring or devaluing cultural aspects will result in partial understanding or misunderstanding of how students learn and cooperate in CL. Cultural differences affect students' cooperation, learning, perceptions, interpretations of the learning environment, participation, motivation and learning behavior. While Johnson et al. reported that cultural diversity offers positive learning outcomes such as better interaction skills, sensitivity and respect toward other cultures, some have argued that stereotypes, prejudices, and hostility may occur in CL groups due to misunderstanding and conflicts arising among students from different cultures. One of the potential reasons is that language barriers may hinder "promotive interaction" in a working group, leading to unnecessary communication conflicts. Thanh et al. highlighted that Asian students tend to pay special attention to personal relationships as a crucial factor in determining group success. In addition, Tan argued that Asians' perceptions and responses to critical thinking differ from those in the West, as Asians view critical thinking as collegial, communal, emphatic, and interpersonal instead. On the other hand, Loh and Teo advocated that Asian learners are open to active and innovative learning approaches. Wong suggested that Confucian heritage is an integrated part of Chinese culture that influences teaching and learning. Bray et al. claimed that in Confucian heritage cultures, there is a high regard for education where teachers usually rank highest in the social hierarchy and students tend to show more respect to them. Biggs and Watkins added that in Chinese culture, teachers are well respected for their wisdom, and the wisdom of teachers is not to be questioned. Additionally, teachers retain much class control with students asking fewer questions to maintain harmony in class, and they speak only when asked to do so since doing so disrupt lessons. To some extent, asking questions is also considered to be a challenge to the authority of teachers, which may explain why some students display a passive attitude in class when they are not encouraged to speak out. Hence, Asian students may prefer a teacher-centered approach, expecting their teachers to be well prepared masters of knowledge delivering content in a coherent, systematic, and structural manner.

3.4   Summary

This review defines the meaning of CL and discusses theories relating to CL. Studies included in our review show that CL is an effective teaching and learning approach in higher education. Findings appear to be consistent with the notion that CL helps to enhance academic, affective, and social development of students. We identified some factors that strengthen or constrain the implementation of CL in higher education. Students, staff readiness, and group formation are considered as strengthening factors, whereas institutional factors are considered as constraining factors. The role of culture is considered as either strengthening or constraining, depending on how CL is valued in a particular cultural context. In terms of limitations, our choice to restrict our research to articles written in English might have led to an overrepresentation of studies from English-speaking countries, which may have influenced our summary. This study might provide some insight for future research to consider different contextual factors in determining the success of CL.

Chapter Four Review of English-majors' Listening Course

4.1 Significance of English-majors' Listening Course

Listening is one of the four basic skills, it should be mastered in the course of learning any language. With the rapid development of economic globalization, every country has to establish communications with other countries, and international communication has become a commonplace. English, the most widely used international working language, is a bridge for people to understand each other. Furthermore, English listening has been one of the most important communicative ways in which people express and exchange their thoughts. With the number of international communications largely increasing in China, the graduates with high proficiency of foreign language ability, especially the ones with high proficiency of listening abilities are badly needed in the nation as well as the society. In English teaching and learning, listening plays an important role. It is an important approach for students to develop language communicative competence and improve their ability of using English in practice. It is stipulated in the English Curriculum Requirements that English teachers should lay emphasis on the development of students' listening ability. According to the Requirements, listening has achieved the leading position in the whole system of language education and become the foundation of other kinds of language competence. So it is necessary for students to improve their listening competence. What's more, listening has accounted scores into the total scores for some colleges in the College Entrance Examination, so the college students are eager to improve their listening skill to get a high mark in the College Entrance Examination, which will be helpful for them to hunt a good job. However, a lot of students claim that the most difficult part belongs to listening comprehension in the College Entrance Examination.

Because some students think listening is too difficult to learn, and they will feel boring after a period of time. Some students even sleep over the class. If you ask them, they will say that they don't know what is being said at all. Of course, most of the students can offer the right answers to the listening exercises successfully, though they are not sure what the meaning of the whole passage is. That's the problem causing the huge gap between the demand and the present situation.

4.2　Significance of Implementing CL in English-majors' Listening Course

Cooperative learning (CL) in education originated in America and becames a widespread topic later in other European countries. In recent years, it has been regarded as an effective way for teaching and learning foreign language. CL can help students to solve the practical problems and develop their learning proficiency. CL has experienced a quick development. And a lot of substantial researches have been conducted at abroad. However, CL is still a new born thing in China. The studies on CL in China only mainly focus on theory instead of the practical advantages and significance. So, it is necessary for teachers to carry out CL in classroom to testify its effectiveness.

Everyone knows listening is very important for us to communicate with others in the daily life. You understand what's meaning of others by listening. So the students should master the skills of the listening. They will gain more, if they apply CL into their listening.

Because of this, more and more English teachers in colleges begin to choose CL approach to teach listening and pay more attention to CL. By interacting with peers, it is hoped that students will increase their listening proficiency, arouse their interest and promote their achievements. So, if CL is widely adopted, it can play a positive role in English listening teaching and become a helpful method for students in the future.

What's more, in China, most of the English listening teachers in colleges school still adopt the traditional teaching method. The students are tending to remain quiet while listening in traditional listening class, though they have got much information from the listening materials. They are reluctant to speak out what they have heard. The English they learn is called as "the dumb and deaf English" in an ironical but vivid way. Therefore, CL approach can change the embarrassing situation in China. CL can provides a better listening study environment for students and make students have a deep understand to what they have heard from their group members by commutation to each other. And CL can meet the requirements of developing students' listening competence and increase students' learning interest on English. Applying CL to college English listening teaching is beneficial to the students' improvement in English proficiency.

Therefore, the approach of CL can be thought of as a positive method for English listening teaching. Cooperative learning is an effective approach to improving college students' listening achievements and listening proficiency, and it also arouses their interest in English listening. It will become the main focus in future English listening teaching in college.

4.3   The Urgency of the Reform of English-majors' Listening Course

College English Curriculum Requirements (abbreviated as Curriculum Requirements hereafter), clearly states that the objective of college English teaching is to develop students' ability to use English in an all-round way, especially in listening and speaking. It has specified that assessment for learning should be divided into formative assessment and summative assessment and clearly defined and explained the features and methods of the formative assessment. This shows that the new model of English teaching will not focus exclusively on the result of teaching, but on the whole process of teaching and learning, and thus the combination of formative assessment and summative assessment will be applied to evaluate students' learning in an all-round way so as to facilitate them to demonstrate their multiple intelligences in learning. Another document to guide college English teaching is College English Teaching Guidelines (draft) developed by the Supervisory Committee for College Foreign Language Teaching in the Ministry of Education. With regard to evaluation and test for the course, it has suggested that various evaluative methods should be applied and the relationship between formative assessment and summative assessment should be well handled in order that the transformation from "summative assessment towards teaching results" into "formative assessment towards promoting course development" can be accomplished. On teaching methods, it is advocated that task-based, cooperative, project-based and exploratory teaching methods be employed in college English teaching to fulfill the teaching principles of "students-centered" and "teacher-leading" and realize the transfer from "teaching objectives-focused" to "students' needs-focused" in the whole teaching process.

Taking the above three governmental guidelines into consideration, college English teaching should meet the present English level of different groups of students and strive to develop students' English ability in an all-round way. However, in teaching practice, there are some conflicts between the guideline and the reality, which hinder the fulfillment of this objective.

Cooperative learning has been proved as an effective teaching strategy, which can take good care of students' different language aptitude and stimulate students' learning motivation, improve their communication skills, and finally enable them to build up a positive learning atmosphere. Formative assessment is a procedural and developmental assessment, which can effectively track and monitor the learning process of students. The application of formative assessment in cooperative learning can facilitate teachers to timely know the real teaching effects and to make corresponding and prompt adjustments if there is some problem arising in the students' cooperative learning.

4.4 Application of Cooperative Learning in English-majors' Listening Course

Cooperative learning has been proved to be effective in different areas and subjects, so this experiment is conducted with the purpose of proving its effectiveness in English listening teaching. How to apply cooperative learning to English listening teaching is the key issue. In addition, the systematic grouping and the reasonable listening stages is the precondition for successful cooperative listening.

4.4.1 Students' Grouping in Cooperative Listening

It is very important to build up a cooperative and dynamic listening group atmosphere in cooperative listening. In a sense, it even decides the whole cooperative classroom environment and the accomplishment of the teaching design. The purpose of group processing is to clarify and improve the effectiveness of the members in contributing to the collaborative efforts to achieve the group's goals. Generally speaking, cooperative learning groups are purposefully heterogeneous. It is usually made up of 2-6 members. Each member of the group is involved in cooperative tasks in order to achieve group goals. Their performances are evaluated by the performance of the whole group. Each one of a group is positively dependent on each other and accountable for the success of the whole group. The grouping process of the cooperative groups depends on students' achievements.

Of course, every student has different aspects, such as students' age, gender, language learning ability, English level, attitude, personality and so on. Teacher can divide students into cooperative groups in terms of their achievements, and take their differences into account for grouping. All in all, teachers should hold one principle: forming the groups depending on students' achievements will motivate students to actively take part in the process of learning, to help each other, to support each other, to cooperate with each other so that they can gain the goals of improving the individual and group study with the teacher's assuring a balanced mix of different groups, female and male, extroverted and introverted, advanced and slower in English. In general, when students are from various backgrounds or have different abilities, it is beneficial to the group.

The known research shows that a group made up of 2 to 6 members can be particularly effective, because they are small enough to encourage all members to participate, but big enough to benefit from multiple ideas and roles of the individual members. It can maximize each student's contributions to the groups and to provide each student with opportunities to learn from other individuals. In terms of one of the essential elements, small group social skills, a teacher needs to teach some specific cooperative skills and useful expressions involving those skills like how to express praise, agreement, suggestion and how to ask questions and respond to others. Group members can be of homogeneous or heterogeneous abilities depending on the kind of students in the class. The former makes the work of the teacher a lot easier, while the latter may require some careful planning on the part of the teacher to decide how to pair up students of high academic ability with those of average or low ability. When the group is made of students of high as well as low abilities, the brighter students can be used as peer tutors to assist the students of low ability. This extra duty should be regarded as a privilege, not an extra burden by the student peer tutors. In this way, the teacher's burden will be shared by all the students. The grouping arrangement does not have to be permanent. If a group works well together, it is fine. If the teacher notices any major personality conflicts or any discipline problems from any group, he or she should not hesitate to re-group them.

4.4.2 Stages of Cooperative Learning in English-majors' Listening Course

On the basis of Mary Underwood's theory, listening process is commonly divided into three stages. That is the 3-phase listening teaching: pre-listening, while-listening, and post-listening. The stages of cooperative learning in listening are similar to this traditional listening process. However, there are lots of differences between the traditional and cooperative listening process.

4.4.2.1 Pre-listening

In traditional pre-listening, teachers help the students prepare to listen. But in cooperative pre-listening stage, the group members try to consult relevant books or search the Internet before the listening class to get the reference information as much as possible.

The process is conducted by group members themselves, not by the teachers any more. Members of each group elect the representative to make a report regarding their group findings in class, which is quite beneficial for all the students to know the reference information. It is helpful to improve their communicative competence and to understand the meaning of the listening materials and promote their cooperative ability with the group members. The purpose is to motivate students, activate their schema, to add context, and make them prepare for necessary language so that the actual listening itself becomes easier. Then, the teacher as a guider should explain the new words, phrases and sentences about the listening material on the listening book. Combining the each group's finding outside class and the teacher's expiations in class is full-scale for students, and beneficial for them to prepare for the following listening.

4.4.2.2 While-listening

In traditional while-listening, the focus of students' attention is led to the listening text and the teachers can guide the students and help them understand it. But in cooperative while-listening stage, there are also cooperative groups in the teaching and learning process. It reflects that the students are the center in the listening class now instead of the teachers. The teachers need to play the recording in order, and tells students specific requirements about listening process.

For the first listening time, the students are not permitted to take notes or write anything. They only listen to the recording and get a general idea about the material. After the recording, the groups are given some minutes to discuss what they have heard and what strategy they have used in the listening just now. Some groups are asked to make the report to the class. Every student should think about the information they have heard and take a proper strategy for the following listening tasks.

For the second listening time, the students can take notes according to the filling-gap-practice about the text. The focus of students' attention is led to the important details or key words to help them with the reconstruction of the text. After listening for the second time, the students can be given a short 5-minute break to discuss their notes and identify the points they need to focus on. They analyze the different ideas and the key points that they have heard to put forward their opinion and make a report to the class and teacher.

For the third listening time students are given a chance to confirm the information and revise the notes if necessary. As a matter of fact, it is sufficient for students to listen to the recording twice. However, according to the different English listening levels of students in the class, the teacher can make the different choices of times to play the recording.

By this while-listening stage, the students are given a purpose to listen, and they can focus on the listening itself. By providing the type of task, students learn to listen for a purpose which better prepares them for listening inside and outside the classroom.

4.4.2.3　Post-listening

In traditional post-listening, the teacher used to help students to solve some questions when they meet in listening and give a proper and reasonable evaluation on the students' performances. And the teacher should give the right answers to the gap fillings and the whole original text. However, in the cooperative listening process, the post-listening is different, during which students are offered with opportunities to integrate what they have learned from the text into their existing knowledge and communicate with others using the information in the listening text. In cooperative post-listening, students work in groups and reconstruct the text based on their notes. Then students in the form of teams discuss what they have heard and attempt to produce a coherent text that closes to the original version.

After that, the teacher needs to select some teams randomly to present their group's workto the class. Finally, the students work together with group members to compare their versions of the text with the original and try to identify mistakes. Then, they need to analyze the reason of making mistakes and correct them. What' more, the students need to read the text again for improving their comprehension on the text. In the cooperative post-listening stage, there are many opportunities to integrate listening with the practice of language. These tasks in post-listening offer students an opportunity to integrate what they have listened with their own knowledge and meanwhile they can show their personal views and reactions towards what they have heard. By this way, it is easier to lead to much more interactions between students and keep their high motivation on listening, which is essential for the real language learning to occur.

4.5　Related Research on Application of Cooperative Learning English-majors' Listening Course Abroad and at Home

From 19th century till now, a large number of language educators and experts have been discussing and doing research on various kinds of language teaching methods. Some prestigious linguists have established several kinds of important language teaching and learning theories as well, among which CL is one of the most controversial and widely applied methods. As an important teaching and learning theory, CL has drawn the attention of numerous famous educators and scholars both from home and abroad in the past decades.

4. 5. 1 Related Research Abroad

In the late 1990s, the application of CL in second language class became pervasive. Numerous researches have proved that CL is of great effectiveness in second language teaching and learning if properly designed and carried out. Some experts also found that CL works a lot in enhancing language learners' learning competence by providing a great number of opportunities for them to interact and cooperate. Language learners are able to practice the target language through various interactive activities. Their language abilities as well as cooperating skills have been greatly improved.

In 1981 the Johnson's and their colleagues published a meta-analysis of 122 studies of cooperative learning using academic achievement as the outcome measure. They find cooperation is much more powerful in producing achievement than the other interaction patterns, and the results are held for several subject areas and a range of age groups from elementary school through adult.

Long and Porter observe and analyze the students work with groups in language teaching and state that CL provides language learners with enough opportunities to negotiate meanings with one another and thereby create the comprehensive input, which is salutary to second language acquisition. Johnson and Johnson investigate 193 studies to prove that cooperative learning is more effective than traditional forms of instruction, using group productivity as an outcome measure. They also find that in the process of CL, participants have high enthusiasm to the cooperative learning.

According to Olsen and Kagan, CL offer more opportunities for getting language development to second language learners than the traditional language teaching and learning pattern do. They said that, on the one hand, CL promote more active use of language when second language students try to apprehend or produce the language within their cooperative groups; on the other hand, CL enhance second language learners' abilities to express their own thoughts. They are more confident and mature to demonstrate, explain, and elaborate their points with free communication within the learning groups.

Slavin makes 99 comparisons of cooperative learning and other control groups. The review reveals that the overall effects of cooperative learning achievement are clearly positive as 63 of comparisons significantly favor cooperative learning and only 5 comparisons significantly favor the control groups. Ghaith argues that CL has a dramatic positive impact on almost all the variables critical to language acquisition including input, output and context. Crandall believes that Cooperative Language Learning promotes and upholds almost all of the favorable elements that correlate to each other positively to achieve language learning. He holds that CL reduces learning anxiety, increases enthusiasm, and promotes the development of positive attitudes toward language learning and the use of language. Cowie and Berdondini make an investigation and find that CL increase understanding of the interpersonal interactions taking place during cooperative group work among children given the opportunity to explore their own and others' feelings and actions to share their emotional responses with other members of the group.

Nunan notes, the new techniques for teaching listening comprehension focus more on training learners to utilize effective strategies for listening. These strategies are best learned in an environment of cooperative learning, which enable students to work jointly with their classmates and then benefit each other by sharing the strategies they employ during the listening. Patrisius presents a technique for teaching listening comprehension that combine cooperative learning with strategic learning, which is considered not only good to communication of learning strategies, but also for creation of a learning atmosphere conducive to feelings of togetherness among the students.

To sum up, CL has been studied and put into practice by a great number of foreign educators, scholars and teachers. Its theoretical system as well as specific teaching methods and learning principles have been improved gradually in the past years. It has proved to be an effective teaching and learning pattern and has been applied to more and more subjects.

4.5.2 Related Research at Home

Cooperative learning has been researched for a long and rich research history in foreign countries. Compared with these countries' investigation into cooperative learning conducted abroad, domestic study in China is much later and much limited.

In the early 1990s, CL was introduced to China. It has received much attention from scholars and teachers. And in the past years a lot of exploration and experimental researches have been made on it, which have been enriching the content of CL.

The first one is in Zhejiang. The earlier attempt of applying cooperative learning is found in the city of Hangzhou, Zhejiang province. The experiment is carried out by the former Hangzhou University, Tianchang Middle School and No. 1 Middle School of Hangzhou. The teachers of the experimental class state that cooperative learning in small groups can add vitality and dynamic to the class. When the experiment is completed, the teacher of the experimental class prove the cooperative learning is efficient to enhance the enthusiasm and interest, then the students increase the achievements.

The second one is an important and typical experiment, cooperative learning and practice which are conducted in 1993 in Shandong province. It is finished by the Chinese and foreign researchers. Many foreign experts take part in this experiment such as professor Slavin of Johns Hopkins University, a representative figure of cooperative learning, Johnson and Johnson from Centre for the Study of Cooperative Learning, University of Minnesota and professor Sharan of Educational Psychology in the School of Education, Tel-Aviv University, Israel. After six years, the experiment passes the province-level evaluation. There is a consensus among the experts about the experiment, which is successful in getting beneficial result in terms of practice and theory.

Wang and Miao advocate the interactive teaching of listening where pair work and teamwork are used between learners. Chen investigates into the effects of cooperative learning instructional approach on Taiwanese ESL students' English listening competencies and notes that cooperative learning approach do positively correlate with an increase in students' listening scores. Zhu proves that cooperative learning is proved to be effective in creating the supportive learning atmosphere and promote the students' motivation for English learning. The students adopting cooperative learning instructions express stronger motivation for listening learning. By using cooperative learning, the students' interpersonal relationship is enhanced and their social skills are also trained.

Zhang claims that cooperative learning situation generally provides a better listening learning environment for students. The most obvious implication for the use of CL in the second language classroom will seem that it will certainly improve students' opportunities for language use. Students will be placed in situations whereby they will be required to use the language as well as hear and comprehend. Wu and Chen argue that cooperative learning of College English Listening Course significantly stimulate the learners' English learning interest and motivation. In this way, they are more likely to learn automatically thus their English language communicative abilities get enhanced a lot. More listening skills can be instructed in this teaching mode. Li and Nie prove that cooperative learning is much more effectively than traditional teaching approaches in fostering some positive affective factors. And cooperative learning have been proven as an effective teaching and learning method in enhancing English learning autonomy, they are obviously relevant. It is beneficial to students for learning English.

Based on the studies mentioned above, cooperative learning is gaining more attention in English teaching. Many researches on CL have been carried out by researchers abroad and in China, but it remains to be seen what the condition of CL is in English classroom of college. Therefore, there is much need to carry out an experimental research on English listening teaching that fits college. At the same time, the researcher will put forward some useful suggestions on how to make English listening teaching more effectively.

With the introduction of cooperative learning to China, relative researches have been conducted in different aspects of teaching on various subjects and achieved positive results since the late 1980s, the early 1990. In recent decade, a growing number of empirical researches on cooperative learning have been carried out in College English teaching, however only a small quantity of researchers have focused completely on English listening teaching. Li put forward a multi-modal of autonomous and cooperative learning for College English listening teaching without making empirical studies. Dai explored the application of Jigsaw, one specific cooperative method, in her English listening teaching experiment with 72 English major students as the subjects. The experiment had proved that the jigsaw listening classroom was more effective and successful than the traditional one. More frequently, researchers just mentioned English listening teaching as a small part of English teaching practice such as Li's research and Peng's research. Currently, Chinese scholars and educators have done much work in the introduction and practice of formative assessment in the field of English teaching, of which the researches on the application of formative assessment in College English listening teaching only take a very small part.

The successful implementation of cooperative learning in English listening teaching largely depends on the design of cooperative tasks, the participation of students and the assessment methods applied by teachers. The innovation of the present research lies in the following two aspects. First, it explores the application of feasible and practical formative assessment methods for cooperative learning activities which are designed for College English listening with non-English major students as the subjects. Second, there are experimental group and controlled group in this research. Both groups will have the same cooperative learning activities in English listening teaching. The formative assessment will be applied in experimental group, while the traditional assessment will be employed in controlled group so that the effects of these two assessment ways can be compared after the experiment and thus the effectiveness of formative assessment in cooperative learning can be verified with facts.

To sum up, the empirical studies cooperative learning can be classified into three types in terms of research designing. First, the integrated application of formative assessment and cooperative learning was adopted in the experimental class, while traditional teaching method and summative assessment were applied in the control class. Second, cooperative learning was used in both the experimental class and the control class, while formative assessment was implemented in the experimental class and summative assessment was employed in the control class. Third, the application of formative assessment and cooperative learning were carried out in the experimental class without any control class. Qualitative and quantitative analysis were made on the data regularly collected from several rounds of teaching action. Common methods of data collection in these empirical studies included questionnaire, interview, test, class observation and various evaluation scales and the data were commonly processed by SPSS. The findings of all these research showed that students in the experimental class had greater progress in their academic achievements than those in the control class. Some positive changes took place on students' learning attitude, interest or cooperative ability. Besides, it was commonly pointed out that formative assessment and cooperative learning were really time-consuming and effort-consuming to both teachers and students. It was suggested by some researchers that the criteria of self-assessment and peer-assessment still needed to be improved and effective solution to the free-rider behaviors in cooperative learning activities had not been worked out.

4.6 Summary

First of all, CL approach in improving students' English listening interests is better than the traditional teaching approach. The CL approach to teaching English listening can stimulates students' interests and arouses their enthusiasm in listening. Meanwhile, it is proved that the CL approach can improve students' English listening proficiency more effectively compared with the traditional English listening teaching approach.

What's more, in cooperative learning, the changed scores of listening tests in heterogeneous groups are different from homogeneous groups. The heterogeneous group can improve students' listening scores more effectively than homogeneous group. So dividing students into the heterogeneous groups can get a better result in a period of time.

However, it needs to do the further research about whether the heterogeneous groups can always get the best result no matter in long-term or short term. Finally, cooperative learning is an effective approach which can make up for the weakness of other teaching approaches. The teacher becomes more enthusiastic and pays more attention to the students' creative ability and the efficiency of study.

Cooperative learning means that it generally provides a better listening study environment for students and the present research holds several meaningful implications for college school English listening teaching and even second language learning in China. CL can meet the requirements of developing students' communicative competence and increase students' learning motivation on English. Applying CL to college English listening teaching is beneficial to the students' improvement in listening proficiency. Therefore, the approach of CL can be thought of as a positive method for college English listening teaching. It will become the main focus in future English listening teaching in college. The result about the cooperative learning also will help students in college school improve their listening proficiency.

Teachers can be enhanced through the listening teaching approach from cooperative learning. This will be believed to be a beneficial attempt for the college school students to improve their language and cooperative learning abilities. At last, the results of heterogeneous groups and homogeneous groups in cooperative learning can give the edification to teachers for applying CL effectively. And this study can make up the gaps in this field and have both theoretical and practical significance.

Chapter Five Review of English-majors' Reading Course

5.1 Review of Reading

In reading process, readers are involved in an active interaction which Goodman called "psycholinguistic guessing game". The information from the materials and the background knowledge the reader brings with him to reading are combined. Many scholars have developed a systematical teaching and learning method in reading skills and models. In this part, the author explains the main theory of skills, reading models and related research of cooperative learning in reading in details.

5.1.1 Definition of Reading

Reading has been becoming the increasing important part in college English curriculum. As for college students, what they have to face is the master of English tasks. Reading has been one of the most urgent tasks in improving college English teaching. We have already built remarkable theories and guidelines in reading. Without any doubt that the combination of the cooperative learning and reading has been aroused intensively studies which focus on maximize its positive role. Jin believed that reading is a kind of ability in understanding and absorbing written information. It is the basic living way in human activity. It is an important way in knowledge acquisition, understanding of objectives and development of intelligence and sensibility. Chi asserts that reading is a tool from which people acquire useful information and understand author's intention. Reading is the process from which readers acquire what they need from materials. It is obvious that reading comprehension lay its foundation on reading; it collects fragments and systematizes them into integrated word information, then collects it with related science and professional knowledge, finally analyzes and constructs these information and knowledge.

Mitchell D C claims that reading can be defined loosely as the ability to make sense of written or printed symbols. And according to Grabe, "reading is a complex information processing skill in which reader interacts with the text in order to recreate meaningful discourses." Generally speaking, reading involves both the text and the reader, namely, the interaction between these two physical entities. It is the interaction between purpose and manner of reading, the interaction through reading strategies and the interaction through schema. To sum up, by reading, the readers can get necessary input to build up vocabulary, develop the strong sense of language, and improve the proficiency of foreign language defined reading as an interactive process in which readers interact with the text using their background knowledge.

5.1.2　Reading Skills and Models

Reading comprehension involves the most basic level of cognition and understanding of the information stated in the text, which is called explicit literal skills. Such kind of comprehension has been called "text explicit", in that information is directly stated in the text. Generally speaking, main ideas are always placed in a topic sentence, which occurred in the first or last sentence of certain paragraph. So just "read the lines" and understand what the author is trying to convey. Main ideas are the hardest one to conquer because it may not be directly provided in one paragraph. Beside cognition of main ideas in a text, detailed information is used to support the main ideas, the information is always stated in several modes, such as some scientific or numeral data that helps clarify the conclusion, gives ways of solving one problem, and shows practical examples that help to explain the concepts. Skilled readers are good at identifying details that lead to a full and accurate understanding of the main idea.

In what ways students can acquire reading skills provide a hard nut to teachers who are responsible for improving students' reading competence. Some relevant questions which are asked before, during and after reading give learners preconceived segment to form the rough sketch of the whole text. It is important to accelerate students' reading skills in cooperative learning. The teachers should prepare questions in advance in order to maximize the effects of CL. Those questions give students distinct guidance in understanding of the text. Students who can not make full use of reading skills show their anxiety and dislike toward reading. Lacking of reading skills in English is of the first fatal factor in college students' English reading.

Implicit skills refer to reasoning and analysis of information which is implied in materials. It requires teachers focus on the facilitation of students' integrated inferential skill and critical competence. Making inferences requires the learners to supply information that the author does not provide directly . However, the problem is that students will not always supply inferences spontaneously or automatically. Most implicit obscurity can not be attained through "reading the lines". Research has shown that this kind of skill can be improved by strategies such as cloze exercise, teacher-student interview, questions aimed at inferential understanding, background discussion that fosters prediction, and encouragement of self-monitoring procedure. Implicit information always emerges when it makes paragraphs more reasonable and understandable, so it better to give close attention to some marked tone in whichreaders are provided what is actually meant. Besides, pre-reading helps students get connection between what they have learnt and what they will complete. It is "reading beyond the lines" which aimed at forming hypothesis and setting related thinking logic.

These two skills in reading should be drilled repeatedly in classroom with researcher's interference. In cooperative learning, the author will pay attention to the training of the two skills, for instance: getting main ideas form the text, listing major details to the main ideas, giving a summary of each paragraph and the text. Some examples will be introduced in the following chapter.

Researchers believed that the models of reading can be divided into three types: bottom-up model, top-down model and interactive model. Some scholars give the definition of reading as decoding process; they think reading is a process which transfers written sign into oral form by visual sense. Some researchers lay emphasis on the process of semantic acquisition, they state that reading is the reconstruction of the new information and the preexisting information that the learners has stored. Learners modify background linguistic points and current predictions with the new information encounter in the assigned materials.

Bottom-up model refers to individuals learn words at first such as syllable letters, morphemes, phrases, discourse markers, grammars etc. and then understand sentences, analysis the whole text meaning is followed. The final stage is the Vocal system, where the reader utters orally what has first been accessed through prints. Because the process starts with sensory and proceeds upwards to more abstract levels, it has been called a bottom-up model of reading. It is the process of decoding individual linguistic units and reconstructs them to the largest unit. However it is less effective if skilled readers are imposed upon bottom-up model.

Top-down model is also called concept-driven processing. Readers analysis the discourse on the basis of background knowledge preoccupied inside reader and certain reading strategies. As they proceed, readers match author's intention with what they expect and hypothesis according to their background knowledge. According to Frank Smith, reading is a psycholinguistic process; he cites four fundamental characteristics of reading: reading is purposeful, selective, anticipatory and based on comprehension. So top-down model give more importance on knowledge related to the text but not just literal meaning. Thus the key point is to strengthen students' cognitive competence and skills in stimulating the ability in analysis the new and background knowledge. Readers are considered as the main force in reading process. Some specific word, sentence, chart or even a sign would possibly activate related knowledge in readers' mind.

Interactive model mixed bottom-up and top-down model in a more reasonable way, that is to say, we can not use only one fixed model in one discourse. It reorganizes and maximizes the positive effects from former two models. Aderson points out that it is the interactive model that describes reading process accurately.

That is to say, interactive model refers to the combination of bottom-up decoding and top' down analysis. Single bottom-up and top-down model can not create satisfactory reading comprehension; only by combining them together can a reader understand reading passages better.

5.1.3 Studies of CL in Reading Teaching

Many researchers have been exploring whether the CL has positive effects on reading through theoretical and empirical studies. Many scholars and teachers have been doing researches into reading instruction.

Slavin contends that CL activities are particularly appropriate in areas such as reading comprehension and social studies. Rasinske and Nathenson Mejia argues that reading instruction should promote cooperative ability and social skills. Some state that "the program which stresses the cooperative and social skills of reading is the most appropriate" as Goodman stated. Wang holds that peers serve as an audience with which students can share what they have read, cooperative learning has been shown to reduce anxiety, increase motivation facilitating the improvement of positive attitudes toward language learning, and encourage perseverance in difficulties of learning language. All of these researches are the confirmation of the positive effects of CL on the learners which provide US solid evidence in implementing CL in classrooms.

Cohen proposes that CL represents a change from teacher-centered teaching model to learner-oriented learning method, raises new problems to educators. From where the author stands, problems do exist in the whole process of CL. Such as group students of different levels in a reasonable way, choose material that can be easily done and so on. Lin and Wang suggests that English teachers of senior high school should comply with three basic principles when implementing cooperative learning: practical cooperative learning activities, proper sequence as well as compromise principles. Practical CL activities refer to the teachers should refrain from the formalism and make sure all plans and activities are in the service of English teaching goal. Teaching plans should cover different levels which accord with different levels of students. That is to say, teaching aims and activity designs should be practical. In proper sequence refers to the teacher should choose appropriate material which inspire students think back previous knowledge with what they just learnt. Compromise principle refers that the teacher should make full use of cooperative learning with other methods in English class. The effects of CL method should not be overly exaggerated.

Though many studies show that cooperative learning improves student's ability in English in middle school or primary school, as to the researches done at home, a few are focus on English reading in college. And fewer are empirical and persuasive study. It still needs to be verified in different aspects in college. English reading in college would have great improvement only when an increasing number of researchers offer their hardships unselfishly.

5. 2   Theoretical basis of CL in Reading Teaching

Cognitive development theory is put forward by Piaget and Vygotsky, through which people obtain a more complicated knowledge from the world. The initiator believes that it is the cooperation in a certain environment that impels social-cognitive conflict occurs and results in cognitive disequilibrium, which in turn stimulates perspective—talking ability and cognitive development.

According to Piaget, cooperative learning has played important role in people's cognitive and intellectual development. Equilibrium occurs when we are aware of new experience, if not, we have to change the idea that we have gained before and use a more complex thinking mechanism in order to avoid disequilibrium. As a result, cognitive development is seeking the balance point between the subjective individual view and the objective world around people. Vygotsky's theories elaborate that knowledge is social, constructed from cooperative efforts to learn, understand, and solve problems. The distance between individuals' actual mental level and the level they reach in solving problems with the assistance of others is the Zone of Proximal Development (ZPD). That is to say, when one person can benefit more from the interaction of cooperative with more capable people, he is in the potential level of the ZPD. So, making full use of cooperative learning in English reading is depend on the interaction with more capable partners rather than by individuals alone.

In cooperative learning classrooms, students should be encouraged to discuss with their partners who can stimulate them to adopt the new and sophisticated knowledge and abandon the wrong. The further and higher level of cognitive development internalizes sophisticated information then uses them in the subsequent reading tasks. Students in cooperative learning should be given more time in solving problems in reading tasks. It is the process of bridging the gap between the students' skill and their potential skill; it is also the process of enhancing their ability in solving the problems alone.

5.3 Reading Ability

Being an important way of obtaining information and knowledge acquisition, reading has been becoming the increasing important part in college English curriculum, especially for English-majors. English reading is not only one of the purposes, but also the main means of learning English. English reading ability is one of the most important language abilities that students must master because it's the basis for the development of other abilities. Reading ability is a comprehensive ability of positive thinking activities. Generally speaking, reading ability should mainly include the following aspects.

5.3.1 Ability of Guessing the Meanings of the New Words

The students should take a guess when they come across new words. They should learn how to find the clues given by the author or sometimes, they can figure out the meaning of a new word by looking for clues provided by context. Context sometimes supplies definition clues or sometimes example clues. It's better for students not to interrupt their reading to look up new words in dictionaries. It will affect the reading speed and break the coherence of the reading materials. The ability of guessing the meanings of the new words can effectively improve the reading efficiency.

5.3.2 Ability of Reading Comprehension

Reading comprehension involves the most basic level of cognition and understanding of the information stated in the text. The students should have two kinds of skills. One is called explicit literal skill. Sometimes the comprehension can be called "text explicit", in that case information is directly stated in the text and students should be able to find it. The other is called implicit skill and it refers to the ability of reasoning and analysis of information which is implied in materials. In this case information is not directly stated in the text and students should make inferences to obtain information that the author does not provide directly. Most implicit obscurity can not be attained through "reading the lines". A good ability of reading comprehension shows the students' integrated inferential skill and critical competence.

5.3.3 Ability of Fast Reading

Fast reading is a vital ability for students to quickly get knowledge and information. It's a fast filtering process of information and a product of knowledge surge era. Fast reading requires the students to be highly concentrated on the reading materials and keep active thinking during the reading process so that they can select the most valuable things from the reading materials as quickly as they can. Fast reading focuses on reading speed and efficiency. The goal is to be fast in three aspects, namely fast reading, fast comprehension and fast memory. It should be silent reading because the symbols are directly reflected to the brain through the visual. Fast reading needs students to combine brains and eyes perfectly and students should master overall reading ability just like watching a picture or a movie.

5.3.4 Ability of Summarizing the Main Ideas

Skilled readers are good at identifying details that lead to a full and accurate understanding of the main idea. Generally speaking, main ideas are always placed in a topic sentence, which often occurred in the first or last sentence of certain paragraph. So students sometimes can just "read the lines" and understand what the author is trying to convey from the topic sentences. But sometimes the main idea is hard to get because it may not be directly provided in one paragraph. In that case students should learn how to identify the main ideas in a paragraph or a text according to the detailed information used to support the main ideas, such as some scientific or numeral data that helps clarify the conclusion, gives ways of solving one problem, and shows practical examples to explain the concepts.

5.4 Significance of Reading Course for English-majors

The numbers of different theories of reading is simply overwhelming: what it is, how it is required and taught, how reading relates to other cognitive and perceptual abilities and so on. All these aspects are important.

Brown states that from the psycholinguistic perspective, the readers are actively involved in the process of deriving and assigning meaning since reading is a problem-solving behavior. In this sense, reading is the interaction between the readers and the text. Reading is a kind of speech, which is used as a tool of communication between readers and authors. Besides, it is a high level mental activity of the nervous system. Cognitive linguistics attaches great importance to the process of the internal mental activity of reading. They believe that reading is the process of interaction between language and thought. They think of reading as an activity in which the readers will try their best to combine their knowledge with the textual information. In a word, reading is general cognitive, problem solving ability.

As one of the four skills of language learning, English reading plays a very important role in English learning. It is viewed as an important standard to assess one's language ability, the most important way to continue to develop one's language knowledge and an essential tool to provide large quantities of input for students with which the expected learning outcomes can come out. Besides, in order not to fall behind the advanced technologies in the world and to master the latest development, most of the people need to read the original information. Students especially need to develop specific English reading skills to understand reading materials. For them, reading is also a basic way to master a language. It is generally acknowledged that by far reading skill is the most important one of the four skills in a second language learning, especially in EFL. By reading, students can not only obtain language input but also expand their vocabulary, more importantly, they can broaden the scope of knowledge and understand western culture. It is no exaggeration to say that learning to read has been the core of education for a long time.

Extensive reading is an obligatory course for English-majors and it plays a very important role in the whole stage of undergraduate. As one of the main skill courses, extensive reading is designed for English-majors for four continuous semesters and the significance can be concluded.

5.5 Requirement of English-majors' Reading Course

The socialist market economy calls for new requirements of professionals withChina's college English training model. To meet the need of the country and society for qualified professionals in the new era and keep up with the new development of higher education in China, the new National English Teaching Syllabus for English Majors was issued by the Ministry of Education in 2000, which gives a detailed description about the cultivation objectives and the course design requirements for English-majors.

According to the new National English Teaching Syllabus for English Majors, extensive reading aims at developing students' reading comprehension and improving students' reading speed as well as developing students' ability of careful observation and logical thinking such as assuming, making judgment, analyzing, summarizing, inferring and testing. Extensive reading also aims at improving students' reading ability including guessing the meanings of words, fast reading, scanning and skimming. Extensive reading helps students to enlarge their vocabulary and absorb the language and background knowledge.

The new National English Teaching Syllabus for English Majors puts forward the following requirements towards students. The first level: To be able to read the plain materials like Thirty-Nine Steeps (abbreviated version) and Reader's Digest at the reading speed of 70-120 words per minute, understanding the main ideas and master the main plot or argument. The second level: To be able to read international news like US Newsweek and the original literary works like Sons and Lovers. On the basis of understanding, the main ideas should be mastered and the correct evaluation should be made. Reading speed is 120-180 words per minute with accurate understanding of not less than 70%. The third level: To be able to read materials of moderate difficulty with about 1000 words within 5 minutes and grasp the main ideas. To be able to read editorials and political essays like Times or New York Times. To be able to read the original literary works like The Great Gatsby and historical biographies like The Rise and Fall of the Third Reich. On the basis of understanding, the main ideas, discourse structure and stylistic should be correctly analyzed. Reading speed is 140-180 words per minute with accurate understanding of not less than 75%. The fourth level: To be able to read materials with about 1300 words and grasp the main ideas. To be able to read editorials and book reviews, biographies and literary works of medium difficulty published in English-speaking countries. The theme, discourse structure, language features and rhetorical devices should be correctly analyzed. The highest level: To be able to read materials with about 1600 words, grasp the main ideas and understand the facts and details.

Extensive reading for English-majors is very important and the requirement for it is really hard to meet. In this case, the effective teaching approach is urgently needed. This research tries to apply CL theory in extensive reading teaching for English-majors to meet the high requirement.

5.6 Summary

This chapter mainly talks about the definition and related studies of the cooperative learning at home and abroad, elements as well as techniques followed to draw the comprehensive outline to research procedures. Many researchers hold that cooperative learning can be a positive motivator in students learning. Large numbers of scholars have put cooperative learning into various subjects. All of these positive results will be used for reference in present research. However, the author would make some adjustment in process of CL. Integrating the use of cooperative learning into college English reading class will be of great value to students' improvement in various aspects. Through the review of the CL and reading, whether cooperative learning method is effective or not to college students still need to be verified.

Chapter Six Review of English-majors' Writing Course

Writing, being an important way of language output and one of the most basic language skills, plays a crucial role in English learning. However, for many Chinese college students, their English writing performance is still not satisfactory. In the light of the present situation, more and more scholars are committed to seeking an effective teaching method for English writing. And lots of researches have indicated that cooperative learning, as a creative and effective teaching theory and strategy, has great influence on improving students' English writing ability. Therefore, it is imperative to carry out the study dealing with the implementation of cooperative learning theory into English writing teaching to improve students' English writing performance.

6.1　Importance of Writing Course

As a main way of language output and one of the most important means of successful communication, writing is an indispensable part in foreign language learning. Swain claimed that, English writing is the reflection of learners' comprehensive English language competence and when the learners compose, the defect of their language ability will be exposed. As a result, English writing is extremely essential for language learners. In view of that, both English teachers and learners in China have spared much effort to improve English writing teaching and learning, but the current situation of Chinese students' English writing ability is still far from satisfactory, especially for non-English majors. In order to solve this problem, researchers have devoted themselves to focusing on teaching strategies and methods. Among them, cooperative learning is proved to be one of the most effective ways for language learners.

Actually, cooperative learning originated in America in the early 1970s. Since the concept was put forward, it has been employed in many aspects of foreign language teaching and learning, such as listening teaching and learning, reading teaching and learning and so on, and lots of successful outcomes showed its effectiveness. Encouraged by the positive results, many researchers have made attempts to apply cooperative learning theory in writing to help students acquire better writing skills and hence improve their writing performance.

According to Swain, applying cooperative learning in writing means that learners are required to work in pairs or small groups to produce one written text cooperatively. That is to say, learners need to work together during the entire writing process, and each member in the same group should be responsible for their final product.

In terms of the importance of cooperative learning in writing, lots of researches have indicated that cooperative learning contributes to language learners' writing ability from different aspects. Specifically, in cooperative learning class, the assigned small groups provide students with a relatively relaxing learning environment and ensure them to have more opportunities to express their own opinions, which can help students reduce their sense of writing anxiety, enhance their writing enthusiasm and thus foster their positive writing attitude. Besides, in the process of cooperative learning in writing, students are expected to consider not only what to write but also how to write, which encourages them to explore different language structures, stimulate their writing inspiration, expand their writing perspectives, and hence improve their writing performance. Furthermore, many researchers also pointed out that applying cooperative learning in writing is efficient in developing students' communication ability, enhancing interpersonal relationship and nurturing cooperation consciousness.

As a matter of fact, with the growing wealth of studies abroad, domestic researchers also begin to investigate the value of cooperative learning in writing. However, looking through the previous relevant studies, it is discovered that the researches concerning cooperative writing in China are not as universal as those in foreign countries, and there are few empirical studies related to the effects of cooperative learning on Chinese students' English writing performance, especially on non-English majors. In view of this, it is essential to carry out such an empirical study, and thus an effective approach to improve non-English majors' English writing ability will be found out.

6.2　Writing Theory

6.2.1　Definitions of Writing

As one of the most important ways for people to communicate, writing is a complicated and creative process of language communication. In terms of its definition, lots of scholars hold their own opinions. In the following part, the author will list some famous scholars and their representative definitions, which are displayed in Table 6.1.

Table 6.1　Definitions of writing Scholars Definitions of writing

Scholars	Definitions of writing
Judyand Judy(1981)	Writing, we believe, is a liberal art-it functions as a source of self-discovery as well as of learning. Writing is a means of learning, often an act of discovery. Writing is not just dressing up thoughts. It is inextricably bound up with the making of ideas. Writing needs not to be just an onerous task of transcribing thoughts to paper. Because it involves human communication and interaction, it should be a pleasurable, personally valuable activity.
Neufeld (1985)	Writing is the process of taking an idea from inside of one's head and putting it into a code so that it can be shared with others.
Grabeand Kaplan (1996)	Writing can be defined as who writes what to whom, for what purpose, why, when, where and how.
Sperling (1996)	Writing, like language in general, is a meaning-making activity that is socially and culturally shaped and individually and socially purposeful.
Hamp-LyonsandKroll (1997)	Writing is an act that takes place within a context, that accomplishes a particular purpose, and that is appropriately shaped for its intended audience.
Hyland (2005)	Writing is the act of making up correct sentences and transmitting them through the visual medium to manifest the graphical and grammatical system of the language.
Xiao Fushou (2007)	Writing is the art of putting words together to form sentences and/or paragraphs in an active, creative, and recursive process of communication in which the writer uses a conventional graphic system to convey a context-based message to a reader in a grammatical and rhetorical manner.

From the definitions above, we can find that although the scholars differ in their words when they make a definition for writing, they agree to the view that writing is a complicated process concerning not only the linguistic activities, but also the communicative activities. That is to say, on the one hand, writing is a linguistic process, which involves its own stages, planning, drafting and revising. On the other hand, writing is an interactive process, which serves as the communication between writers and readers with particular purposes.

6.2.2　Main Writing Approaches

Though writing is so important in language communication, the writing ability of most EFL learners is not satisfactory. To improve their writing performance, more and more researchers have devoted themselves to studying writing approaches in recent years, and three main writing approaches have attracted their attention. They are product approach, process approach and genre approach. Each of them emphasizes different aspects of writing and has its particular advantages and disadvantages. The three main writing approaches and their characteristics are presented as follows.

6.2.2.1　Product approach

As the most common approach of traditional writing teaching, product approach was widely used before the mid 1960s based on the behaviorism theory, which regards writing as a process of stimulus and response. That is to say, the teacher provides students with a stimulus, and then students make a response by imitation. In 1982, Pincas pointed out that the implementation of product approach consists of the following four steps: familiarization, controlled writing, guided writing, and free writing. During familiarization stage, learners are expected to be conscious of certain features of a chosen composition. In the controlled and guided writing stage, learners are trained to practice the writing skills and then imitate. After this stage, in which students receive enough training and master essential writing skills, they can enter the last stage in which they are expected to write freely. In Chinese college English writing class, product approach usually includes three steps as follows. Firstly, the teacher offers a writing sample, analyzes it and explains certain writing skills. Secondly, students are asked to write sentences, paragraphs and compositions through imitating the writing sample. Finally, the teacher evaluates students' writings and gives them some comments mainly on spelling, grammar, and the usage of words.

From the steps described above, we can see that product approach has obvious disadvantages. On the one hand, it regards imitation as the basic way of writing and lays much stress on the final products, so that it ignores writing process. On the other hand, in this approach, teachers are the center of the class who control the whole writing process, while learners are only passive recipients lacking the writing creativity, which not only reduces learners' writing interest but also hinders the communication between teachers and learners in writing process.

6.2.2.2   Process approach

Process approach was proposed by Wallace Douglas in the 1970s based on the interactive theory, which regards writing as an interactive activity instead of an individual activity. Unlike product approach, what process approach emphasizes is the creative process of writing rather than the final products. According to Tribble, the implementation of process approach includes the following four steps: pre-writing, drafting, revising, and editing. Among them, pre-writing is the first stage for learners to make some preparatory activities to collect writing material as much as possible. Drafting is the second stage for learners to write the first draft according to the writing material collected in the pre-writing stage. Revising is the third stage for learners to discuss with peers and revise their first drafts based on the teachers' feedback and peers' advice. The last one is editing stage, in which learners finish and hand in their final products.

To sum up, process approach attaches importance to the writing process, and the active participation of learners instead of the dominant role of teachers, which contributes to stimulating learners' writing enthusiasm and promoting the interaction between learners and teachers in writing process. However, every coin has two sides. Process approach also has its disadvantages. Firstly, it overemphasizes writing process but doesn't give enough attention to the basic language knowledge, such as the appropriate usage of words, grammar, and organization in writing. Secondly, process approach requires learners to experience four writing steps, which is time-consuming and not suitable in Chinese college English writing class. Thirdly, it's rather difficult for teachers to give instruction and evaluation to every student in a large class.

6.2.2.3   Genre Approach

Genre approach was put forward by Jim Martin and the otherAustralia scholars in the mid 1980s based on genre theory, which emphasizes on teaching different types of writing genres. This approach is viewed as the combination of product approach and process approach. It not only focuses on learners' language knowledge, but also stresses the writing purpose in particular language situation and social environment. The main procedures of genre approach consist of the following three steps: modeling, joint negotiation, and independent construction. At modeling stage, the teacher introduces a genre by providing a model text, analyzes the schematic structure of the genre, and then points out the social purpose of the text. At joint negotiation stage, the teacher and students write together by using the same genre of model text, including reading, studying, collecting and collating writing materials. And at independent construction stage, students are required to choose a title, analyze it and write individually by using the same genre of model text.

In summary, genre approach helps learners to understand the texts deeply and comprehensively, acquire the characteristics of different kinds of writing genres, and realize various writing communicative purposes. However, this approach may lead to the repeated use of the same writing patterns, which will make learners feel boring and dull in writing class. What's more, genre approach attaches great importance to the analysis of writing genre instead of giving sufficient attention to language accuracy and language skills.

6.3 Relationship Between Cooperative Learning and Writing

From the review of main writing approaches above, it is easy to find that the three writing approaches all have their disadvantages and are not very efficient methods to improve learners' writing performance. Thus, in this paper, the author tries to apply cooperative learning theory in writing and spares no effort to find a better way to improve Chinese college non-English majors' English writing ability.

As we all know, cooperative learning is more than just a kind of small group activity, but an organized, systematic teaching and learning strategy in which group members work together to achieve a common goal. As one of the most effective instructional strategies, cooperative learning has been widely used in many disciplines. In order to improve learners' writing performance, in recent years, more and more researchers make efforts to apply cooperative learning in writing, and many researches have been done to study the relationship between cooperative learning and writing. And applying cooperative learning in writing is also named as cooperative writing.

In Flower and Hayes' viewpoints, writing is a process of socialization. They advocated cooperative learning and encouraged students to discuss writing topics actively, share knowledge and support group members in the writing process. Through cooperative writing, students can realize how to revise and evaluate their own and other students' compositions, and how to communicate and cooperate with others more efficiently.

Similarly, Zamel also regarded writing as a cooperative and collective process instead of single behaviors. In 1984, Damon proposed that cooperative learning contributed to promoting students' self-esteem, arousing their writing interest and improving their writing achievements. And Hyland also pointed out that, in the process of cooperative writing, students had the opportunities to read and evaluate other group members' compositions, find errors and give them peer feedback, so that they could avoid making the same errors in their own compositions in the future study. Besides, Jacobs and Ball carried out a survey to study the effect of group activities, and the results of the survey also revealed that group activities can better cultivate the sense of cooperation among students.

In addition, at home, Wang did an experiment and proved that cooperative learning is helpful to improve the reading and writing achievement of high school students. Dang Long made an empirical study of cooperative learning in writing and confirmed that cooperative learning is beneficial for classroom organization in the writing class. He also deemed that in the process of cooperative writing, group members discuss with each other and learn from each other, which is conducive to developing their habit of thinking and reducing their writing anxiety.

Based on the review above, it is clear that cooperative learning in writing is an effective method for writing teaching and learning. Firstly, it is helpful for improving students' writing ability, because in the writing process, the group members can assist and encourage each other, learn others' strong points and apply what they have learned in writing to promote themselves. Secondly, it transforms the traditional teacher-centered teaching mode to student-centered. That's because in small groups, students are encouraged to discuss, to express, to communicate and to cooperate, which changes the teacher's leading position and facilitates the interaction between teachers and students.

What's more, cooperative learning provides students with a harmonious and active classroom atmosphere, which is beneficial to reduce writing anxiety, motivate writing enthusiasm and hence cultivate positive attitude towards writing.

6.4　Previous Relevant Studies both at Home and Abroad

Ever since it emerged inAmerica in the early 1970s, cooperative learning has become one of the most creative and practical teaching and learning theories and has been widely employed in many countries. Slavin once said, "research on cooperative learning is one of the greatest successful stories in the history of educational research."

Because of the significant effect of cooperative leaning on second language acquisition, lots of scholars both at home and abroad have been devoting to conducting researches from different perspectives to investigate this learning mode. In view of the importance of writing, more and more researchers have been involved in applying cooperative learning in writing and achieved excellent effects. In this part, a brief review of the previous relevant studies both at home and abroad will be presented.

6.4.1　Relevant Studies Abroad

Studies on cooperative writing in western countries began in the 1980s. Since the concept was put forward, a large number of researches have been carried out by many scholars who are committed to finding efficient ways to improve learners' writing performance. The researches can be shown in the following three aspects.

6.4.1.1　Studies on cooperative learning

In the last few decades, cooperative learning has aroused much attention in the western countries. A great many researches concerning the effects of cooperative learning on learners' performance have been done with different subjects and perspectives. In addition, a number of researchers make efforts to explore learners' attitude towards cooperative learning. Kagan deemed that second language acquisition is determined by a complicated interaction of many factors, such as, numerous of input, output, and different context variables, and in this process, cooperative learning has a significant positive effect on almost all the factors related to language acquisition. Therefore, it can be concluded that cooperative learning is a suitable and practical method for second language acquisition.

Ghaith and Yaghi maintained that cooperative learning provided language learners with a well-suited classroom atmosphere, so as to encourage them to communicate, cooperate, solve problem, and think creatively.

Storch investigated the effect of cooperative learning on learners' grammatical accuracy by using three different tasks: a cloze task, a text reconstruction task, and a composition task. The results indicated that students working in groups had more opportunities to discuss their answers, and their productions were more accurate than those who wrote individually, which proved that cooperative learning made more contribution to the improvement of learners' grammatical proficiency than individual learning.

Kim chose 32 Korean students as subjects to examine the impact of cooperative learning on second language vocabulary acquisition, and the results revealed that learners who worked in groups preformed better in vocabulary post-test than those individually, which proved that cooperative learning helped to facilitate learners' vocabulary acquisition.

6.4.1.2 Effects of cooperative learning on learners' writing performance

Concerning the effects of cooperative learning on learners' writing performance, a lot of scholars devoted themselves to exploring the studies in this field and carrying out the researches for students with different levels, so as to find an effective way to improve learners' writing ability. Zammuner investigated the differences of draft and revision conditions between cooperative groups and individual students, and then concluded that cooperative learning in writing could help to enhance students' overall writing quality. Wigglesworth and Storch compared cooperative writing with individual writing through an argumentative essay. The results revealed that though the groups spent more time finishing the writing task than individual students, the essays produced by cooperative groups were more accurate than those written by individual students. Narges did an experiment to explore the effect of cooperative learning on Iranian EFL learners' writing accuracy. The research results showed that the learners in experimental group performed better than those in control group, which demonstrated the important role of cooperation in writing.

What's more, Masoumeh investigated the effect of cooperative learning and group work on EFL learners' writing performance at elementary level. The results indicated that the writing performance of students in experimental group and control group was both promoted. But the students in experimental group improved more significantly than those in control group. Therefore, the researcher concluded that cooperative learning and group work was conducive to enhancing EFL learners' writing performance at elementary level.

6.4.1.3 Learners' attitude towards cooperative learning in writing

In addition to the study of the effect of cooperative learning in writing, students' attitude towards cooperative learning in writing also has attracted great attention by numerous of scholar. Storch required 23 students to finish a writing task with 18 students in pairs and 5 students alone, aiming to investigate students' attitude towards cooperative learning in writing. In an interview, most of the students in pairs reacted positively. They thought that cooperative learning in writing gave them opportunities to share each others' ideas, broaden their knowledge and learn how to cooperate with others. In particular, they believed that writing in pairs was beneficial for their grammatical accuracy and vocabulary learning.

Elola and Oskoz used web-based social tools wikis and chats to study the attitude of senior Spanish students towards cooperative writing task. Most of the learners in this study agreed that writing in pairs helped them enhance their writing content and organization. Besides, they felt that the process of cooperative writing was an enjoyable experience. Ali Shehadeh also conducted an empirical study to explore the students' attitude towards cooperative learning in writing. In this study, 38 freshmen in two intact classes at a university were chosen as subjects, and most of the 18 students who wrote in groups held a positive attitude towards cooperative learning in writing. They insisted that cooperative learning in writing enabled them to generate ideas, pool ideas together, discuss and plan, generate their text collaboratively, give feedback immediately to each other, and put their text in better shape. In addition, some students deemed that cooperative learning in writing not only helped them promote their writing skills, but also enhanced their self-confidence.

6.4.2 Relevant Studies at Home

Compared with the researches abroad, studies on cooperative learning in China are comparatively later and rarer. It is in the late 1980s and the early 1990s that cooperative learning was first introduced into China and the value about applying cooperative learning in teaching began to be explored. The earliest provinces attempt to implement cooperative learning in China were Zhejiang and Shandong.

Wang Tan, supported by some famous foreign experts in cooperative learning field, such as professor Slavin, Johnson and Johnson and professor Sharan, presided over the project—the Research and Experiment of Cooperative Learning in Shandong province, which spread theimplementation of cooperative learning in the elementary and middle schools in provinces like Shandong, Zhejiang, Beijing, Tianjin, and so on. Gao F P investigated whether it was feasible to apply cooperative learning into college English majors' writing, and hence found out that cooperative learning could stimulate students' writing enthusiasm and encourage them to participate in English writing class actively. Chen Y L employed cooperative learning approach into a college English writing classroom, and found out that the writing performance of both high-level students and low-level ones was enhanced. Thus the researcher concluded that compared with traditional writing approach, cooperative learning was an efficient and beneficial method to raise students' writing achievements. Zhang X L conducted an experiment lasting for one year with the purpose of investigating whether cooperative learning was a useful way to improve college English majors' EFL writing ability. In this study, 123 English majors of four classes were divided into two control classes and two experimental classes, which employed traditional writing method and cooperative writing method respectively. After analyzing the students' writing tests, the researcher discovered that the pass rates of two experimental classes were 73. 8% and 91. 8% while the pass rates of two control classes were 64. 5% and 80. 6%, which proved that cooperative learning significantly improve students' writing ability. Besides, through the analysis and comparison of the results gained from the questionnaires and interviews, the researcher found out that cooperative writing could help the students enhance interpersonal relationship, care and encourage each other, and thus strengthen their writing interest.

Zheng G R studied the effectiveness of cooperative learning in writing and concluded that this kind of writing approach was helpful to stimulate students' thinking, encourage them to discuss actively and learn from each other in vocabulary, organization, and grammar. In addition, taking the argumentative essays as an example, he clarified how to use cooperative learning to improve the quality of college English writing teaching and the students' English writing ability, so as to build a new, effective and student-centered teaching mode for college English writing. Wu Y H and Gu Weixing used the second language writing anxiety scale to conduct a questionnaire survey for 454 non-English major college students, aiming to examine the effect of cooperative learning on students' English writing anxiety. The results before teaching experiment presented that the English writing anxiety of non-English majors was in a high level. However, from the comparative analysis of paired samples before and after the teaching experiment, they found out that cooperative learning could significantly reduce the general anxiety, physical anxiety ($P < 0.05$) and the evaluation anxiety ($P < 0.01$) for non-English major students in their English writing. In addition, the interview results of 12 experimental students showed that students held a positive attitude towards cooperative writing.

Wu R H and He Gaoda did a writing teaching experiment, which lasted for 15 weeks among 120 freshmen in one college to explore the impact of cooperative learning on EFL writing. And the research results revealed that cooperative learning could help students overcome writing anxiety, reduce writing errors, enrich writing contents, and then improve students' language skills and writing strategies. In addition, it could also promote the realization of the three functions of language output.

6.5　Principles of Implementing CL in Writing Course

6.5.1　Reasonable Grouping and Dynamic Management

The grouping principles should be followed: (a) Same group but different quality: group students of different learning levels, help each other in a homogeneous group to achieve common learning goals, which is conducive to mutual help and mutual promotion between students; (b) Group homogeneity: Maintain the balance between the group and the group, choose a good group leader. (c) Adopt a dynamic management approach, which is to allow every student to have the opportunity to be a group leader and group member. The adjustment of group members can expand the contact surface of different students, and then allow students to learn from each other.

6.5.2　Equal Participation and Timely Regulation

Cooperative learning is not a unilateral cooperation of students. Teachers should also participate in students' learning activities. Discussions between teachers and students are one of the important principles of cooperative learning. Teachers must change their traditional concepts, change the original command-based teaching to discussion-based teaching, shift the focus down, stand on the same starting line with the students, and truly become the guides and friends of the students' learning.

6.5.3　Equal Opportunities and Diverse Forms

To carry out cooperative learning in classroom teaching, teachers should provide every student with equal opportunities to participate in the various classroom teaching processes, and ensure that every student actively participates and exercises in the cooperative learning process. This will not only exercise the courage of students, but also can improve students' expressive ability and sense of cooperation. While giving equal opportunities to students, teachers should organize a variety of classroom activities so that students who don't like to talk, have difficulty speaking, are introverted, and dare not boldly express themselves have the opportunity to speak, express themselves, and exercise themselves. After experiencing the first success, students have the confidence and courage to continue learning.

6.5.4　Combination of Individual Study and Group Cooperation

In the process of cooperative learning, each student assumes certain responsibilities and tasks, and at the same time shoulders the tasks of the entire group. This requires each student to study on their own, but also not to ignore the cooperation with group members, that is, to combine individual study and group cooperation to achieve the original purpose of cooperative learning: the common improvement of the performance of the individual students and the group members.

6.6 Three steps of Implementing CL in Writing Course

6.6.1 Pre-writing

Before writing, the teacher should group the students according to their comprehensive English ability, and then select topics of interest to the students and assign the writing tasks to the students, let the group brainstorm ideas, and respectively state their personal ideas on the topic of the composition, and State the advantages and disadvantages separately, and finally reach an agreement based on the best.

6.6.2 While-writing

The members of each group discuss the subject matter, paragraphs, and logic of the article, express their positions and opinions, and then a classmate writes the outline of the paragraph of the article, and then supplements and polishes the article based on the writing materials given by the teacher. During the discussion, each student should separately state their writing skills on the topic of the essay that has been given, for example, what topic is better and easy to score, and what position should be adopted in the essay to capture the teacher's psychology and be closer to social reality. Which kind of related words are more likely to get high scores, how to avoid words that you can't write or call them correctly, etc. During the composition process, each student conducts a collective comparison and discussion on each sentence, analyzes which sentence or sentence pattern and word score the highest, and finally writes the most perfect sentence under the premise of unifying opinions. Finally, some cohesive words are used to integrate the article. In the writing process, students can use divergent thinking to combine the viewpoints of the article with social hot issues, and write from multiple angles and Omni-directional ways to make the article stand out.

6.6.3　Post-writing

After writing, each group exchanges essays and conducts mutual approval. When incorrect vocabulary and grammar are involved, they are marked out, and then the group evaluates the essays of other groups. When evaluating other groups, other students listened carefully to the evaluation, and then self-evaluated the composition of their group. After the correction and evaluation are completed, the composition is handed over to the teacher. The teacher then revises, reviews, marks errors and grammatical rules, and makes a final comprehensive evaluation of each stage and each student's performance in the entire teaching model process, and finally distributes the composition to each group. The relevant group finally discussed how to make the modification more perfect, and the final draft was finalized. Although the cooperative learning theory emphasizes the cooperation between students and teachers, it does not deny the cultivation and exertion of students' individual thinking ability. It is a teaching method and learning method and behavior of writing using the principle of cooperative learning.

6.6.3.1　To stimulate students' interest in writing

Writing itself is boring and boring. Teachers can only fully mobilize students' enthusiasm for writing by letting students be interested in the content of writing. If you want students to effectively exert their subjective initiative to carry out meaningful learning and writing in a cooperative learning atmosphere in a group, then, first, the teacher's teaching attitude must be serious, and the teaching must be passionate and effective. Teachers should motivate every student and let them actively participate in English writing; Second, the teacher's introduction to writing must be close to the students' real learning and life, so that students can effectively use what they have learned in the classroom. The center and main body of the article should be integrated. so that the articles written by students come from life and are higher than life; third, through scientific and reasonable grouping methods, every student can actively participate in writing activities. Teachers should create a democratic and harmonious learning atmosphere and teaching environment, so that writing becomes an activity, not a task; fourth, teachers should pay attention to the small progress made by each group or even each student in the writing process, and appropriately ask and praise, and cannot ignore the questions, it will effectively let students experience the joy of learning and the joy of success, thereby enhancing students' interest, enthusiasm and confidence in English writing.

6.6.3.2　To develop writing skills as a guarantee

English writing teaching using cooperative learning theory should start from the three stages of pre-writing, in-writing and post-writing, and scientifically and rationally integrate the relevant skills of English writing through the three stages of writing, and cultivate students' mastery and use of writing skills as well as generative ability, through the language output process of writing, students will be trained to accurately apply the input writing skills to the future writing process, and to train students' comprehensive skills of writing.

6.6.3.3　To improve students' writing ability

The ultimate goal of using cooperative learning theory in writing teaching is to improve students' writing ability. No matter what kind of teaching method the teacher adopts, the ultimate goal is to improve students' writing ability, with a view to improving writing scores and total English scores. In the process of cooperative learning, the discussion among students helps to broaden the students' thinking ability and enrich the writing content. Group cooperative learning enables students to study together, discuss together, and improve together in a relaxed and pleasant classroom atmosphere, which not only improves students' writing ability, but also improves students' cooperative ability. Multiple evaluations also provide students with great space and opportunities for learning exchanges and ability improvement.

6.6.3.4　To focus on multiple evaluations

The writing teaching of cooperative learning is a way of multi-person participation and group cooperation, so the teacher's evaluation methods are particularly important. For teachers, it is necessary to affirm and praise each student's learning attitude and ability as well as the positive role played in the group, but also to affirm and praise the group's learning attitude and coordination ability. In the process of group discussion among students, teachers should carefully observe the performance of each group or even each student in each group in the process of class discussion and group discussion, such as whether they actively participate and whether they actively speak. While using simple language to guide, teachers should also make positive evaluations for the purpose of encouragement and appreciation through various methods and channels. Since it is the teaching of writing in cooperative learning, in the evaluation, the teacher should guide the students to conduct self-evaluation, intra-group evaluation and inter-group evaluation. In the process of evaluation, a positive evaluation method is used to create a harmonious learning atmosphere for students, which not only cultivates students' sense of competition, but also cultivates students' spirit of cooperation, enhances the ability of individual learning and group learning, so that students can practice their own sense of collective honor.

6.7   Summary

In this chapter, we have made a general overview on the theories relevant to the current study. Firstly, a comprehensive summary of the definitions and characteristics of cooperative learning are made. Secondly, a thorough review of the definitions of writing and three main writing approaches are introduced. Thirdly, an in-depth analysis on the relationship between cooperative learning and writing is presented. And these three sections will serve as a theoretical foundation for the present study. Lastly, a large number of previous relevant studies with different focuses both at home and abroad are illustrated.

Writing and stimulates students' writing motivation. After the implementation of the cooperative learning writing mode, the group discussions organized by teachers greatly aroused the students' enthusiasm for writing, allowing students to actively participate in the discussion in the writing class, discovering their shortcomings and mistakes in a timely manner, and correcting them in time. It greatly stimulated the students' enthusiasm for learning; increased the frequency of students' frequently used words. The use of cooperative learning in the writing classroom has significantly increased the frequency of using common words in writing; and improved students' writing skills. Through cooperative learning, students' writing skills have been improved. In the classroom, the teacher provides every student with many opportunities to learn the writing knowledge and skills of others, so that every student gains the writing wisdom of everyone invisibly, thus improving every student's writing ability. Cooperation can promote the development of students' intelligence and help students with poor learning ability learn to learn. Cooperation contributes to the development of individual students, and it also contributes to the improvement of collective cohesion.

To sum up, there is no doubt that the previous studies have laid a solid theoretical and pedagogical foundation for future researches. However, from the overall review above, we can easily find that though the studies both at home and abroad related to cooperative learning and writing are relatively extensive, the researches about cooperative writing are quite limited and rare. What's more, compared with previous studies abroad, the studies on cooperative writing conducted in China began late and more empirical studies need to be carried out. In view of this, it's still necessary for the author to make up for the gaps and confirm the research findings of former studies by implementing the empirical study to investigate the effects of cooperative learning in writing performance for non-English majors, so as to find an efficient way to improve their writing ability.

Chapter Seven Review of College English-majors' Translation Course

7. 1　The Importance of Cooperative Learning in English-majors' Translation Course

7. 1. 1　Improving the Efficiency of Students' English Translation

Cooperative learning is to strengthen communication between students, enhance team awareness and overall collaboration. Through group assignment, it can improve students' problem-solving ability. English translation is a difficult point in learning. Through cooperation between students, problems can be solved more easily, thereby improving students' learning efficiency.

7. 1. 2　Improving the Initiative and Enthusiasm of Students' English Translation

In the previous English classes, teachers used more mechanical methods to educate students. English as a foreign language, students have been using Chinese since childhood. When they first came into contact with English, they naturally seemed relatively unfamiliar. The fall has caused the difficulty of promoting college English in the classroom, and the translation level of students is not good enough. Faced with such problems, through new methods and the use of teacher-student interaction methods, students communicate with teachers in the classroom to gain knowledge. This method conforms to the playful nature of modern students, and allows students to play in the process of entertainment. Students can feel the happiness that English brings to them, which will help improve the learning atmosphere in the English classroom, and the students' enthusiasm for learning English will increase, and their academic performance will also be improved.

7.1.3　Facilitating the Development of Teachers' Teaching Tasks

The use of teacher-student interaction methods in college English classrooms can attract students' enthusiasm for learning English. In the classroom, there is no longer any phenomenon such as students messing up or sleeping in class. The atmosphere in the classroom has been improved between teachers and students. The dialogue between teachers and students can shorten the distance between teachers and students. Studentswill feel that taking English class is just like playing games with the teacher. They are more willing to take English class. At the same time, students will say goodbye to mechanical memory. Words, after all, those traditional teaching methods have completely failed to keep up with the development of modern education. Students are keen on learning English. This is also the development of English teachers' teaching work, and the teaching work becomes more relaxed.

7.2　Application Steps of CL in English-majors' Translation Course

There are many teaching modes in translation teaching, and different teaching goals correspond to different teaching methods. Cooperative learning is a commonly used teaching mode in higher vocational translation teaching. This teaching mode is usually divided into the following six links in teaching practice:

7.2.1　Preparation Before Class

Cooperative learning means that the teacher assigns learning tasks, and the students cooperate with each other to complete the learning tasks. The teacher first divides the students in the class into groups of the same number. The number of groups should be as even as possible. If there are groups with fewer people than other groups, teachers should make up for small groups in terms of grading. Each group chooses a leader to assist the teacher in teaching tasks. At the beginning of the semester, if the teacher is unfamiliar with the students in the class, you can first group according to the number of students. At the middle of the semester, then adjust the group members according to the specific situation of the students. The preparation work also includes the preview of the text. The day before the class, the teacher releases the learning task to the group leader, and the group leader subdivides the learning task to each group member or leader. To complete together, the learning tasks are usually based on pre-study texts and familiar words.

7.2.2 New Lesson Import

The main reason for dividing students into groups is to improve the ability of students to unite and cooperate. Therefore, teachers should set aside time for the group to report on the learning situation before each class. This can not only check the group's preview status, but also make the students like group learning. Learning is not a display but has practical significance. After the student representative reports, the teacher will ask questions about the pre-study task to further check the pre-study situation, and at the same time, it can also help the students to learn with questions.

7.2.3 Group Exercises

Students learning in a group can learn from each other's learning methods and ideas, and members can also point out each other's strengths and weaknesses, which is conducive to the progress of students. In addition, completing translation tasks in groups can save the class time when practicing.

Before starting, the teacher will distribute translation materials to each group, and then give the specified completion time. The materials that the teacher sends to each group are selected, the difficulty is moderate, the length is the same, and the group of a class. The materials used are usually separated by an article. If they are not selected from the same article, the topics of the materials will be similar. The same materials are used in every two groups to facilitate comparison between the translations. After reaching the material, you can choose whether each member translates a short paragraph and finally integrates it together or all members translate the whole material together. When the group members are practicing individually, the teacher should move around the class more and pay attention to the situation of each group. The group conducts guidance.

7.2.4　Group Report

After the exercise, representatives of each group will report the results of the exercises and read the translation results of the group. Teachers can display the original text through multimedia teaching tools so that students can compare the details. After the group representatives have finished reading, members of other groups will do the work. Comment out, if you have any questions, you can also ask. After a group's report is over, a group member representative who translates the same material will make the report. Other students can understand the difference in translation styles between the two groups. The representatives of the two groups can also explain the translation ideas of the group. After the group report, the teacher will comment, point out the highlights and shortcomings in the translation of each group, and finally explain and guide the complete material. Teachers must first introduce the source and background of the article, and then teach students the corresponding skills. In cooperative learning, students can first get inspiration and ideas from the group members, and get knowledge supplements. After the teacher's explanation, the students' knowledge and skills will be further improved. Cooperative learning can bring double progress to students. Everyone's thinking activity is limited, and the amount of knowledge is also limited. If you let each student do an exercise individually, the student's speed will be very slow. Moreover, due to the existence of knowledge blind spots, the final translation will not be of good quality. And through cooperative learning, students can make up for each other's technical deficiencies, gain new inspirations in discussions, and find the right methods. Cooperative learning can improve learning efficiency, and students' thinking sparks can collide with each other in cooperation. However, the communication between students will also cause differences and collisions due to their own habits and personalities. These are the possible results of cooperative learning. In group study, each member should learn to put the interests of the group as the most important thing, and be patient for this. In this process, students can become mature and understand the meaning of teamwork.

7.2.5　Class Summary

After each class is over, the teacher should guide the students to summarize the content of the class. A complete class summary has a very important role. On the one hand, it can deepen students' understanding of teaching content and promote the absorption of English translation knowledge.

On the other hand, teachers reviewing knowledge points can also cultivate students' ability to refine key points, thereby promoting the improvement of students' learning ability.

7.2.6　Homework

Teachers should assign appropriate homework is an important method and means to test students' learning situation and expand students' learning content. Although the formal class is over, for students, the study of English translation is far from over. Teachers should arrange some extracurricular homework reasonably, starting from two points when assigning them: First, the teacher should be able to examine the content of the classroom and the absorption of students; second, the teacher should be able to extend the knowledge of students appropriately.

7.3　Problems of Cooperative Learning in English-majors' Translation Course

Practice has proved that the application of cooperative learning to college English translation teaching has a positive effect on the improvement of teaching effects and the improvement of students' learning ability. However, affected by the traditional education and teaching model, there are still some problems in the implementation of cooperative learning in college English teaching.

7.3.1　Inadequate Prepare of Teachers

Traditional college English translation teaching can be completed by teachers relying on textbooks, teaching plans, blackboards, chalk and theoretical lectures plus exercises after class. Teachers play a leading role, and teaching and learning are unilateral acts. Affected by this kind of educational philosophy, teachers have problems such as lack of initiative, insufficient curriculum preparation, or insufficient reserves of their own Internet technology capabilities when implementing cooperative learning. The selection and push of video or PPT content before English translation classes is the key to the implementation of English translation cooperative learning. Although the Internet provides a wealth of translation teaching resources, very few can adapt to the courses taught and the level of students. It requires processing, editing, and processing, which requires a lot of time and effort. Teachers themselves have heavy teaching and research tasks, so many English translation teachers are unwilling to try cooperative learning, or they are not sufficiently prepared in the implementation process. In addition, cooperative learning has changed the dominant position of teachers. With the student as the center, the authority of teachers has been challenged. Especially in English translation, there may be multiple translation methods for the translation of a sentence or paragraph. Although the answer given by the teacher is standard, it may not be the best. In the discussion and revision of the students, it may even subvert the answer of the teacher. English translation teachers have brought challenges.

7.3.2 Lack of Motivation for Students to Write

Although cooperative learning is student-centered and emphasizes the student's dominant position, it also requires students' active cooperation while giving students freedom, and requires students to have a certain ability to learn independently. However, under the influence of traditional exam-oriented education, college students in our country have always been passive learning and lack the awareness of active learning. Therefore, some students do not take the initiative to learn the teaching content pushed by the teacher before class in the English cooperative learning teaching, and cannot complete the learning tasks on time, so that they cannot integrate well with other students in the classroom learning and discussion stage. The translation task is temporarily played in the classroom, and even the teacher's teaching process cannot be implemented smoothly. Some students also subjectively evaluate the teaching level of teachers in the after-class feedback stage, which brings interference to the true evaluation of the teaching effect of cooperative learning in English translation.

110

7.3.3　Unscientific Curriculum Design

Many translation courses aren't systematic and forward-looking, and extremely important translation practice courses account for a small proportion, neglecting the translation training of Chinese classics and culture. Some colleges and universities even lack courses on English and Chinese language comparison and cultural comparison. These unreasonable courses are not conducive to students' knowledge structure and future development. Secondly, and many textbooks for translation majors are outdated and have not included new language terms, translation software equipment is outdated, and the utilization rate is not high. Students cannot feel the convenience of machine translation and the shock of big data operations.

7.3.4　Outdated Teaching Methods

In previous translation classrooms, teachers required students to practice translation within the specified time, and then used the reference translation as a template to explain translation skills. This kind of teaching only uses the reference translation as a ruler, allowing students to mechanically master translation skills and theories. His translation behavior is very passive, and it is difficult to integrate translation skills and theories and apply them flexibly. Translation teaching is limited to the classroom and does notfully expand extracurricular resources.

7.3.5　Lack of Practical Learning Opportunities

The social practice of translation majors is very important. However, due to the lack of relevant practical opportunities and the limited ability of graduates, translation majors often choose English teaching as their practice activity, even if they enter translation companies and other institutions. The difficulty level is not suitable or the industry terminology and translation technology are not understood, and the company is not entrusted with important tasks, and can only do some sorting and proofreading work.

7.3.6　Lack of Language Test Objectives

As a professional assessment method, the translation qualification examination is also a nationally recognized talent evaluation system. It is not only a stepping stone for graduates to enter the industry, but also a touchstone for testing the translation ability and quality of translation staff. In actual teaching, teaching and language testing should be "seamlessly" connected, so that the two complement each other to achieve common development.

7.4　Strategies of Cooperative Learning in English-majors' Translation Course

7.4.1　Training Professional Teachers

In addition to translation teachers who need a solid foundation in English language knowledge, common translation skills and theoretical professional knowledge are also necessary for the course. At present, many translationteachers in China are graduates from teachers majors and have not undergone systematic translation learning and translation practice. The experience is very limited. Therefore, relevant colleges and universities can provide translation professional teachers with opportunities to go out to learn and communicate, sothat teachers' knowledge system can be updated in time and effectively used in teaching practice activities.

7.4.2　Making Scientific and Practical Curriculum

The purpose of translation teaching is to cultivate students' bilingual conversion ability through the teaching of theory and practice courses. The setting of translation courses should serve the cultivation of translation ability, and the means used should be continuous "teaching" and "practice". In view of this, relevant colleges and universities can carry out practical courses such as "translation training" and "translation skills training" according to students of different grades and different professional levels. During the teaching process, teachers need to submit electronic versions of all students in accordance with the new translation test requirements. Homework, let students find the feeling of CATTI test machine test. Only through a lot of translation training can students internalize the steps, methods and theories of translation. Applying what you have learned is an eternal learning theme. In the practice of dynamic translation, students' practical ability and the spirit of mutual assistance and cooperation can be cultivated.

7. 4. 3   Increasing students' Practical Opportunities

For translation colleges, translation majors must have abundant and sufficient practical activities to improve students' knowledge structure. Schools can actively use the Internet and real-world resources, actively seek opportunities to cooperate with the website, and allow students to conduct group assignments on website content classification, translation, and revision. These practices have greatly broadened students' learning horizons and promoted their translation interests.

According to the " Outline Requirements " of the translation qualification certificate, CATTI level 3 is quite difficult to be between professional level 4 and college English level 6, and students are required to have a certain amount of practical experience in interpretation and translation. Undergraduate translation colleges should actively take into account the actual situation of their students, launch CATTI exam courses or related elective courses in the junior year or earlier, focusing on the question types and the setting of points, and should also pay attention to the examination process and Mastery of skills.

7. 4. 4   Standardizing the Teaching Process

In order to ensure the smooth implementation of cooperative learning in college English translation teaching and the standardization of teaching, the teaching process should be unified and standardized. The teaching and research section should regulate which teaching platform and duration range of the teaching materials that teachers use in advance when implementing cooperative learning teaching, and promptly and actively answer students' questions to form effective communication and interaction. In the internalization stage of classroom knowledge, the teaching department needs to standardize the teaching department how to play the guiding role of the teacher in the discussion and interaction between the English translation teacher and the students, and whether to give reference answers to the discussed questions. Due to the diversity of college English translation, if teachers do not strengthen guidance, it is difficult for students to distinguish what is an excellent translation sample, and they do not know the true level of their translation. For the reflection and evaluation after class, the teaching department should also standardize, such as how to use feedback, and the standards of assessment. Only by standardizing the teaching process can we effectively ensure the application of cooperative learning in English translation teaching, and thus ensure the improvement of teaching effects.

7.4.5 Optimizing Teaching Content

Although our country has been learning English in the basic education stage, English translation is less involved, and there is a large gap in the level of translation among students. Students with a better foundation can complete basic paragraph translation, while students with poor foundation have problems even in single-sentence translation. Traditional translation teaching adopts a "one size fits all" approach, and all students receive the same translation teaching content. The introduction of cooperative learning in college English translation teaching can send different levels of teaching content in the pre-class stage according to the actual level of students, and students can perform selective translation learning according to their actual situation, so as to meet the actual needs of students of different levels Demand, to avoid the phenomenon that some students with poor foundations gradually become bored with translation learning because they can't keep up with the teaching progress. Teachers should pay special attention to the selection of pre-class materials when conducting cooperative learning teaching. According to the actual selection of teaching, not all knowledge points are suitable for cooperative learning. Materials are integrated into thematic education, so as to achieve the optimization of teaching content.

7.4.6 Making Teaching Goals Clear

In order to cultivate excellent English language and literature professional translators, college teachers must change the traditional teaching methods, and set clear teaching goals for the actual classroom teaching content, so that students can learn the knowledge of English language and literature professional translation and consciously To cultivate students' literary literacy, students also need to learn more English translation skills in actual teaching. In addition, the school should also develop an effective training plan, through this method to train interdisciplinary English language and literature professional translators. Let teachers and students know that the main reason why the school arranges this course is to enable them to become outstanding talents who are helpful to the development of the country after graduation, and to know how much they will promote the development of society in the future.

In the context of the new era, teachers should absorb the essence of traditional translation teaching models, and combine constructivism as the theoretical basis of interactive translation teaching. For example, in teaching, teachers can use the "Translation Workshop" training method that is well received by teachers and students, allowing students to understand and familiarize themselves with the requirements of the translation business environment through group cooperation, and let students experience the process of teaching methods. Translators need to have a solid foundation in bilingualism and inter-language translation skills. These abilities can be cultivated through a variety of extracurricular activities, such as translating news on campus radio stations into English, because students have participated in these activities personally.

7.4.7 Improving the Evaluation System

Scientific and reasonable teaching evaluation is helpful for teachers to clarify the problems in the teaching process, and then improve them, and it is also very helpful for the improvement of students' learning ability. The teaching effect of cooperative learning in college English translation teaching should be evaluated from both teachers and students. After completing the teaching of a certain knowledge point, teachers should reflect on whether their own teaching concepts, teaching methods, knowledge reserves and teaching implementation process are perfect, and should also communicate with other teachers, and discover their own problems through the comments between teachers to further improve the curriculum. For students, according to their own learning situation, whether the cooperative learning teaching adopted by teachers really improves their own translation ability, and making an objective and true evaluation is not only conducive to the teaching of teachers, but also conducive to the improvement of their own translation level. Of course, the best learning feedback is to consolidate the basic translation knowledge you have learned before class. The process of teacher-student interaction in the classroom can help students solve difficult problems encountered before and improve their own translation capabilities.

7.5   Translation Capabilities of English Majors

With the development of economic globalization, the frequency of exchanges between my country and other countries has also increased. The society puts forward higher standards for training translators. Therefore, it is necessary for teachers of various universities to explore a set of effective teaching methods to train English majors into professional translators who meet the needs of social development. At present, due to the outdated training model, the translations of graduates cannot meet the needs of the translation industry. In the context of the new era, the society's demand for translation works has increased dramatically, and at the same time, new requirements have been put forward for the training of translation talents. "Bilingual plus skills" compound talents have become the characteristics of the new era. The new requirements have also promoted innovation in the training methods of colleges and universities, including cultivating teachers' teaching ability, innovating teaching methods, increasing students' practical opportunities, and setting language test goals, etc., in order to improve the quality of training translation talents.

The translation field is service-oriented that has emerged with social development and needs. Due to the in-depth advancement of the "Belt and Road" initiative, the exchanges between China and the countries along the route have become more frequent. As a bridge between people of different languages, translation has its social important position self-evident. The society's demand for translators exceeds the speed and quality of training talents. Compound translators have become the school's training goal. How to scientifically and systematically improve the quality of translators' training is a practical problem that colleges and universities need to solve.

In the new era, the demand for language translation has exploded, and the demand for legal translation, classic translation and other industries has increased. Translation works are diversified and complicated. The translation capabilities of talents must shift to complex capabilities, including the following aspects.

7.5.1 Sound Physical and Mental Quality

As a qualified translator, a healthy body and mind is very important. With the further advancement of globalization, the amount of tasks for various cross-industry translations is increasing day by day. Translators need to face a large number of high-quality translation tasks. Without a healthy body, they will not be able to complete all kinds of interpreting tasks. Without strong resistance to pressure, one is not able to cope with high-concentration interpreting work. Good psychological resilience and adaptability are also required by translators.

7.5.2 High Ideological and Political Awareness

Good ideological and political awareness determines the translator's values, world outlook and professional outlook. Facing various translation tasks, the translator needs to have a clear political stand and a high degree of political sensitivity. It is necessary to maintain positive energy in the communication activities so that translation tasks can be completed well.

7.5.3 Proficiency in the Implementation of Translation Theories and Techniques

Translation theories and language use are the in-depth laws of any language transformation, which play a directional guiding role in the translation process of the translator. In addition, the technical penetration of various translation materials makes translation theories and techniques useful.

7.5.4 Solid Translation Skills

In the past, translators only needed to master the text conversion software Word, but now the continuous introduction and use of big data and terminology databases require translators to work efficiently and accurately in line with technology. A qualified translator needs extensive information searching capabilities. Modern translation technology equipment and software operation skills are the working methods and tools for translators in the new era.

7.5.5　Comprehensive Professional Ability

It is widely known that, translation work also has industry codes of conduct and ethics. When dealing with translation tasks and translation teaching, translators need to have a high degree of professional responsibility and a serious and rigorous work attitude, good communication skills and a team. The spirit of cooperation is also the requirement of the translation team for talents.

7.6　Summary

As the cooperative learning model has been developed in many universities, the advantages of this teaching model have become more and more obvious. For the English translation teaching of higher vocational colleges, the application of the cooperative teaching model has brought the following inspirations:

First of all, it is necessary to broadly understand cooperative learning. Cooperative learning aims to improve students' practical ability and teamwork ability, so that students can integrate into the team more easily. Therefore, higher vocational colleges must be aware of the advantages of cooperative learning and apply it to daily teaching. Secondly, according to the characteristics of professional teaching, this teaching mode should be appropriately adopted. For English translation teaching, due to its own unique characteristics, students cannot be encouraged to fully adopt cooperative learning methods during translation teaching. For example, when students are completing their own thesis, this method is not very suitable. Finally, add a part of the comments on the cooperative learning process, that is, in the process of cooperative learning, students are usually the main body and the teacher is the assistant. However, some students may lack team adaptablity or cooperative communication skills, making it difficult to gain more in the entire cooperative learning. Therefore, teachers should guide students to comment on each other after cooperative learning, and provide targeted supplements after students' comments, so as to promote the improvement of students' cooperative learning ability.

Although the cooperative learning model has many advantages that can improve student performance and classroom learning, most vocational students are still accustomed to the teacher-centered passive learning model. Therefore, there is some resistance in the implementation process. First of all, in the initial stage of the implementation of the common education model, some students often did not cooperate, resulting in slow progress in classroom teaching, and sometimes activities could not even be carried out. At this time, teachers should be patient and correctly guide students to actively participate, so as to successfully implement the cooperative teaching model in the subsequent teaching process. At the same time, teachers should adjust the teaching plan in time according to the characteristics of the students. After a certain adjustment period, the students will gradually realize the benefits of cooperative learning. Second, the cooperative learning model emphasizes collective learning, and the learning effect of a single student is easily overlooked. When teaching translation, the teacher is not only the disseminator of translation skills, but also the leader of cooperative learning training. Teachers should not only help students set clear learning goals, but also focus on adjusting learning content, learning progress, and teaching methods. In teaching, teachers should gradually adapt to the change of roles, that is, from the initial evaluator to the task organizer, integrate into the teaching process and communicate with students on an equal footing. Since the cooperative learning model emphasizes the orientation of students, teachers only play the role of macro-control, and these adjustments are usually implicit.

In translation teaching, the role of a teacher is not only a trainer of translation skills, but also a mentor and collaborator of students' learning. It cannot be superficial work. For example, teachers should arrange teaching time reasonably. They should not sing a one-man show, nor can they symbolically ask a few outstanding students to answer questions to show that there is an interaction between teachers and students in the classroom. Teachers should clarify learning tasks and allocate them reasonably according to the needs of students and the actual situation of learning, and strive to meet the requirements of all students, and strive to be for all students, teach students in accordance with their aptitude, classify guidance, and comprehensively improve students' translation level based on group cooperation The learning mode has changed the inherent teaching mode that the class was used as a"static collective background" in the past, making all students a "dynamic collective force" for completing learning tasks and playing their respective roles. Through teaching practice, the cooperative learning teaching model can indeed improve students' English translation ability, and at the same time effectively improve their ability and awareness in communication, management, collaboration, innovation, and the spirit of unity and cooperation. Research on this topic has established effective collective learning strategies in the practice of English translation teaching, and it has been confirmed that the teaching model based on cooperative learning can provide students with more learning motivation and clearer learning goals. By mobilizing students' internal factors, they can develop their independent learning and joint learning abilities, and give full play to their dominant position in the learning process, effectively improving students' ability to use English.

All in all, in the English translation teaching of many universities, the teaching mode of cooperative learning has been partially promoted. The cooperative learning model can not only create a learning environment for mutual exchange and discussion, and continuously deepen students' understanding of knowledge points, but also teach students how to learn effectively in practice, thereby fostering good habits of lifelong learning and interesting learning. In the future, as some restrictive problems are solved, the practice of cooperative learning will be more perfect.

Chapter Eight Implementing CL in English Majors' Reading Courses

English is a challenging task in education where students read lots of specific information related to their major studies. Engineering students need English as means of efficient communication not only for their jobs but also to connect with a world where the English language is one of the official languages of the science community. Therefore, there is a need to provide students with opportunities to use the language and to have a more active participation inside the classroom. Developing reading skills is a complex process considering that students should understand what they are reading, and apply that information on their area of knowledge. According to Maria "For engineers, English is primarily a library language meaning that the student must understand enough to gain access to knowledge contained in textbooks and particularly in periodicals and journals in order to extract information and keep abreast with latest technologies". It means that there is a constant need for effective reading skills across the curriculum which will contribute not only to foster reading but also to improve the engineering education by exposing learners to authentic knowledge and real situations.

Considering the relevance of improving students' reading proficiency in this public university, this research study discusses the effectiveness of cooperative learning projects to foster reading skills of a group of students. The university adopts a communicative approach however; it is blended with other teaching methods which depend on the teacher's perspective. Students have to take six mandatory English language levels which do not affect students' grade-point averages (GPA) since English is not part of every program curriculum. The fact that English is a mandatory subject has led students to become passive learners who do not regularly attend to English classes, students just come when a test is administered, and according to Saber Pro testing most of the students' English level is A2. Despite this situation, students are aware of their need to improve the English level because in the content subjects they are required to read texts in English with specific technical language not seen before in the English classes, in order to keep updated with the different processes, tendencies and technologies in Engineering and industrialized countries.

In this way cooperative learning projects were chosen as a new strategy for them because of their multiple benefits, methods and strategies to use in the classroom, students have different learning styles and that is why they may have different strengths, some of them might be good at grammar or some others might be fluent or feel confident talking in public, this is why students can support each other with their strengths in cooperative activities that help them learn and improve their abilities not only in terms of language proficiency but also in terms of personal skills like teamwork or problem-solving. In this way, a motivation emerged to contribute with strategies to foster students' reading skills as they need to become effective and efficient learners on their engineering programs since English is required to acquire knowledge and learn new information, bearing also in mind that the six levels are necessary to graduate.

8.1   Changes in Teaching and Learning Modes

Cooperation, competition, and individualization are the three main ways of working in human society, as well as the three most common learning methods in the school education process. As far as social production is concerned, individualization is the most basic mode of production. Cooperation is the core element of contemporary society, while competition is a means to promote continuous social progress. However, competition in contemporary society is team competition based on cooperation. As far as school education and classroom learning are concerned, only based on individualized efforts, centered on cooperative learning, and guided by the idea of moderate competition to promote development, can we effectively promote the development of individual students and school groups.

The traditional classroom in my country emphasizes competition and individualized learning, and completing homework independently is a typical embodiment of this idea. These two learning methods are characterized by the mutual dependence between learners. Individualized learning means that there is no interdependence between learners. To complete the learning content and evaluation separately, the knowledge comes from two channels: one is teachers and students, and the other is students and learning resources. There is a negative dependence between learners. The success of anyone means the failure of others. The academic circles have been arguing about the advantages and disadvantages of competitive learning. So researchers began to attempt to build a positive interdependence relationship between learners.

At the same time, with the development of smart learning terminals and the rise of big data and learning analysis technology, researchers have begun to pay attention to personalized learning, that is, based on individual learners' or group's cognitive starting point, learning interest, learning style and other individual factors. Create a smart learning environment and design learning activities. The individual is the basic unit of personalization. Personalization is the manifestation of the individual. There is a world of difference between personalized learning and individualized learning.

(1) Personalized learning emphasizes the individual differentiation of learners, including many factors such as learning style, learning attitude, and learning motivation. Individualized learning only emphasizes the existence of individuals.

(2) Personalized learning can also include groups with similar characteristics, not just a single individual. The same is to establish a positive interdependence between learners, and personalized learning does not completely deny the element of cooperation. In the current classroom teaching, while teachers pay attention to individualization, they often ignore the cooperation between learners. When teachers pay attention to cooperative learning, they often ignore the individual differences between learners. Purely competitive learning has been abandoned by the academic world from the perspective of ideas, and cooperative and personalized learning is the general trend.

8.2 Theoretical Foundation of the Implementing of CL in Reading Courses

8.2.1 Motivation Theory

Motivation is defined as a series of behaviors that can impel people and instruct people. Some researchers believe that motivation plays an important role in individual cognition. If learners have strong motivation in learning a language, they can learn it better and make greater progress.

Motivation perspectives on CL mainly focus on the goals and rewards. Group cooperation is reinforced through the goals and rewards. From this aspect, CL creates such an environment that the only way the group members can reach the goals is through cooperation among them and everyone should try their best. Therefore, motivation is created based upon the fact that students are induced by group incentives to work towards the goal within the group. Methods that are developed from motivation theory are related to group rewards.

Johnson et al. give scores according to group performance. On the contrary, Slavin points out that the distribution of rewards must be based on the individual learning of all group members. Each team member should learn hard to ensure the team to succeed. According to Slavin, this is important because in this way it can be avoided that one or two students do all the work while others just sit around.

In reading class with CL, the students' achievement goals are closely related. When one of the students reaches the goal, the others cooperating with him naturally reach theirs. The students' intrinsic learning motivation is reinforced and they're driven by external force.

8.2.2 Social Cohesion Theory

According to social cohesion theory, individuals form groups based on how much they want to meet mutual needs. The formation and maintenance of the groups is due to the individual interaction during which individual needs realize.

The Jigsaw method that was mentioned in the previous chapter can be viewed from the social cohesion perspective. Activities of teambuilding and cohesiveness building are important to cohesion theory. Students simply present to each other, without getting any reward.

The forming of the learning groups has many elements that can be included into the social cohesion perspective. In this model, some characteristics are focused on, such as desired behaviors, positive interdependence and roles of group members, who focus on building a good team which will work well. However, this model also offers incentives, often in the form of giving group grades, so the motivational perspective can also be included by in this theory.

Social cohesion theory is very similar to the motivation theory because they both emphasize motivational explanations for the effectiveness of CL. However, there is also difference between them. Motivation theorists believe that students are motivated for themselves, while social cohesion theorists believe that students are motivated for mutual benefit.

8.2.3 Cognitive Theories

This perspective mainly focuses on the cognitive processing in individuals brains. Through CL, the students are provided with opportunities to review and process what they've learned so as to better master it. The cognitive perspectives include the following two variations of perspectives.

8.2.3.1 Developmental Perspective

Piaget held the view that knowledge is obtained during the interaction activities with others. Learning through interaction among peers is the core element to develop their learning ability. Peers have similar cognitive structure and they can give information and feedback in the construction of logical system. So the education strategies tend to be in favor of solving problems through interaction and cooperation among peers. According to this theory, learning first occur during the students' interaction and cooperation, and it even occur prior to individual thinking process of brains. That is to say, when learners receive certain help, language learning is sure to happen. So in the reading process, students can learn more and promote their potential learning ability through CL.

8.2.3.2 Cognitive Elaboration Perspective

This perspective is based on research in cognitive psychology, which holds the view that if a learner wants to keep in mind some information related to something else already stored in memory and combine them, he must reconstruct the information. The most efficient way is to explain or teach the learning materials to others. During the process of explaining and listening, both the one who expresses and the one who listen get benefit.

In summary, these two types of cognitive theories are similar in that they both lay emphasis on the necessity and importance of interaction among students for mental processing. However, they do look at cognitive learning slightly differently.

8.2.4 Multicultural Education Theory

Multicultural education is the educational strategy in which the student's cultural background is viewed as positive and essential in developing classroom instruction and a desirable school environment. Students bring to class different historical backgrounds, individual belief, day-to-day living experiences, and studying styles. These experiences direct the way student behaves in school. As students interact cooperatively, they can learn from each other, understanding is mole likely to occur for they are required to explain, elaborate, or defend their positions to each other. Sometimes, peer explanations are more helpful to students than adult's explanations because they are given by someone at a similar cognitive developmental level.

Ross J and Smythe E stated that multicultural education is trying to change schools and other educational institutions so that students from all social class, gender, racial, and cultural groups will have all equal opportunity to learn. Students learn to get along and to respect each other. Banks suggested that multiethnic and multicultural education programs can help students expend their cultural knowledge.

Multicultural education tries to ensure better learning and equity for all students. In other words, multicultural education addresses cultural diversity and the provision of equal educational opportunity in schools. The cultural backgrounds of students are as important in developing effective instructional strategies as their physical and mental capabilities.

Slavin and Madden found that teacher workshops, multiethnic texts, minority history, heterogeneous groups, and classroom discussions of race relations had very 1imited effects on students' social attitudes and behavior. On the other hand, the assignment of students of different races to work with each other and the participation of students in multiracial sports teams had strong, consistent, positive effects on race relations.

A Johnson and Johnson study, using 51 fourth-graders divided into Cooperative and individualistic groups, showed significantly greater cross-ethnic interaction in the CL group during both instructional and free time. Attitude scores also supported the finding that CL experiences benefit intergroup relations. Studies designed to increase the acceptance of mainstreamed academically handicapped students demonstrate a similar facilitative effect on students' acceptance.

8.3   Rationale for Implementing CL in English-majors' Courses

Halliday regards, language serves two main functions allowing the language users to (a) interact communicatively and (b) to interpret experience by organizing it into meaning.

In other words, language serves as both communicative and cognitive toolsto convey and organize meanings. If a language serves these main functions, being able to use a language means, then, to have competence in "using" the language rather than "knowing about" the language. To be competent in communicative use of the foreign language, one has to know how to use grammar and vocabulary of the language, how to conduct conversations, how to use and respond to different types of speech acts (such as request, apologies, thanks, etc.), and how to use the language appropriately at different situations. In courses for English majors, the emphases are traditionally laid upon the knowledge of grammar and vocabulary. However, for the facilitation should be, "It would be beneficial to provide the learners the opportunities to " use " the language to perform various tasks that require meaningful communication".

8.3.1   Input

According to Kagan, language is best acquired when input is comprehensible, developmentally appropriate, abundant and accurate. In cooperative group settings, students need to make them understood so they adjust their language to suit the members of that group. As a result, there is a much higher proportion of comprehensible input. Students can check for understanding and adjust their speech much easier in a small group than a teacher can in front of the class, simply due to number. Language also needs to be developmentally appropriate.

According to Vygotsky L S, the zone of proximal development is difference between what a student can do alone and what he/she can do with supportive collaboration. The next step in language acquisition will be stimulated if it is in the zone of proximal development.

CL helps bring students to the proximal level due to its very nature of collaboration. Kagan states that CL is a "natural source of redundant communication". Students will all speak in different ways on some topics, thus ensuring that input is received repeatedly from various sources. Although lack of accuracy is a disadvantage in CL groups due to peers' output being less accurate than teachers' output, Kagan feels that it should not be a deciding factor in choosing a traditional approach over a cooperative approach. It is more important to have frequent opportunities to produce output than formal accurate input provided by the teacher as this has a greater chance of producing speech acquisition.

8.3.2 Output

Kagan proposed: "language acquisition is fostered by output that is functional and communicative, frequent, redundant, and consistent with the identity of the speaker". CL is the ideal situation for communicative output. Language is best acquiredwhen it is used in a way that is meaningful to the students. CL provides opportunities for students to express themselves in a functional manner which is personally relevant to them. Students are using the language for a specific purpose, usually to meet certain group goals. The CL setting also provides for frequent use of the language. The fact that students are in small group settings allows for many greater opportunities for language use than the traditional classroom.

Redundancy is important with regards to output as well as input. Students who are speaking on a topic get many more chances to speak about some topics than they would in a traditional classroom. Kagan also refers to output needing to be "identity congruent". The cooperative groups provide for less formal language use which is closer to the identity of many students than that of the traditional, formal classroom.

8.3.3 Context

The third variable that Kagan refersto is context. Language which occurs in a context that is "supportive and motivating, communicative and referential, developmentally appropriate and feedback rich" will be much more likely to be acquired.

Kagan lists a number of reasons of why students are more motivated and feel more supports in a cooperative classroom. (a) They are more frequently asked questions; (b) They need to communicate to accomplish the CL projects; (c) Peers are far more supportive than in the traditional classroom because they are all on the same side; (d) CL structures demand speeches; (e) Students are taught to learn to praise and encourage each other; and (f) Students are made interdependent so they need to know what the others know. It is obvious, therefore, that CL situations generally provide for a better learning environment for foreign language acquisition. A communicative/referential context is much the same as the meaningful situations which was mentioned earlier.

To summarize, CL provides opportunities for students to develop and improve their second language acquisition. Because language acquisition is determined by input, output, and context variables, and because CL provides for variables, second language acquisition and CL are, as Kagan puts it, a "natural marriage".

8.4　Research Status

8.4.1 Research Status Abroad

Slavin points out that the history of CL can be traced back as early as the seventeenth century. He cites such educational theorists as Comenius in the seventeenth century, Rousseau in the eighteenth century, Pestalozzi in the nineteenth century and Dewey in the early twentieth century who held some form of cooperation among students as essential to learning. Yet strictly speaking, the origin of modern CL dates from 1896 when John Dewey advocated that teachers are not the only sources of knowledge and students should be able to help each other and learn in all interdependent way. Slavin also refers to Piaget and Vygotsky's developmental theories which emphasized the importance of discussion and joint problem solving among peers. Social interdependence theory, according to Johnson et al. , can trace its roots back to Koffka in the early 1900s.

CL, therefore, is not new to education. Although the term may not have been used, CL in some form has been happening for decades. However, CL, as an instructional strategy first rose in USA during late 60s to early 70s, had made great progress and become a teaching theory and strategy by mid 80s. With the development of jigsaw and other teaching methods in the late 1970s and the 1980s, this approach became more and more popular all over the world. It has been applied to the teaching of various subjects and age groups by teachers in more than fifty countries.

With respect to the social cohesion perspective, achievement outcomes are unclear. Research on jigsaw has not generally found positive effects on achievement. However, studies of forms of jigsaw that have added some type of group rewards have found positive achievement outcomes.

Group investigation has been found to significantly increase student achievement. However, Slavin attributes the success of group investigation to the fact that groups are evaluated based on their group products, which are composed of unique contributions made by each group member. As a result, this method may be using a form of the group goals and individual accountability which is viewed as essential by motivation theorists.

From the cognitive development perspective, Slavin points out that there is little evidence from classroom experiments that cooperative methods which depend solely on interaction will produce higher achievement. However, he also states that these processes are important "mediating variables" to explain the effects of group goals and tasks on achievement.

Littlewood W T conducted all informal study of CL in a Spanish honors foreign language classroom. She found that the point system designed by Slavin did not work well due to the students' high marks to begin with. She suggested that the "intrinsic rewards of working together successfully" seemed to be enough. Krashen S D found that although all groups showed improvements in oral performance and aural comprehension, CL benefited weaker and average ability students more than higher ability students. This study compared CL and traditional classroom methods. The study also showed that students of all levels in the CL groups acquired significantly more vocabulary than that of the traditional method. More importantly, the use of the language increased in the CL situation. Johnson et al. also state that nearly 600 experiments and over 100 studies have been conducted on cooperative, competitive and individualistic efforts to learn since 1898. According to the statistics in the meta-analysis of 164 studies conducted by Johnson, the consistency of the results and the diversity of CL methods provide strong validation for its effectiveness.

8.4.2 Research Status in China

The research on CL is considered one of the greatest successful studies in the history of educational research. Some Chinese educators and teachers also notice the successful outcomes and positive effects derived from CL and begin to introduce it to China. Nowadays, an increasingly number of introductions are made and lots of attempts are tried to apply CL to English languages learning at educational institutions of all levels, including elementary schools, middle schools and colleges in China. The statistics in the above table is gotten from CNKI by way of searching for titles of articles. According to the above table, from 2000 to 2014, there are 14025 articles published concerning CL theory. There are 2258 articles concerning the implementation of CL theory in English teaching. There are 640 articles concerning the implementation of CL theory in college English teaching. There are twenty-six articles concerning the implementation of CL theory in college English reading teaching. There is none concerning the implementation of CL theory in courses teaching for English-majors.

From this data we can see that CL theory is a very mature one and has been widely used and studied in the teaching of many subjects, among which English teaching esp. college English teaching makes up a large proportion.

Around 2000, CL was still a rather new concept in Chinese educational field and some educators were interested in it and eager to introduce it. Articles are published to explore the theoretical basis, features, techniques, and advantages of CL. Guo S M in his article "On the Theory and Skills of CL and the Reform of EFL Teaching" studied the theory and skills of CL and tried to apply it to the teaching reform of English as a foreign language. Pei Tina in her article "The Teaching Strategies of CL" discussed some different teaching strategies of CL. Gao X B, in his article "Some Basic Problems in CL Teaching", put forward that different subjects should have different features when using CL. Wang T in his book Cooperative Learning-Principles and Strategies Compared the Different Definitions of CL given by many theorists. Wang T published the book named Theory and Implement of Cooperative Learning, stating the general introduction, history development, theoretical foundations, models, and implementing strategies. Ma H L in his article "Connotation, Elements and Significance of Cooperative Learning" believed that essential elements of cooperative learning include positive interdependence, face to face interaction, individual responsibility, interpersonal skills and team working. Wang Hang in his article "Cognitive Research of Cooperative Learning" divided cooperative learning into two stages. One is stage of individual knowledge construction and the other is group knowledge construction.

Then some language teachers made some attempts to apply CL in their teaching. Guo Y B in his article "Implementation and Evaluation of Cooperative Learning in English Class" discussed how to carry out the design and how to improve students' learning through cooperation learning. Lin L in his book "The Implementation of Cooperative Learning" also discussed the implementation of CL in English teaching. Ma X X in her graduate thesis "Research of Cooperative Learning and the Enlightenment on College English Teaching" performed research of CL and explored the effects on college English teaching. Sheng Q L and Zheng S Z in their book "Design of Cooperative Learning" discussed the design of CL to the teaching of English. Liu W in her graduate thesis "Task-based Classroom Activities in College English Teaching" argued how to use the CL principles to organize the college English class. Quan H X in her article "Cooperative Learning in English Teaching" stated that the implementation of cooperative learning effectively stimulated the students' learning enthusiasm and initiative. Luo X L's article "Problems and Improvements of Cooperative Learning in the Implementation" described the implementation of CL in classes of middles schools and summarized some problems and improvements. Han Y H in her article "Problems and Solutions of Cooperative Learning in Teaching" thought that in teaching practice, CL could inject fresh vitality into teaching and play a very important role in training students in non-cognitive psychology. Wu R H and He G D in their article "Effects of Cooperative Learning on College English Writing Teaching" put forward that CL could help students to overcome their writing anxiety and writing difficulties.

8.5 Key Patterns of CL Implementation in English Majors' Reading Courses

8.5.1 Teacher-led Cooperation Pattern

This kind of pattern was structured on the basis of the cooperative type of teacher-student. The teaching task will be completed and reached under the teachers' guidance through the student-student and group-group cooperation. And the specific cooperative procedures are as follows:

(1) Teachers' guidance.

(2) Group discussion.

(3) Collective communication.

(4) The students' self-assessment and teachers' processing.

8.5.2 Student-autonomy Cooperation Pattern

This pattern of CL is structured on the basis of the type of student-student CL, and it is the pattern in which the students are divided into several fixed groups. Following this pattern, learning tasks being accomplished and goals being reached, are all through student-student cooperation or group-group cooperation according to the goal of the course learning appointed by the teacher. The procedures are usually included below:

(1) Goal presenting.

(2) Together inquiring.

(3) Communicating and discussing.

(4) Exercising and applying.

8.5.3　Computer-assisted Cooperation Pattern

Computer-assisted cooperation pattern is also called human-computer cooperation pattern. Now the world is changing and technology is developing fast. More and more new things appear in our daily life. The teacher must follow the trend of the times, meet the students' interest and keep as a qualified teacher. He/She sets a certain teaching surroundings in which the students can participate in the class activities and creates new ways to help the students form good qualities. On the basis of knowledge learned in classroom, the students should learn how to learn English in natural surroundings themselves. There are not only all kinds of English newspapers, English magazines, English written information, but also English broadcast, English programs on TV and etc.

With the development of science and technology, multimedia is widely used in English teaching classes. It brings in more teaching effects than those in other teaching ways; it can make abstract knowledge into concrete one and lots of knowledge contents concentrate and enrich the students' knowledge; it can get the students to find, discuss and solve questions, to develop self-study ability. Using the teaching method of human-computers cooperation pattern, the students can make good use of these English media to enlarge their amount of intake, to input naturally, to absorb naturally, to deepen the students' impression of what they have learned; not to remember and recite forcefully. The amount of intake in English learning is similar to the children's native language acquisition in some degree. It can relax the students' anxiety. With the help of computer multimedia, the aim of using language is finally reached; their listening and speaking skills are further practiced. The students learn English well subconsciously. By using this method, we can save much time so that the students can be given much time to practice and make the students feel the reality of language. Thus it can completely change the traditional learning style and the students are expected to discuss the contents of teaching materials and the plot of the story in groups. The students can learn how to be a real man. In that way the atmosphere of the lesson reaches the maximum. Other teaching methods can't match it for this. Thus this pattern combines the teaching processes with the learning processes, and forms a new compound among teachers, students, textbooks and teaching methods.

Now, multimedia aid teaching such as radios, computers and so on are widely used in teaching, which makes teaching activities direct, lively and vivid. They help enlarge the teaching contents, quicken the teaching rhythm and help the students understand the materials more easily. English teachers should learn to take advantage of these new teaching aids to make their lessons more vivid, rich and interesting.

8.6   Major Methods

The major models of CL will be introduced, which are pervasively adoptedby a large number of educators. But first of all, let's re-mention the major leaders in the field of CL. They are:

(1) Robert Slavin, Director of the Elementary School Program at the Center for Research on Elementary and Middle Schools, John Hopkins University.

(2) David W. Johnson, Professor of Educational Psychology, and Roger T Johnson, Professor of Curriculum and Instruction, both Co-Directors of the CL Center, University of Minesota.

(3) Spencer Kagan, Director, Resources for Teachers, San Juan Capistrano, California. Generally speaking, there are dozens of variations within the CL approaches. Among those variations, researchers generally group them into four types: Group Investigation, Student Team Achievement Divisions, Jigsaw and Learning Together.

8.6.1   Group Investigation

The Group Investigation (GI) method was developed by Sharan. In this method, groups take on topics within a unit studied by the entire class. The groups break these topics into tasks for each individual within the group and carry out the activities necessary to prepare group reports, which are presented to the class as a whole. This method could lend itself to creative projects in the second language classroom.

Group would be given a theme to prepare and would be required to break that theme into smaller topics for research and discussion. Many opportunities for meaningful language use would take place.

Group investigation is a highly structured method with six specific stagesif implementation. Students' involvement occurs in every stage, from topic selection for study to evaluation of students' learning. The stages are as follows:

(a) identifying the topicand organizing students into research groups; (b) planning the learning tasks; (c) carrying out the investigation; (d) preparing for the final report; (e) presenting the final report; (f) evaluation.

8.6.2　Student Teams Achievement Divisions

Student Teams Achievement Divisions (STAD), developed by Slavin, is commented to be assigned in groups of four which are totally heterogeneous. The teacher presents a lesson, and then students work within their groups, helping one another, to make sure that all team members have mastered the lesson. All students' individual scores of their individual quizzes contribute to the team score.

The main idea behind STAD is to motivate students to encourage and help each other master skills and to accelerate the achievements of all students. In teaching of English-majors' courses, STAD is most appropriate for teaching basic skills such as mastering grammatical rules, words, phrases and etc. So STAD is made up of five interlocking components: Class presentations, teams, quizzes, individual improvement scores, and team recognition.

8.6.3　Jigsaw

Jigsaw was first developed by Elliot Aronson et al. in 1978. Conducting this method, the faculty member divides an assignment or topic into four parts with all students from each learning group volunteering to become "experts" on one of the parts. Expert group then work together to master their portion of the material and also to discover the best way to help others learn it. Upon returning to their groups, the expert students take turns teaching their own learning group about their topics. Ultimately, students are quizzed on all aspects of the topic.

There exist only individual grades, but no group score. Jigsaw, as the most widely used collaborative language learning and teaching activity, is used to create a real "information gap" in the classroom and encourage communication, which will be suitable for reading and listening tasks.

The elements of original Jigsaw include:

(1) Specially designed curriculum materials;

(2) Team building and communication training;

(3) Group leader;

(4) Teams;

(5) Expert groups;

(6) Individual assessment and reward.

8.6.4 Learning Together

When Johnson D W et al. developed their method of CL, often called Learning Together (LT), it was quite general in terms of implementation. Conducting LT, students work in small groups on assignments to produce a single project. Students are instructed to seek help from one another before asking for the teachers' assistance. They will be rewarded based on both individual and the overall performance of the group. LT is a quite efficient way to help students go to research work. Johnson and Johnson called their method Circles of Learning and have delineated the following eighteen specific steps for implementation (some of which are optional). They are divided into five main types, as follows:

(1) Specifying objectives;

(2) Making decisions;

(3) Communicating the task, goal structure, and learning activity;

(4) Explaining the academic task;

(5) Monitoring and intervening;

(6) Evaluating and processing.

8.7 Implementation of CL for Three Forms

8.7.1 Implementation of CL for Intensive Reading

Intensive reading, as its name suggests, is a type of reading practice, training students' various reading skills of skimming, scanning, summarizing, inferring and evaluating; on the other hand, it aims to enhance learners' language proficiency, thus it also encompasses the training of other language skills, such as listening, speaking, reading, writing and translating.

In addition to the training of linguistic competence, communicative, social and strategic competence are, due to be trained through collaborative efforts in identifying, analyzing and solving problems and fulfilling learning tasks. The approach of CL, therefore, has enormous potentialities in this type of class.

Under the guidance of Group Investigation (GI) which is suitable for the teaching of Intensive Reading in Chinese teaching of English-majors' courses and will be adopted by the author in the following experiments, the learning of one unit in the book of Intensive Reading presented from teaching of English-majors' courses generally follows the procedures below:

(1) Collaborative preparation work before the actual classroom learning. (a) Cooperative members go out to find resources so as to provide relevant background information about the coming reading passage. (b) Cooperative members divide work among them, consult the dictionary or other reference books available to them, learn new or difficult words and structures together and get ready for presenting them in class.

This type of language-related learning activity constitutes a crucial part of Intensive Reading. As done in collaborative effort to consult background information, each group would in turn take the responsibility for consulting the dictionary about words and structures assigned by the teacher and make preparations for presenting their findings to the whole-class in the following step.

(2) CL in the classroom. (a) Collaborative teams present their findings in front of the whole class. (b) Collaborative learning activities are designed to guarantee students' comprehension of the reading passage and to promote communicative output among cooperative members. (c) Comprehension of the reading passage and promotion of communicative output is among cooperative members.

(3) Collaborative written work after class. Those activities are principally designed for students to practice communicative output in forms of summary reporting, evaluation or suggestion making, and role-play sometimes. Therefore, it is possible for several cooperative tasks to be performed simultaneously. Group Investigation (GI),

again, can be employed at this stage.

At this stage, students are provided opportunities to demonstrate their talent for imagination and creation by adding more detailed suggestions. Each group receives its specific problem together with one suggestion provided by the teacher as a guide.

8.7.2 Implementation of CL for Courses

Learning Together (LT) and its subsequent competitive mechanism are the most frequently employed method in finding out the main idea, rearranging jumbled sentences and so on. Perhaps due to the inclusion of competition among various groups, learners are so eager to be the first to finish their duties in their discussions. Dealing with these kinds of tasks, a variety of concrete forms of CL activities are needed, i. e. role-play, debate and etc. Through such an activity, communicative competence which requires students to understand both linguistic forms and their respective functional meanings can be trained.

8.7.3 Implementation of CL for Exercises

Exercise class is relatively difficult to carry out due to the fact that Teachers' Book is available in the library and in bookstores everywhere. In addition, two hours' mechanic checking from vocabulary exercise to translation practice is boring. Cooperative mode of learning, therefore, is also attempted in this type of class. Jigsaw, Learning Together (LT), and Group Investigation (GI) can all be conducted in dealing with the exercises.

The cooperative groups would do the work of consulting the dictionary. In order to prevent students from directly copying from Teachers' Book, students are required to have correct pronunciation and be ready to answer questions proposed by either the teacher or other students. Students gradually learn to initiate explanations rather than be questioned by others.

Translation exercise in each unit also has great potential for collaborativeeffort. Individual work of translation and handing in to be evaluated by the teacher may easily result in mere copying from Teachers' Book and a heavy load of grading work on the part of the teacher. However, cooperative translation in class, on the contrary, can not only avoid such drawbacks but also be less boring. Through cooperative effort, translation task can be fulfilled in a more relaxed atmosphere; additionally, positive interdependence, together with individual accountability and competitive mechanism can be incorporated.

8.8 Teachers' Functions in the Implementation of CL for English-majors' Courses

In a CL classroom, the teacher is a guide on the floor rather than a sage on the stage, a learning facilitator rather than a learning disseminator. His primary role is to set up the appropriate context for the students to learn together as well as to seek opportunities to share the responsibility for interaction and learning, which have been placed on his shoulders with the students. This partial transfer of control from the traditional style (teacher lecturing) to peer teaching has proven itself through bountiful research to be a significant factor in learning and motivational gains. As a famous cognitive psychologist Vygosky L S maintained, "The only time people really learn anything is when they internalize it through social interaction with others". Although the teacher may move from the foreground to the background during class time, he actually has much more expanded roles in the CL process: organizer, monitor, stimulator, and facilitator.

In CL, the role of the teacher can be very effectively summarized in the following words of Dr. Spencer Kagan: "Teachers in a CL classroom are freed from the responsibility of always lecturing and directing. They can become consultants and attract the most to those students who can benefit most from their attention." And Dr. Spencer Kagan also considers: "The teacher in the cooperative classroom is on the same side as the students, serving not to dam up their natural expressiveness, but rather to channel it in positive directions."

8.8.1 Making Pre-instructional Decisions

There are five basic decisions teachers will make before finalizing his lesson.

(1) The teacher must first decide how big each group should be to efficiently and effectively run one lesson. The optimal size of a cooperative group will vary according to resources needed to complete the assignment (the larger the group is, the more

resources are available); the cooperative skills of the group members (the less skillful the members are, the smaller the group should be); and the nature of the task. If the purpose is for the group members to review, rehearse information, or practice, 4 to 6 students is about the right size. But if the goal is to encourage each student to participate in discussions, problem solving, then groups of 2 to 4 members work best.

(2) The secondimportant decision for the teacher is how to assign students to their groups. A lot of the powers for learning in cooperative groups come from the need for discussion, explanation, justification, and shared resolution on the material being learned. At the beginning, it is usually better for the teacher to assign the students to groups. Teachers may want to assign students by interest, by mixed ability, by homogeneous ability, or randomly, depending on the task at hand. Students should know from the beginning that every student would work with every other student in the class on a somewhat regular basis over the course of school year.

(3) Arranging the room is the activity being done. If students need to discuss materials, placing the groups far apart to allow for more privacy is important. Other concerns like whether or not there will be a good deal of movement are important to consider before the class begins. Teachers can define the workspace boundaries in a classroom by moving furniture, using lighting, using labels and signs that designate areas.

(4) What materials will be needed and how they will be organized are the next decision. Using appropriate materials is only the first part of this decision-making process. The teacher needs to consider the logistics of organizing the material, passing out the material, and collecting and storing the material. Lack of these factors can make a great lesson become a nightmare.

(5) Finally, the teacher has to consider which students to hold what roles during the lesson. When assigning group roles, the teacher needs to be sure that each group includes the students possessing four types of skills: forming skills, functioning skills, formulating skills, and fermenting skills. The student with forming skills will be the one to monitor turn taking in the group. The roles for the group members with functioning skills will be the one to record the discussion, encourage all to participate, clarify/paraphrase the group discussion, and work to seek a group consensus. Formulating skills require a student to generate discussion and to summarize the group's work.

Finally, the students with the fermenting role works to ask for justification of the group's outcome and also helps to give a rationale for the group's activities.

8.8.2 Setting the Task and Positive Interdependence

The teacher's job here is to make sure that all of the students understand what they are supposed to accomplish during a CL activity. The teacher explains to the students in clear terms of what their academic goals are, specifies the criteria for success, explains positive interdependence, structures individual accountability, structures inter-group cooperation, and specifies expected behaviors. When student groups are given clear directions, they are more likely to arrive at the expected destination. The opposite is also true: without a clear map, they tend to go nowhere.

8.8.2.1 Explaining the academic task

The teacher needs to tell the class (a) what to do to complete the assignment and (b) how to do it. A few steps should be followed in explaining the academic task. First, the teacher must explain the assignment which should be a clear and measurable task, and explain lesson objectives. Next the teacher explains the concepts, principles, and strategies that the students will use during the lesson and relates them to students' past experience and prior knowledge. The teacher also explains the procedures students are to follow in completing the assignment. The teacher asks the class members to specific questions to check their understanding of the assignment. The last step is to ask students to answer in pairs or triads the questions the text will focus on.

8.8.2.2 Specifying the criteria for success

CL requires criterion-based evaluation, which means adopting a fixed set of standards and judging the achievement of each student against these standards. A common version of criterion-referenced grading involves assigning grades on the basis of the percentage of test item answered correctly. Or the teacher might say: "Before the group is finished, every member must demonstrate mastery." To promote inter-group cooperation, the teacher can say: "If the whole class can score over 80% correct on our English test, each student will receive three bonus points".

8.8.2.3 Explaining positive interdependence

Positive interdependence exists when a mutual joint goal is established so that individuals perceive they can attain their goals if their group mates attain their goals. Without positive interdependence, cooperation does not exist. First, the teacher structures positive goal interdependence. According to Johnson D W, "We, not me," the teacher says to students: "You have three responsibilities. You are responsible for learning the assigned material. You are responsible for making sure that all other members of your group learn the assigned material. And you are responsible for making sure that all other class members successfully learn the assigned material." Secondly, the teacher supplements positive goal interdependence with other type of positive interdependence, such as reward, role, resource, or identity.

8.8.2.4 Structuring individual accountability

Johnson D W et al. stated "An underlying purpose of CL is to make each group member a stronger individual in his or her own right. This is accomplished by holding all members accountable to learn the assigned materials and help other group members learn". Teacher can structure individual accountability in the classroom by assessing the performance of each individual member and by giving the results back to the individual and the group to compare to established criteria. The feedback makes students recognize and celebrate contributions to group-mates' learning, provides immediate remediation and any needed assistance or encouragement, and reassigns responsibilities to avoid redundant efforts by students.

8.8.2.5 Structuring inter-group cooperation

The teacher establishes class goals as well as group and individual goals. The teacher encourages the members of a group, who have finished their work, to help other groups who have not finished work to complete the assignment successful or to compare answers and strategies.

8.8.2.6 Specifying expected behaviors

In CL, the teacher has to specify desired behaviors such as group skills and individual techniques. Because students are simultaneously encouraged in task and teamwork, they must learn both. When specifying the expected behaviors, the teachers have to be specific with defining each social skill, start group work by emphasizing no more than one or two behaviors at a time, and emphasize over-learning by having the students practice the skills until they become automatic.

8.8.3　Monitoring and Intervening

It is important to observe the interaction among group members toassess students' academic progress and appropriate use of interpersonal and small-group's skills. The teacher needs to make sure that students benefit from face-to-face interaction. Monitoring, which means checking continuously, has four stages: (a) preparing to observe the learning groups, (b) observing to assess the quality of cooperative efforts in the learning groups, (c) intervening when necessary, and (d) having students assess the quality of their own individual participation to encourage self-monitoring. Since the teacher has set very specific and clear academic and social goals. It is clear what the teacher should be monitoring. The teacher plans a route to use so that each group has an equal amount of data gathered during their work. The teacher creates a chart in order to collect the king data for each student. Again, the teacher is looking for progress towards the academic goal and towards the social goal.

Intervening occurs for two purposes: (a) if the students are having issues with the academic goals; (b) when they are learning the material to be mastered properly. If they are getting off track, the teacher facilitates the process by helping the students understand the assignment and the material. This is usually done by asking the students to probe questions.

When the students are having problems with the social skills, the teacher asks them to put aside the academic side of the process for a little while, so that they can learn/rectify the issues they are having with the social goals. The teacher asks the students to: (a) identify the problem, (b) develop at least three ways to resolve the problem, and (c) choose one of the solutions to try.

8.8.4　Evaluating and Reflecting

Assessing the quantity and quality of students' learning is another very important task for the teacher. It is also important to involve the students in assessing and reflecting each other's favor of learning. Reflections do not have to be long or complex; but they should occur on a regular basis. It is usually a good idea to emphasize with students how to give positive comments about their peers' performances first and then to add specific suggestions for improvements. Regarding group

144

processing, the teacher makes sure that all the students receive feedback on their work, analyze the data on group functioning, set an improvement goal, and participate in a team celebration.

8.9 Teachers' Roles in the Implementation of CL for English-majors' Courses

8.9.1 Formal Cooperative Learning

Formal cooperative learning consists of students working together, for one class period to several weeks, to achieve shared learning goals and complete jointly specific tasks and assignments. In formal cooperative learning groups the teachers' role includes:

(1) Making pre-instructional decisions. Teachers (a) formulate both academic and social skills objectives, (b) decide on the size of groups, (c) choose a method for assigning students to groups, (d) decide which roles to assign group members, (e) arrange the room, and (f) arrange the materials students need to complete the assignment. In these pre-instructional decisions, the social skills objectives specify the interpersonal and small group skills students are to learn. By assigning students roles, role interdependence is established. The way in which materials are distributed can create resource interdependence. The arrangement of the room can create environmental interdependence and provide the teacher with easy access to observe each group, which increases individual accountability and provides data for group processing.

(2) Explaining the instructional task and cooperative structure. Teachers (a) explain the academic assignment to students, (b) explain the criteria for success, (c) structure positive interdependence, (d) structure individual accountability, (e) explain the behaviors (i. e., social skills) students are expected to use, and (f) emphasize intergroup cooperation (this eliminates the possibility of competition among students and extends positive goal interdependence to the class as a whole). Teachers may also teach the concepts and strategies required to complete the assignment. By explaining the social skills emphasized in the lesson, teachers explain

(a) the social skill objectives of the lesson and (b) the interaction patterns (such as oral rehearsal and jointly building conceptual frameworks) teachers wish to create.

(3) Monitoring students' learning and intervening to provide assistance in completing the task successfully or using the targeted interpersonal and group skills effectively. While conducting the lesson, teachers monitor each learning group and intervene when needed to improve task-work and teamwork. Monitoring the learning groups creates individual accountability; whenever a teacher observes a group, members tend to feel accountable to be constructive members. In addition, teachers collect specific data on interaction, the use of targeted social skills, and the engagement in the desired interaction patterns. This data is used to intervene in groups and to guide group processing.

(4) Assessing students' learning and helping students process how well their groups functioned. Teachers (a) bring closure to the lesson, (b) assess and evaluate the quality and quantity of student achievement, (c) ensure students carefully discuss how effectively they worked together (i. e., process the effectiveness of their learning groups), (d) have students make a plan for improvement, and (e) have students celebrate the hard work of group members. The assessment of student achievement highlights individual and group accountability (i. e., how well each student performed) and indicates whether the group achieved its goals (i. e., focusing on positive goal interdependence). The group celebration is a form of reward interdependence. The feedback received during group processing is aimed at improving the use of social skills and is a form of individual accountability. Discussing the processes the group used to function, furthermore, emphasizes the continuous improvement of primitives interaction and the patterns of interaction need to maximize student learning and retention.

8.9.2 Informal Cooperative Learning

Informal cooperative learning consists of having students work together to achieve a joint learning goal in temporary, ad-hoc groups that last from a few minutes to one class period. During a lecture, demonstration, or film, informal cooperative learning can be used to focus student attention on the material to be learned, set a mood conducive to learning, help set expectations as to what will be covered in a class session, ensure that students cognitively process and rehearse the material being taught, summarize what was learned and prepare the next session, and provide closure to an instructional session. The teacher's role for using informal cooperative learning to keep students more actively engaged intellectually entails having focused discussions before and after the lesson (i. e., bookends) and interspersing pair discussions throughout the lesson. Two important aspects of using informal cooperative learning groups are to (a) make the task and the instructions explicit and precise and (b) require the groups to produce a specific product (such as a written answer). The procedure is as follows.

(1) Introductory Focused Discussion. Teachers assign students to pairs or triads and explain (a) the task of answering the questions in a four to five minute time period and (b) the positive goal interdependence of reaching consensus. The discussion task is aimed at promoting advance organizing of what the students know about the topic to be presented and establishing expectations about what the lecture will cover. Individual accountability is ensured by the small size of the group. A basic interaction pattern of eliciting oral rehearsal, higher-level reasoning, and consensus building is required.

(2) Intermittent Focused Discussions. Teachers divide the lectureinto 10 to 15 minute segments. This is about the length of time a motivated adult can concentrate on information being presented. After each segment, students are asked to turn to the person next to them and work cooperatively in answering a question (specific enough so that students can answer it in about three minutes) that requires students to cognitively process the material just presented. The procedure is:

(1) Each student formulates his or her answer.

(2) Students share their answer with their partner.

(3) Students listen carefully to their partner's answer.

(4) The pairs create a new answer that is superior to each member's initial formulation by integrating the two answers, building on each other's thoughts, and synthesizing.

The question may require students to:

(1) Summarize the material just presented.

(2) Give a reaction to the theory, concepts, or information presented.

(3) Predict what is going to be presented next; hypothesize.

(4) Solve a problem.

(5) Relate material to past learning and integrate it into conceptual frameworks.

(6) Resolve conceptual conflict created by presentation.

Teachers should ensure that students are seeking to reach an agreement on the answers to the questions (i. e., ensure positive goal interdependence is established), not just share their ideas with each other. Randomly choose two or three students to give 30 second summaries of their discussions. Such individual accountability ensures that the pairs take the tasks seriously and check each other to ensure that both are prepared to answer. Periodically, the teacher should structure a discussion of how effectively the pairs are working together (i. e., group processing). Group celebrations add reward interdependence to the pairs.

8.9.3 Closure Focused Discussion

Teachers give students an ending discussion task lasting four to five minutes. The task requires students to summarize what they have learned from the lecture and integrate it into existing conceptual frameworks. The task may also point students toward what the homework will cover or what will be presented in the next class session. This provides closure to the lecture.

Informal cooperative learning ensures students are actively involved in understanding what is being presented. It also provides time for teachers to move around the class listening to what students are saying. Listening to student discussions can give instructors direction and insight into how well students understand the concepts and material being as well as increase the individual accountability of participating in the discussions.

8.10 Key Points of Cooperative Learning Theory in English-majors' Reading Course

8.10.1 Standardizing Learning Mode

Regarding the standardization of learning mode, teachers need to guide students to form an efficient learning method, and in the development and research of specific English reading course projects, through the adjustment of standardized group learning methods, in the collection of English materials and logical outlines In a series of tasks such as filling of English content, organizing drills, etc., students can apply the learning mode in the group in a standardized mode, and gradually complete the innovation of this standard mode in the continuous practice of learning and running-in. Find a learning method suitable for your group implementation.

8.10.2 Clarifying the Purpose of Reading

The purpose of reading is mainly divided into two categories: obtaining information and satisfying interest. "Talking Books" mentioned "Reading dead books is useless, only which books can be swallowed, only extreme books are worth chewing." Mao Dun also said: "Reading dead books is useless, only how Use your eyes to observe and use your brain to think about your talents." Teachers also have the responsibility to help students understand how to determine reading goals and use reading skills when reading different types of texts; guide students on the basis of increasing vocabulary and basic knowledge reserves Increase the amount of reading. At present, cooperative learning theory has become a trend. How to coexist and mutually benefit the traditional reading mode of the green light yellow scroll and online reading and browsing is a problem that deserves the attention and discussion of contemporary educators. There is nothing wrong with shallow reading for entertainment, but if you are addicted to it, there is no trace after reading, it is a waste of time. Therefore, teachers should guide students to conduct self-disciplined in-depth reading.

8.10.3 Studying Multimodal Discourse Analysis Theory

Cooperative learning polymorphic discourse analysis is the focal theoretical model in the field of discourse analysis today, forming three main symbolic models. The first is represented by Kressand Leeuwen, starting from the perspective of social methodology, theoretically constructing a framework based on the research of functional linguistics, which is usually called "systemic functional multimodal discourse analysis". The second is "multimodal interaction analysis" represented by Norris. The third is the combination of multimodal discourse analysis and corpus language proposed by Gu Y G. Combine learning to form a "learning multimodal corpus".

8.10.4 Enhancing Interaction Between Students

After rationally dividing the members of the group, the most important thing is the process of group cooperative learning. Cooperative learning needs to strengthen the interaction between students and through role-playing, group discussion and other forms, the observation and analysis of students' cooperative learning situation can improve students Understanding of reading skills and key content of reading. First of all, in the process of strengthening the interaction between students, teachers can allow students to cooperate in learning and thinking about a certain paragraph of English reading content, and improve the reading level of students through the forms of role play and sentence reading by group members. It can also allow students to divide the work in the group to integrate reading materials and search, etc., to give students more opportunities for discussion and cultivate students' good cooperation ability. Cooperative learning also includes cooperation between students and teachers, giving play to the leading role of teachers, guiding students in cooperative learning, and cultivating students' English reading ability. In addition, in the process of cooperative interaction and learning with students, modern teaching technology can also be used to show students the key and difficult knowledge of English reading in this class through multimedia, and then raise relevant English reading questions, allowing students to develop group cooperative learning, comprehensive Analyze the problems, look for strategies to solve the problems, and finally send a student representative to give a reasonable explanation of the answers to the questions, so as to indirectly cultivate the students' cooperative thinking and problem-solving ability, and realize the diverse interaction between students and students and teachers. In the process of combining multimedia teaching, in order to cultivate students' knowledge-building ability, teachers can also carry out cooperative competition activities for English reading teaching, mobilize the enthusiasm of members in different groups to participate in cooperation and competition, thereby enhancing students' awareness of cooperation and competition and cooperative learning, to better improve reading and comprehension in competition and interaction.

8.11 Reading strategies

The use of reading strategies in this research study resides in the need of students to improve their reading skills. These strategies were implemented as steps during the development of each of the projects starting by predicting, then making connections, passing to the inference step, later questioning and finally summarizing, they were chosen to help students not only to read texts, but also to interpret diagrams, figures, tables, find main objectives, question the functionality of some devices, summarize and make conclusions of specific content. There are different views of the use of reading strategies depending on the context and the population. Barnett defines a reading strategy as the understanding processes that a person carries out when reading as a means to comprehend what they read. In this process the teachers' role is essential to make reading strategies useful for students, it is required a clear, guiding and scaffolding orientation, which lets achieve the understanding process when reading. The reading strategies implemented are:

8.11.1 Predicting

The first step to become an effective reader is setting a purpose for reading and depending on it, looking for details becomes vital to acquire knowledge. According to Küçükolu, "Some of the approaches for teaching predicting are teacher modeling, predicting throughout the text; with partners, with a graphic organizer, or using post-it notes throughout the text. Using the title, table of contents, pictures, and key words is one prediction strategy". When implementing these strategies the brain prepares for the reading process activating previous knowledge to be ready for the text.

8.11.2 Making Connections

This second step is very essential because it is at this stage where students connect what they read to what they already know. Effective readers always make connections to the purpose of their reading and with the academic context they are involved. According to McNamara, "Good readers attempt to bridge incoming sentences with previous text content and with their background knowledge". When readers process a text in a deep way, such as answering WH questions they would start building a meaning which is seen as a comprehension and reflection process.

8.11.3 Inferring

Inferring means reading through lines. Effective reading requires making a prediction, learners use their background knowledge to infer what is coming up in the text. Serafini stated that "If readers could decode the words on a page, they would be able to monitor what was being read to themselves orally and understand what they were reading". This step allows learners to have a more complex process of reading, it requires students to predict, make connections to finally draw their own conclusions.

8.11.4 Questioning

This step can be used before, during or after reading. Its purpose is to guide students to find answers, solve a problem or find out new information. "Question-answering instruction encourages students to learn to answer questions better and, therefore, to learn more as they read"as Adler stated in 2001. It also implies learners to make use of all the previous reading strategies mentioned, to achieve an enriching understanding process of the text.

8.11.5 Summarizing

During the summarizing step readers should select and highlight the most relevant information or details of the text read. "The interpretation of the information in the text, the use of prior knowledge to interpret this information and, ultimately, the construction of a coherent representation or picture in the reader's mind of what the text is about"as McNamara stated in 2012.

8.11.6 Reading Strategies and Students' Reading Skills Interaction

The principal aim of this research study was to foster reading skills through the integration of cooperative learning into the regular English classes. Then, the first aspect to be discussed is how reading skills evolved or changed during the research process. In the initial survey a 100% of the students affirmed that they did not read in English for pleasure, all of them answered that they just read because they had an assignment to develop in their content subjects. From that perspective, it was understood that the incorporation of authentic reading material motivated students to start reading in English because they were interested in knowing what the text was about as it is noted by Dukeand Pearson, "providing experience reading real texts for real reasons and creating an environment rich in high-quality talk about text-will undoubtedly help". During the first group interview applied at the end of the first cooperative learning project, students asserted the importance of knowing how to implement different reading strategies as well as reading other kinds of texts. Student F said: "In my English classes I always read articles from a book, they always talk about things that happen in other countries. During these four weeks I read about engineering topics which called my attention and I spent much time predicting what the writer tried to say... it was very interesting, and I worked with classmates from other programs, it was fun" (Researchers' translation).

This perception from a student indicated that it was required the integration of reading strategies or techniques to explore a text in detail. It was imperative for learners not only to read a text but also to comprehend what is behind it and going beyond the words that are written; all these aspects can be achieved by the implementation of authentic material and a good use of reading strategies since "discovering the best methods and techniques or processes, the learners choose to access, is the goal of research in reading strategies"as Karbalaei described in 2010.

Participants acknowledged the advantages of discussing the way they used to work on reading activities in English classes compared with the way the reading instruction was done during the implementation of this project. These students interacted to ask each other about not only the texts in depth but especially how they approached every text. The teacher-researchers wrote in the teachers' journal: "Today, I noticed that students liked to discuss what the article probably would talk about just by reading the title. They started to talk about engineering requirements nowadays. Another group of students talked about the importance of predicting because it helps them to remember prior knowledge. "

8. 12 Summary

In the process of teaching reform and the process of developing cooperative learning mode, we should always take the actual situation of students and the needs of the current society as the basic criteria, and cultivate the comprehensive and applied talents that our country currently urgently needs. In the process of college English teaching, the use of cooperative learning mode can not only establish a relatively good learning atmosphere, but also help students learn from each other's strengths. By changing the traditional learning mode and diversifying the teaching methods and content, we can create diverse, authentic, relevant, practical and participatory situations for students, and create an "immersive" experience for them. The second language learning environment is the essence of the cooperative learning model. Every language has its own ingenious features, as well as its characteristics. Therefore, if you want to learn a language well, you need to understand the language. The real purpose of teaching is to enable students to apply what they have learned. The previous college English courses focused on the introduction of Western culture. The era of globalization requires us not only to learn Western culture, but also to understand our own culture. The cooperative learning mode can help students express their native language culture in English, to help our culture go to the world, and to promote exchanges and mutual trust between different cultures.

To apply CL theory in courses teaching for English-majors has its theoretical foundation, such as motivation theory, social cohesion theory, cognitive theory and multicultural education theory. Many researchers abroad and in China have done much about the theoretical and practical researches, but there is no relevant article combining CL theory with courses teaching for English-majors. This means on the one hand there has been a lot of good experience that the researcher can refer to, and on the other hand the research has an exciting innovation.

There is well documented evidence that CL is an effective method for increasing second language acquisition. CL is more than just asking students to form groups and cooperate with each other to do tasks, it is a formal instructional approach and strategy that students actively work together to complete the task according to the instruction from their teachers. Several main activities can be adopted in CL, including jigsaw, STAD, TGT, group investigation and Kagan's CL structures. However, not all activities are suitable and effective in language teaching classroom. Teachers should make adjustment according to different learners and teaching objectives. Courses are a very important course for English-majors. But the traditional teaching method can't meet the need for it. In recent years, many researchers have been exploring the effective method of courses teaching.

Chapter Nine Design of the Experiment on Implementing CL in English-majors' Reading Course

9.1　Goal of the Experiment

The goal of this experiment is to explore the effectiveness of CL theory on extensive reading teaching for English-majors. This study may first explore the professional views on CL, self-assessment of current teaching practice as well as the classroom context of the students participating in the project, and then further pursue the possibilities of implementing CL into English-majors' courses. CL rationales and methods applicable to EFL context would be introduced through the key patterns presented in Chapter Three. The aim is to demonstrate the effectiveness of CL, to discuss how CL could be implemented in their particular teaching environment, to guide the teachers in showing them how to play a more effective role implementing small group work in their classes as well as to encourage teachers to choose models and methods that best match their particular teaching styles and student populations. It aims to answer the two questions: (a) Can the implementation of CL theory improve students' reading ability? (b) Can the implementation of CL theory improve students' reading interest?

9.2　Subjects

The subjects are two classes of students in Jilin Agricultural Science and Technology College. Judged from their English scores in the College Entrance Examination, most of the students are at average and under-average level in their English competence. There are two natural classes that are formed randomly. Class

One is assigned to be the experimental class (EC) and Class Two is assigned to be the control class (CC). There are forty students in the EC and the CC respectively. Of the forty students in the EC, six are male and of the forty students in the CC, seven are male. The majority of the students are from eighteen to nineteen years old. All the students are from grade of 2014 who have studied English for at least six years when the experiment starts so that they have certain basic language competence that is the foundation of the experiment. In addition, they have nearly the same English learning experiences. According to the first questionnaire, most of them took English classes in traditional teacher-lectured environment before entering the college so the experiment can attract their interest and they are glad to cooperate. Both classes involved in the study are under the researcher's instruction so that the experiment can be carried out with much convenience. Both classes use the same text book.

CL method was adopted in the EC where most of the focus is on student-teacher and student-student interactions. Traditional teaching method was adopted in the CC. The two classes met their teacher once a week with two class periods each time (each period lasts for forty-five minutes) for sixteen weeks.

9. 3　Instruments

9. 3. 1　Tests

A pretest and a posttest were designed in this research. The pretest and the posttest were carried out both the in EC and in the CC. The pretest was carried out in the first week of September, 2014. The posttest was carried out in the last week of December, 2014. The pretest and the posttest have the same question variety and total scores, which can ensure the difficulty level remains almost the same in the two tests so that objective, reliable and accurate data for comparing the subjects' progress can be collected. The pretest and the posttest both consist of four parts: (a) Guessing the meanings of words. This part is adopted from Unit one and Unit 16 respectively from New Extensive Reading, Book I, compiled by Wang S H in 2005. This part accounts for eight scores. (b) Reading comprehension. This part is adopted from CET Band Four. It consists of four passages, each of which has five items. This part accounts for sixty scores. (c) Summarizing the main idea of a passage. This part is adopted from the Internet. It is a short passage about 300 words. This part accounts for twelve scores. (d) Fast Reading. This part is adopted from CET Band Four. It consists of one passage, which has ten items. This part accounts for twenty scores. The pretest and the posttest were designed to test the students' reading ability.

9.3.2　Questionnaires

Two questionnaires were designed in this research. They were addressed only in the EC in the first week of September, 2014 and in the last week of December, 2014. The first questionnaire contains twelve items, each having three choices. The students were questioned about their former learning experiences, interest, attitude, motivation, their feelings about the classroom behaviors and atmosphere, feelings towards each other and the teacher, and their expectations of the coming extensive reading course etc. The second questionnaire contains twelve items, each having three choices. The students were questioned about their feelings about the present extensive reading class, their learning interest and their attitudes towards CL. The questionnaires mainly helped the researcher to get the information about the changes of students' learning habits and interest. The questionnaires were given out to the students and collected back by the researcher herself. Before answering the questionnaires, the students were asked repeatedly to be careful and serious about the survey to ensure the answers were as authentic and reliable as possible.

9.3.3　Interviews

Some interviews were designed to know more objectively about students' English learning and their impression on the implementation of CL theory so that the researcher could make some adjustments and improvements. Interviews were occasionally done by the researcher in the EC during the class break or after the class in a casual way so that students may feel easy to tell the teacher their existing problems, suggestions for the current implementation and their expectations for future English teaching.

9. 4　Procedures of the Experiment

9. 4. 1　Preparation

CL is an instructive strategy that has been planned and designed carefully. It's very necessary to make some important preparation to ensure the experiment to be successful.

9. 4. 1. 1　Setting a Positive Environment to Encourage Participation

While many students are eager to have the opportunity to learn with and from their peers, there are still a few students who're reluctant to take part in group activities, and most of the students have never heard of CL before. So how to make the students ready for the experiment, and turn them into a community member of learners are huge challenges for the implementation of CL. The first thing that the teacher should do is to work on creating a caring classroom climate.

Therefore, in this research, in the initial weeks, the researcher tried to establish a warm and caring atmosphere in the EC so that students could feel free to be engaged in activities without worrying that classmates would laugh at them. In doing so, the researcher started from personalizing the learning environment and demanded the students to use each other's first name. It was difficult to remember all students' names in a short period of time but it did work well to make student-teacher relationship closer, especially, in the initial time. To get students familiar with each other, the following activities were used. (a) Pair Interviews-the activity was conducted in pairs. The pair took turns to ask each other information that he or she wants to know, for example: favorite food, birthplace, hobbies, favorite sports, etc. (b) Students were encouraged to volunteer to introduce their partners or the teacher randomly selected students to make introductions.

9. 4. 1. 2　Informing the Students of CL

At the beginning of the experiment, it's necessary and important for the teacher to clearly inform the students of CL and demonstrate it by means of simple, well-structured cooperative activities, since it helps to improve the efficiency of the implementation.

So, in this research, at the beginning of the semester, the researcher told the students what she was going to do, why she decided to use this approach, they were going to do team activities in class, and they were going to do most of the homework in teams. The researcher also talked enough about the proof and benefits of CL to the students to make it clear that she was not doing this for her own good. She was doing it because there is something in it for them. Some students might not like it at first, but as long as they found the benefits by themselves, they would be willing to cooperate.

9.4.1.3 Teaching the Students Some Skills of Cooperation

Johnson thought there was nothing more important than cooperation to human being, which was the basic mutual interaction. Successful cooperation skills are important for everyone to master to enforce the learning efficiency.

In this research, some necessary skills of CL were summarized as follows: (a) Skill of organization. When a member is learning with his or her group, he or she shouldn't make noise to disturb others. Each member should speak gently and encourage others to be involved in the activities of CL and pay close attention to every speaker. (b) Skill of control. This skill is used effectively to manage the activities to make sure the expected task to be fulfilled and the members to cooperate smoothly. The members should show their support by verbal or nonverbal means and help each other to explain and clarify when necessary. When other members become less motivated, try some humorous methods to stimulate their motivation. (c) Skill of illustration. It is used to deeply understand the reading materials. It can help the students to illustrate what they've read or discussed as completely as possible. The members should be able to make the illustration more specific by enquiring and correcting the other members. The members should be able to find the effective ways to illustrate some important information.

9.4.1.4 Forming Groups

In 1994 Johnson put forward some advice on forming groups. (a) The number of each group should be controlled within eight persons; (b) The groups should be formed according to competence, sex and races to keep balance; (c) The members in each group should assign roles properly; (d) Every member's responsibility should be clarified to motivate them to work hard towards the same aim; (e) The standard or requirement of every task should be clarified. The standard must be objective and fair; (f) Appropriate monitor and instruction should be given to the members and help them to solve some problems they encounter; (g) The learning content should be summarized. Both teachers and students can do this: (h) Proper evaluations about the performance of individuals and groups should be made.

In this research, there are forty students in the EC. The students were divided into five groups and each group was composed of eight students mainly on the basis of their English scores in the Entrance Examination to College, their scores in the pretest, their character and sex. Students in a group stayed together for a semester. After the groups were formed, students were informed that each one of them should take a different role in tasks and activities to promote their learning. The role of the group leader and other specific roles were rotated, so each one has an opportunity. At first, the leader of a group was appointed by the teacher. When students got acquainted with each other, they selected their own leader and the other specific roles of a group were decided by the leader, or by students themselves according to their own preference and strength. The other roles included recorder, reporter, checker and so on. The leader's work was mainly to organize the teamwork, decide how to do a task, distribute roles, mediate conflicts and make sure the team was cohesive and well developing.

9.4.2   Implementing

With the efforts of CL scholars and researchers, a lot of CL activities have been developed. However, not all activities are suitable and effective in language teaching classroom. Teachers should make adjustment according to different learners and teaching objectives, just as Bejarno stated that different group activities complement one another when they serve different teaching objectives in the language class. Therefore, this research adopted different activities considering the teaching content and the needs of the students. The following are some activities adopted in this research.

9.4.2.1   Sample Activities before Reading

Activities before reading were usually named "Leading-in". There are four major purposes for this. First, to help students know more about background knowledge and to better understand the passage; Second, to provide some necessary information; Third, to arouse students' reading interest; Fourth, to instruct students to use proper reading strategies.

The following example is one sample of activities before reading. It is predicting the content of the passage.

Predicting is an important reading strategy. The reading efficiency of reading with predicting is much better than that of direct reading. No matter the predicting is right or wrong, the reader's thoughts will be closer to the theme of the passage. The following reading will confirm or deny what readers have predicted. Predicting is feasible because the thinking models of the author and the readers are similar or even identical to some degree. Meanwhile, the structures of some styles of passages are predictable, especially for some experienced readers. Predicting can be performed by many means, such as predicting according to the title or subtitle of a passage, the author's background, the pictures, and so on. Through the activity of CL, the students can lower the reading difficulty and improve the reading ability.

The reading material of this example is from Unit 2, Text A of New Extensive Reading, Book I. The passage is about culture shock. It introduces some differences between cultures. The activity was organized in the following way.

Step 1. Forming Teams. Teams were formed in the process of preparation.

Step 2. Assigning the tasks. The teacher asked the students to predict the main content of the passage.

Step 3. Individual predicting. The teacher demanded that everyone should try his best to find the clues that could be helpful to predict the main content of the passage, including the title, some key words and topic sentences. Everyone should make an attempt to predict.

Step 4. Group discussion. The members of each group shared their opinions in the group. The one in charge of recording took down everyone's main idea, the process of the discussion and the conclusion. The teacher moved around the groups and gave encouragement, advice and necessary help.

Step 5. Group presentation. The teacher asked two groups to illustrate their learning results through CL. Because of time limitation, the other three groups could replenish their results or give some correction or advice.

Step 6. Concluding the activity. The teacher made a conclusion about the predicting based on students' presentation.

Step 7. Evaluating students' performances in the activity. The teacher and the students made a sensible evaluation about every member's performance in CL. The performance in group discussion and in group presentation were both evaluated.

9.4.2.2 Sample Activities during Reading

The following example is one sample of activities during reading. It is asking and answering questions among students.

Asking and answering questions among students is a good way to make teachers be aware of their true feelings. In traditional teaching, it's usually the teacher who asks questions and students answer them. The students don't have chances to creatively put forward questions because they don't need to do so. In class of CL, students ask and answer questions among themselves so as to better understand the details of the passage and improve their reading ability. But the reading material shouldn't be too difficult or it's not suitable for doing that. In that case students can't put forward questions of high quality.

The reading material of this example is from Unit 10, Text A of New Extensive Reading, Book I. The passage is about festivals and holidays. It introduces some festivals and holidays abroad. The activity was organized in the following way.

Step 1. Forming Teams. Teams were formed in the process of preparation.

Step 2. Reading the passage. The teacher gave students several minutes to read through the passage. The passage is of medium difficulty so the students can finish the task.

Step 3. Putting forward questions. The teacher asked every member to write down the questions they wanted to ask according to the passage. The teacher corrected the mistakes of the questions if there were any.

Step 4. Asking and answering questions among members in the groups. Every member asked his or her questions to the other seven members in the group. The members answered the questions in cooperation. Every group wrote down all the questions and picked 8 most valuable questions.

Step 5. Group presentation. One member of each group asked what they thought the most valuable questions to the other groups. Then the one who asked the question determined the best answer.

Step 6. Evaluating students' performances in the activity. The teacher made a sensible evaluation about every member's performance in CL. The evaluation was mainly based on students' pronunciation, the quality of the questions and the correctness of the answers.

9.4.2.3　Sample Activities after Reading

The following example is one sample of activities after reading. It is group investigation.

Usually, in group investigation, every group undertakes part of the whole investigation task. Then members in each group assign the task again to make sure everyone has definite task. The members support and help each other to fulfill the tasks so that the anxiety can be reduced and interest can be increased. Group investigation as an activity of CL can help to stir interaction and communication among members.

The reading material of this example is from Unit 11, Text A from New Extensive Reading, Book I. The passage is about advertisements, including the history, the effects on people's life, and so on. The activity was organized in the following way.

Step 1. Forming Teams. Teams were formed in the process of preparation.

Step 2. Assigning the tasks. The teacher asked each group to make a survey in the campus. They should investigate how many people think advertisements are beneficial and how many people think they are useless. And the reasons.

Step 3. Assigning the tasks among each group. Each member took his or her own responsibility. Someone was in charge of interviews, someone was in charge of recording, someone was in charge of gathering statistics, and so on. The tasks should be detailed and proper.

Step 4. Investigation. This was the most time-consuming activity. The members had to work hard and cooperatively to finish this.

Step 5. Analyzing the statistics among each group. The members in each group organized and analyzed the collected statistics. Finally they should cooperatively write a report.

Step 6. Group presentation. One selected member of each group read the report to the other groups.

Step 7. Evaluating students' performances in the activity. The teacher made an evaluation about every group's report. The evaluation was mainly based on students' working attitude, the writing quality of the reports and the depth of the investigation.

9.5　Summary

To see if the implementation of CL theory can improve students' reading ability and reading interest is the clear goal of the experiment. The researcher chose two classes of students in Jilin Agricultural Science and Technology College as the experiment subjects, with one class being the EC and the other being the CC. The researcher used three instruments: tests, questionnaires and interviews. Two tests were given to both the EC and the CC. Two questionnaires were given to the EC at the beginning of the experiment and at the end of it. Interviews were occasionally done by the researcher in the EC. The experiment was carefully prepared and designed. During the implementing, various of activities of CL were used. The researcher gave three examples to show how CL was applied in extensive reading teaching for English-majors.

The experiment lasted for a term, during which both the researcher and the subjects enjoyed the experiment. Both classes are under the researcher's instruction so the experiment could be carried conveniently and effectively. The students gave the researcher great support and trust. The experiment was also strongly supported by the leaders of English Department of in Jilin Agricultural Science and Technology College. All of these ensured the experiment was smoothly conducted.

Chapter Ten Data Analysis

10.1   Analysis of Test Scores

To test the effects of CL theory applied in extensive reading teaching for English-majors, the researcher used the traditional teaching method and the CL method in the CC and the EC respectively. Then the researcher measured their English reading ability by a pretest at the beginning of the semester and a posttest at the end of the semester.

Data of the test scores were from the official record of the English Department of Jilin Agricultural Science and Technology College (Figure 10. 1). In the process of data computation,

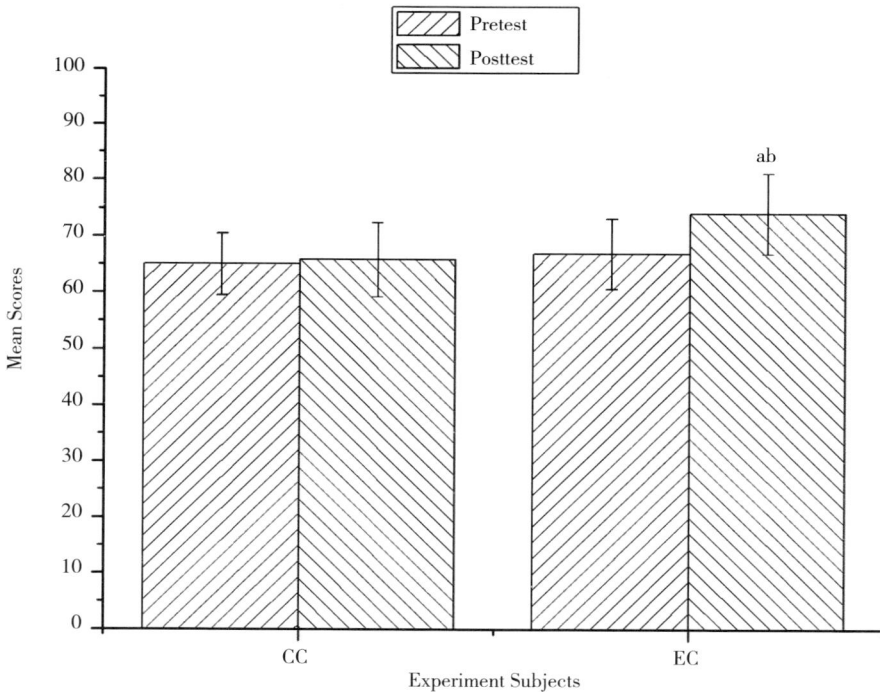

Figure 10. 1   Mean Scores Comparison of the CC and the EC in the Pretest and the Posttest.

the SPSS—statistical package of social science for windows product was used. In using the SPSS, values are expressed as the means ± SD. $^aP < 0.05$, compared with the EC. $^bP < 0.05$, compared with the CC.

As shown in Figure 10.1, in the pretest, the mean score of the CC was 64.95 and the mean score of the EC is 65.825. It's evident that before the experiment, the two classes have no significant difference in the scores ($P > 0.05$). After one semester's experiment of applying CL theory in the EC, the mean score of the CC is 66.85 and the mean score of the EC is 74.05. The mean score in the EC is significantly higher compared with that in the CC group ($P < 0.05$). Besides, in the EC, the mean score in the posttest is significantly higher compared with that in the pretest ($P < 0.05$), while in the CC, the mean score in the posttest has no significant difference compared with that in the pretest ($P > 0.05$).

Besides mean scores, the researcher used another detailed score sections to analyze the statistics.

As shown in Table 10.1, in the pretest, nine students in the CC get scores below sixty, which takes up 22.5% of the total students. In the EC, eight students get scores below sixty, which takes up 20% of the total students. The numbers of students who get scores of sixty to seventy are fifteen and sixteen in the CC and in the EC respectively, and the percentages are 37.5% and 40% respectively. In the CC, twelve students get scores of seventy-one to eighty, which takes up 30% of the total students. In the EC, the number is eleven and the percentage is 27.5%. In the CC and in the EC, four students get scores of eighty-one to ninety, which takes up 10% of the total students. No one gets scores above ninety in the CC, and in the EC, one student get scores above ninety.

Table 10.1   Scores Comparison of the CC and the EC in the Pretest

S N&P	Below 60	60~70	71~80	81~90	Above 90
CC	9 22.5%	15 37.5%	12 30%	4 10%	0
EC	8 20 %	16 40%	11 27.5%	4 10%	1 2.5%

(S: Scores N&P: Number and percentage)

In total, the scores in the EC are a little higher than those in the CC, but there was no significant difference.

As shown in Table 10. 2, in the pretest, six students in the CC get scores below sixty, which takes up 15% of the total students. In the EC, two students get scores below sixty, which takes up 5% of the total students. The numbers of students who get scores of sixty to seventy are fourteen and thirteen in the CC and in the EC respectively, and the percentages are 35% and 32. 5% respectively. In the CC, sixteen students get scores of seventy-one to eighty, which takes up 40% of the total students. In the EC, the number is fifteen and the percentage is 37. 5%. In the CC, three students get scores of eighty-one to ninety, which takes up 7. 5% of the total students and in the EC, seven students get scores of eighty-one to ninety, which takes up 17. 5% of the total students. In the CC, one student get scores above ninety, and in the EC, three students get scores above ninety.

Table 10. 2　Scores Comparison of the CC and the EC in the Posttest

S N&P	Below 60	60~70	71~80	81~90	Above 90
CC	6 15%	14 35 %	16 40%	3 7.5%	1 2.5%
EC	2 5 %	13 32.5%	15 37.5%	7 17.5%	3 7.5%

(S: Scores N&P: Number and percentage)

In total, in the CC, the scores in the posttest are a little higher than those in the pretest but there is no significant difference, while the scores in the EC are significantly higher compared with those in the CC as well as those in the pretest.

According to the above data, we can conclude that before the experiment, the students in the CC and in the EC don't have significant differences in their reading ability. After the experiment, the EC has outperformed the CC in reading ability. CL theory does have positive influence on students' English learning and it confirms that the implementation of it can improve students' reading ability.

10. 2　Analysis of Questionnaires

Two questionnaires were designed in this research. They were addressed only in the EC before and after this experiment.

10.2.1 Analysis of Questionnaires Before the Experiment

The data in Table 10.3 draws a clear picture of the students' former English learning experiences, their learning interest, attitude, motivation, classroom behaviors and feelings toward each other and the teacher.

Table 10.3   The Result of the Questionnaire before the Experiment

I N&P	1	2	3	4	5	6	7	8	9	10	11	12
N A%	0 0	0 0	2 5	34 82.5	3 7.5	8 20	31 77.5	8 20	32 80	35 87.5	7 17.5	2 5
N B%	5 12.5	19 47.5	22 55	4 10	13 32.5	28 70	0 0	29 72.5	5 12.5	2 5	28 70	29 72.5
N C%	35 87.5	21 52.5	16 40	3 7.5	24 60	4 10	9 22.5	3 7.5	3 7.5	3 7.5	5 12.5	5 12.5

(I: item N: number P: percentage A. B. C: the choice items for each question)

Item one is about students' former CL experiences. As the researcher predicts before conducting the questionnaire, most of the students don't have any experience of CL. Only 12.5% of them once took CL class occasionally. Thirty-five students report that they don't have any experiences in CL and have no idea what CL is. The percentage is 87.5%.

Item two is about the instruction model of their former English classes. It reveals that nobody among the students have ever attended student-centered English classes. Forty-seven point five percent of the students feel that their teachers dominated the classes. Fifty-two point five percent of the students report that there were a few interaction activities in their English classes.

Item three and Item four are about students' classroom behaviors in their former English classes. To the researcher's great surprise, only 5% of them often volunteer to answer questions. Fifty-five percent of the students claim that they are not willing to answer any questions unless they are asked by the teacher to do so. There are 40% of the students who even hope not to be called by the teacher. In item four, when being asked the most anxious moment they feel in their English classes, 82.52% of the students feel so when they are asked to answer a question alone facing the whole class.

The result of item five shows that 60% of the students hope they can have classes in an active and relaxing atmosphere.

Item six, seven, eight and nine are about peer roles in English learning. In item six, when meeting difficulties or problems in learning, 70% of the students choose to turn to their classmates for help. In item seven, 77.5% of them try to help others to solve the problems if others seek help from them, because they consider it as a beneficial process. In spite of that, the result of item eight shows that only 20% of them often share learning experience with their classmates. In item nine, when being asked if they'd like to share learning experience with others, 80% of the students give positive answers.

Item ten, eleven and twelve are about their expectations for future English learning. In item ten, when being asked what they think is the most important thing that an English teacher should do in class, 87.5% of students think it should be motivating students' interest in learning English, and developing students' learning ability. In item eleven, 70% of them express that what they want to improve most in their future learning is their language speaking and listening ability, and in item twelve, 72.5% of them hope their English classes will properly combine students' activities with teacher's instruction.

From the above result of the questionnaire, the researcher can conclude as follows: Before entering the university, most of the students had their English classes in a traditional teacher-lectured way. Many students felt very anxious when they were asked to answer questions, much less did they initiatively interacted with the teacher or other classmates. During most of the class time, they would rather listen to the teacher passively and silently. The atmosphere in the classroom was not active. Although students longed for communicating with the teacher and their classmates in English, they seldom had chances or comfortable environment to do so. In spite of these, they still have optimistic attitudes towards their future English learning. They are willing to improve their communicative competence in English. They hope to have English classes in relaxing atmosphere and learn English through interesting interaction activities. In a word, there's a sharp contrast between what the students expected in their mind and what they actually experienced in English classes.

10.2.2　Analysis of Questionnaires After the Experiment

Table 10.4 shows the outcomes of the questions in the questionnaire after the experiment, which is also for the students in the EC. These questions aim to reflect the students' English learning with CL instruction from different aspects, such as the changes of their knowledge about CL, their feelings in learning, the classroom atmosphere and their attitudes towards English learning, etc.

Table 10. 4   The Result of the Questionnaire after the Experiment

I N&P	1	2	3	4	5	6	7	8	9	10	11	12
N	0	33	38	7	30	31	33	34	0	33	34	33
A%	0	82. 5	95	17. 5	75	77. 5	82. 5	85	0	82. 5	85	82. 5
N	36	5	0	31	5	3	3	5	37	7	5	2
B%	90	12. 5	0	77. 5	12. 5	7. 5	7. 5	12. 5	92. 5	17. 5	12. 5	5
N	4	2	2	2	5	6	4	1	3	0	1	5
C%	10	5	5	5	12. 5	15	10	2. 5	7. 5	0	2. 5	12. 5

(I: item N: number P: percentage A. B. C: the choice items for each question)

According to the questions to item one, thirty-six students in the EC think the atmosphere of the extensive reading class is relaxing and harmonious so that they feel more relaxed to learn. The percentage is as high as 90%.

Item two is designed to know the relationship among the students. To the researcher's great delight, 82. 5% of the students agree that they help and support each other to make mutual progress.

Item three is designed to know the relationship between the students and the teacher. The students give positive answers. Ninety-five of them think they have a harmonious relationship with their teacher.

Item four is about the feelings when the students answer questions. Seventy-seven point five percent of the students don't feel as anxious as before and they want to behave well to express themselves. It shows that after the experiment they are learning with much more enthusiasm.

Item five and six are designed to know the students' behaviors in group work. Seventy-five percent of them are willing to participate in group work actively and try their best to fulfill their tasks. Seventy-seven point five percent of them manage to reach an agreement with others through peaceful discussions when they have different opinions.

In item seven, when being asked about others' opinions, 82. 5% of the students claim that views and information from others are helpful to them. In fact, through the sharing of the information, the students in the EC can broaden their knowledge and learn to view things from different angles, which directly leads to the result of item eight. About the effect of CL, eighty-five of the students think that they have a better understanding of what they have learned.

In item nine, 92.5% of the students claim that through CL, they learn to understand how others feel, accept different opinions and communicate with others better. These are all necessary qualities in language learning.

In item ten, 82.5% of the students are willing to complete the assignments the teacher arranges in classes and outside of classes.

In item eleven, thirty-four students think that their interest in extensive reading improves a lot. The percentage is as high as 85%.

In item twelve, about the expectations in future study, 82.5% of the students think CL is necessary enough to go on.

The above positive results indicate that the implementation of CL theory does promote students' individual responsibility and learning interest as well as their attitudes, feelings and behaviors in the learning process. When answering the questions, the students in the EC feel more relaxed than before, which can be attributed to their increased and confidence in addition to the improved classroom atmosphere in which they feel easier to express themselves. In CL class, students have more opportunities to talk in English with peers and make preparations for the questions. Therefore, students tend to have a better understanding of what they have learned. Besides, the students in the EC learn how to deal with conflicts in their cooperation properly and how to communicate with others skillfully so that they have better teacher-student relationship and peer relationships than before.

10.3 Analysis of Interviews

Through the interviews, the researcher found that students had a steady increasing satisfaction toward the implementation of CL theory.

At the very beginning of the experiment, when the researcher interviewed students about CL, only five students eagerly expressed their likeness and expectations toward it. With the experiment going on, all the students knew more about CL but some of them were not very accustomed to it. They complained about some problems and worries they met in the process of CL. For example, because of lack of experience, sometimes they couldn't organize their group work properly. Some students had trouble in speaking English and understanding others. However, with time passing by, more and more students got accustomed to CL, began to love it and confirmed the effectiveness of CL. Positive comments from the students in the EC focused mostly on their satisfaction about the improvement in their English proficiency, reading interest, and communicative skills. They also expressed their appreciation for the chances to exchange opinions with peers. What's more, almost all the students mentioned that they liked the current extensive reading class and the teacher very much.

The following are some samples of students' response to the questions from the researcher in the interviews.

Student A: CL brings extensive reading more fun and gives me the opportunity of more exchanges and discussions. In this environment, I am encouraged to communicate so as to learn more. Each student has the opportunity to express himself or herself. English learning becomes more effective so I feel my reading ability is improving. But the classroom is a little noisy.

Student B: I like group activities that make our English classes active and relaxing. In my former English classes, teachers were always explaining the text paragraph by paragraph which made the teachers and us very tired. Now I have the opportunity to share my opinions in the classroom. When I encounter difficulties, I can discuss with others and I become relaxed. I improve the reading ability and I become more independent in learning than before.

Student C: CL improves our communication skills, and it also allows us to know how to effectively work with other students. But its disadvantage is that some students consciously escape the tasks, leaving what he should do to the group leader because they are lazy. Another disadvantage is that if your partner does not understand the information I provided, I have to slow down and explain again and again. Anyway I think the advantages of CL are more than its disadvantages, so it's worth using.

Student D: When I do not understand some of the learning content, my companion can help me. It makes me feel good. Now only extensive reading teacher is using CL but I hope all the teachers can use this approach. I think this approach is very effective, when I discuss with classmates around me, I feel relaxed. I can concentrate on learning.

Student E: Working with others improves my ability to complete the learning task, or to do what I can't do by myself. CL allows me to listen to the opinions of others, which makes me consider the issue from another angle, so my horizons are widen. I think during the process of CL, I can learn more and understand the materials better.

Student F: When working with others, I think my confidence has increased. Through group discussions I can quickly understand the learning content, and I'm not as nervous as before. Everyone has their own strengths and weaknesses, so we can learn from each other. By observing others, we learn from each other to improve our communication skills. Sometimes when I find I have the same opinions with others, I feel it's really interesting. Sometimes I find I can understand explanation from peers more easily because we are at the same level of thinking.

Student G: Now I know teachers' feeling when the students' do not listen to them. When I am making the presentation, I feel terrible if others do not listen to me carefully. But when the others understand my explanation and positively respond to my presentation, I'm so excited. I experience both difficulties and pleasure in CL and I can understand my teachers more. I am more interested in learning English than before.

These subcategories make reference to the cooperative behaviors that participants evidenced during the project implementation; it also presents the benefits, advantages and difficulties. To begin with, it is important to mention that behaviors that emerged during the incorporation of cooperative learning to foster reading skills were: communication, interaction, cooperative planning, sharing ideas, decision making, leadership and motivation. In the same way, confidence also appeared along the project since students had to solve problems and dealt with them in a proper way, it is worthy to see how trust is built when students can see their partners' ability to figure out a solution. Similarly, the value of the student's contribution to learning in a group was a vital element evidenced during the second group interview, one of the students said he liked working with people who wanted to win, he also noted how working together to reach a goal made him feel great when other members helped him understand the text and explained ideas when he did not understand certain vocabulary, he feels he knows a lot more now.

As it was indicated by this student, collaborative learning gave them an opportunity to socialize, they changed their attitude towards group work and positive interdependence which is a main component of cooperative learning and this was evident during the project implementation. "Positive interdependence exists when individuals perceive that they can reach their goals if and only if the other individuals with whom they are cooperatively linked also reach their goals and, therefore, promote each other's efforts to achieve the goals" as Johnson, et al. stated in 2007, this means that showing a mutual interest of winning which indirectly implies learning and interacting is one of the most important cooperative social behaviors.

When students talked about the difficulties and challenges of improving reading through cooperative learning activities they highlighted the importance of carrying out activities that were more dynamic rather than going through a text several times, because these allowed them to feel safer and their self-confidence increased as indicated in the following excerpt: "We felt different from the previous English classes; we felt that we are important and that we can contribute so the group can have better results. We don't have a good English level but when we read an article and we go through it by pieces it is easy to understand and learn new words. That kind of learning made me participate in the classes and now we are not ashamed or shy to work. "

Providing a confident and safe environment helped students to make better contributions to their learning process in spite of the differences among the members of the group (language level, academic major, learning styles, etc.), this is how we can see that "CL offers learners the opportunity to harness these differences in the pursuit of learning goals in an environment that shows respect for all contributions to learning and in which learners will be more inclined to value themselves and others".

Data also revealed that peer feedback played an important role on students' English language performance because it demonstrated that when students were motivated to work in groups and made important efforts to success, their academic results and participation were higher. In this view, it can be noted that "opportunities for students to discuss, to argue, and to present and hear one another's viewpoints are the critical element of cooperative learning with respect to student achievement".

At the last stage of the implementation of cooperative learning activities to foster reading skills, data illustrated that problem solving was the most challenging factor because students had to deal with assigning roles, accomplishing responsibilities and decision levels. One of the teacher's journal entries said that students spent more than 15 minutes deciding roles such as who is going to be the manager, the reporter, etc. When they did not make a fast decision they started complaining and their voice turned loud. Likewise, during an interview a student argued that it was difficult to agree with his partners as all of them wanted to give orders, this extra time they spent discussing letting the other groups finish first.

It can be seen that this kind of interaction that represented a challenge for students was very useful because it allowed them to manage thinking and social abilities at the same time as well as reinforce the idea that the teacher or instructor must be a learning facilitator to help students to keep working effectively in groups to accomplish the tasks, such a role of facilitator can make a difference when trying to improve learners' skills as Sangadji points out: "Teachers also play a role to help students to plan, implement the plan, and organize group, and serve as academic counselor."After analyzing the core categories, it is possible to say that motivation, interpersonal and group skills, goal achievement, communication among students and teachers, and a safe learning environment provide students with security and confidence to work and learn. This improvement of social skills evidenced excellent student's performance in class considering that when they took a final test and were exposed to different reading activities to assess their knowledge, they obtained good results.

To sum up, most of the students admitted that their communicative ability is improved through CL. They felt relaxing atmosphere so their learning interest increased. Discussions between the students broadened their horizons, exchanges between students caused a psychological change and communication between peers improved their communication skills. They learned to respect and learn from each other. Most of them showed great enthusiasm on CL. It can be seen from the students' evaluation that CL was accepted and loved by most of the students and positive outcomes could be expected to achieve.

10. 4   Achievements of Implementing CL for English-majors' Reading Course

Fruitful results have apparently emerged through the implementation of CL in English-majors' courses. Below are some typical appearances happening. The experimental class experiences the following outcomes.

10. 4. 1   Student-centered Teaching Model

CL makes a complete reform on the teaching model from the traditional teacher-centered model to student-centered model. Students are now the owner of the class, while the teachers are no longer the only central lecturers inEnglish-majors' courses. The class time is properly devoted to students. Teachers are no longer the only resources providers. Both 'tutor' and 'tutee' benefit, since "he who teaches others, teaches himself " as Rodgers stated in 1988. Instead, the teachers are assigned more duties, i. e., to circulate, listen, and assess learning, facilitate interaction, and provide guidance through the process. Of course, not all the class time is devoted to activities, the lectures, demonstrations and teacher-student interaction is still likely to be a important part of instruction. The exact time allocation depends on the particular need and requirements of each lesson.

10. 4. 2   Active and Harmonious Learning Atmosphere

Frequent interactions and communications make the English-majors' courses more attractive than before. Just as one student said, "I found the class more interesting than before. " When they are all properly organized, English-majors' courses are often approached as a union, with plenty of interactions and information provided actively both by the teacher and students. Through the experiment, collaborative learning with its special rich group activities helps promote active learning and create a kind and harmonious atmosphere. The experimental class is reshaped by breaking the whole class into smaller ones. Through offering various interaction chances, students no longer feel dull and sleepy. Instead, they feel the learning process exciting and interesting. The distance between the teacher and students has been shortened and each learner is regarded as an individual, who receives attention from the teacher and other peers as well. The whole experimental class behaves talented and active.

10.4.3 Students' Awareness of Participation

In previousteaching of English-majors' courses, the students have troubles in answering questions and communicating with both the teacher and students in different degree according to Questionnaire 1. However, with the introduction of CL in teaching of English-majors' courses, the safety of small group not only encourages the students' participation, but also ultimately changes the students' psychology. Students become less worried about behaving foolish, about performing naive, about not being quick in learning new knowledge and fluent in answering questions. The clearly defied roles help ensure that the participation is equally distributed so that more advanced, extroverted, self-confident learners are less likely to dominate. Without the worries of being humiliated, the students are willing to have more chances to communicate with each other. And the harmonious atmosphere promotes the students' activeness of participating in English-majors' courses. Also, the other learners equally acquire the confidence and opportunities to speak. This change makes students benefit a lot for their future study.

10.4.4 Students' Psychological Changes

(1) Students' Self-confidence.

Fear of failing or appearing foolish is a constant threat in the language classroom, especially when teachers ask questions which only a few students can answer. Exceedingly, students lack self-confidenceduring the process of learning English in traditional English-majors' courses.

However, when working together to accomplish a task, the students in a group have the responsibilities to plan, organize, and solve problems. Naturally, they gradually get used to undertake a certain role in CL. The anxiety or fear is reduced when the possibility of providing a correct or acceptable answer is increased and when students have had an opportunity to try out their contributions with each other before being asked to offer them to the entire class. In this way, the foreseeable anxiety and lack of self-confidence can be reduced by means of time to think, opportunities to rehearse and feedback to receive. Simultaneously, group mates become the main body of learning and the center of class so that all students can put forward their ideas freely and equally in a relevant relaxed atmosphere of English-majors' courses.

(2) Strengthening Senses of Collective Responsibility and Collective Honor.

In CL, group accountability brings students some pressure andmotivation. Cooperative groups have a common goal, and each learner has an essential role to play. The success of each group member depends on the performance of all its individual members in the group. It is impossible to complete a task or develop product without the contribution from each of the members. The benign and mutual communication and feedback are also developed through evaluating the performance of each group member. In this way, senses of collective responsibility and collective honor are strengthened.

10.4.5 Reform of the Students' Learning Habits

Traditionally, in the teacher-centered class, students' learning habits were as follows: (a) Students usually listened to the teacher, took notes, and did whatever the teacher wanted them to do in classes. (b) Textbook was the only source of knowledge in classes. (c) Rare classroom communications and interdependence happened among the students in class.

However, implementing CL arouses thorough changes in classes. Students are qualified to have theresponsibility to plan, organize, and solve problems in group work.

Naturally, the students' learning habits change: (a) Students learn actively through various forms of group work. Meanwhile, the teacher is no longer the lecture-center, but is supposed to supervise group activity and give help when necessary. (b) Students can learn not only from the textbooks, but also from group mates and classmates. (c) The class is full of love, because students communicate and help each other in the group, even in the whole class.

10.5 Obstacles of Implementing CL for Teaching of English-majors' Courses

Just like the other side of a coin, implementing CL into teaching of English-majors' courses does exist some obstacles such as the limitation of classroom facilities, the classroom chaos, individual differences, and hardness of group communication.

10.5.1 Limitation of the Classroom Facilities

In English-majors' classes, the classroom is usually equipped with fixed desks and chairs, which largely reduces students' face-to-face interaction and the performance of collaborative activities. Though the teacher tried different ways to solve the problem, the difficulties brought to the conducting of CL in teaching of English-majors' courses still exist. In this way, as an objective reason, the implementation of CL in Chinese education must have a long way to go.

10.5.2 Chaos Derived from Grouping

At the very beginning, implementation of CL arouses chaos in classes, e. g. , the students may run about from one seat to another; and shouts and noisescould be heard in every corner of the classroom. As a common phenomena based on previous research, these occurs frequently in CL arranged especially by some inexperienced teachers who are not familiar with CL approach. All this chaos, derived from grouping that is inevitable in implementing CL, are predicable. Therefore, they are called one indispensable part in group processing according to CL. The students admitted that at the beginning they got too excited to concentrate on their learning task when they were grouped, because most of them needed to change their seats. Generally speaking, the reasons of chaos are summarized: (a) Students are not familiar with CL approach; (b) It takes time to study how to learn cooperatively with other classmates.

10.5.3 Individual Differences Among Students

Individual difference also affects the efficacy of CL. In CL classroom, it's easy to find that a small number of students showed indifference to this approach, e. g. , they don't communicate with group mates on learning tasks, but prefer to think over questions independently, complete learning tasks independently. Even if they encounter difficulties in learning, they are likely to turn to dictionary and other references instead of asking help from other group mates. From the interview, some students thought task distribution in CL was not beneficial, because it was hard for students to master overall knowledge. In addition, learning relied mainly on individual effort, and needed continuous accumulation, so cooperation in classroom was not meaningful. Some students stated directly that they were fit for individual learning, not CL with others.

10.5.4 Problems of Group Communication

Although studentsare required to use English as much as possible both in oral and writing work in the divided group, which present a hard nut for them, it occurs that the expressions in Chinese often shift faster and easier than in English, especially meeting with some difficulties or facing greater depth of expression which are hard to explain clearly to partners. Also, most of the students, as we know, speak not good English with poor pronunciation and limited vocabulary. To some extent, this bothers the teacher to implement the CL effectively in English-majors' class.

10.6 Pedagogical Implication

Concerning the achievementsand obstacles in implementing CL in classes, the teachers can attain some pedagogical implications which will be benefit for their future teaching. In another word, collaborative learning will be a good alternative for teaching of English-majors' courses. With the strong witness from the pretest and posttest, and questionnaires, the hypothesis, that implementing CL in class is effective, has been proved true in this thesis, with the comparison between the control group and experimental group. This success owes to the rationale and correct implementation of CL.

Firstly, it is necessary to develop Chinese teachers' awareness of adopting CL for teaching of English-majors' courses comparing to the traditional teaching method.

Acceptance of the reality can help lead to the awareness of the realistic problems inteaching of English-majors' courses. Obviously, the critical factor of language teaching is to provide learners with an occasion to use" the language in real life situation. Language acquisition requires meaningful interaction in the target language, which does not require extensive use of conscious grammatical rules, and does not require tedious drill. The best methods are therefore to supply much more "comprehensible input", in low anxiety situations, under which students can hear more, learn more, and in turn, can make more "comprehensible output". However it is hard to offer such a beneficial condition for learners if the old traditional teaching method is still continuing. In the same way, a learner cannot learn flawless English with limited exposure to the language. Through the experiment, we can see that collaborative learning offers students the opportunity and sufficient time to interact and negotiate with classmates to develop a range of cognitive skills, as well as linguistic skills.

Secondly, it is recommended that CL leads a thorough teaching method change. No doubt, the implementation of CL in English-majors' classes demands systematic and effective classroom management methods. The management differs radically from that in the traditional classroom. From group building, then to leader selecting, last to activity organizing, every step should be carefully designed. The CL encourages students to "sink or swim" together under a clear goal. For each member in the divided small groups has an awareness that the whole group can't succeed without sharing resources, helping, supporting, and inspiring one another, the individuals develop not only linguistic knowledge, but also social skills which facilitate teamwork, create trust and enhance communication, leadership, problem-solving and decision-making abilities in group interaction. Thus, a student-centered class model is instead of the teacher-centered model. In these circumstances, the teacher should not only enjoy the good design of this method, but also implementing it without hesitation in classes.

Thirdly, it is realistic that achievements and obstacles existing side-by-side.

(1) Through themeaningful experiments, the experimental class has been proved more active and effective than the control class. With the new method, the experimental class has been changed from teacher-centered to student-centered dramatically. It is obvious that frequent interactions and communications make the

class more attractive for students than before. In this way, a new and harmonious atmosphere has aroused the students' interests in learning English, which leads the students to master the knowledge voluntarily, instead of passively taking notes and listening to the teacher during class time. Students' psychology also benefits from CL. In cooperative learning group, accountability brings students some pressure and motivation. Meanwhile, it strengthens their senses of collective responsibility and collective honor. Gradually, students' learning habits are changed ultimately.

(2) At the same time, this experiment may also reflect the problems troubling teachers, i. e. the limitation of classroom facilities, the classroom chaos, individual differences, and hardness of group communication. Therefore, this experiment can serve as an opening for other researchers to draw useful experiences and lessons, and in the meantime make out more powerful measures to solve the problems and manage the class with CL effectively.

To sum up, CL approach is a challenge to a number of students. It moves them towards relying on their own judgments and conclusions, so that they become gradually independent.

On the other hand, as a teacher, relegatinglearning tasks and responsibilities to students involves an element of risk. This is not an easy task for teachers who are used to completely control the class. However, despite the barriers and difficulties, the students' responses and enthusiasm will lend a lot of support. Their increased achievement in output and productivity become a reward to the teacher's hard work. Collaborative learning will be a good alternative for teaching of English-majors'courses.

10. 7　Perception of Teacher on Cooperative Learning in the Experiment

Education plays an important role in developing countries to achieve the status of a developed country. This is because education can act a catalyst to produce creative, innovative and knowledgeable students. It can be a determinant of civilization for every country. Therefore, our government intervenes to improve the quality of education in our country to ensure that we can accomplish economic development.

Nowadays, education inMalaysia can furnish students with knowledge and it can also help them develop interpersonal skills, soft skill, and generic skills. We should incorporate appropriate teaching and learning methods in school curriculum in order to improve students' academic performance and enhance their soft skills such as communication skills, leadership and generic skills, simultaneously. One of the methods is cooperative learning.

According to the purpose of cooperative learning is to avail students of the opportunity to think on their own. Therefore, teachers should play an important role in ensuring this method can be successfully and effectively implemented in school. Also, according to the study, teachers can encourage curiosity of students by asking them questions. Thus, the students can make connections between the questions and ideas that have been generated in their mind.

In addition, Che Mansor stated that teachers should encourage students to think effectively in class in order to produce future generation who are able to think creatively and innovatively. Hence, educators do not only deliver their lesson, but emphasize cooperative learning in their class. Students also need to participate in the leaning process so that they can expand their mind.

Nevertheless, this method cannot be successfully and effectively implemented if teachers have scant knowledge about how to use it. The good quality of the implementation should come from teachers who have positive perception and strong awareness about the benefits of cooperative learning. This is because teachers are the individuals who will perceive the learning outcomes as well as the one who will design the learning process including activities and methods used in class. The teaching plan in using cooperative learning methods is important. A good plan can help students realize about the importance of knowing the group and their respective functions thus ensuring the effectiveness of the learning process.

Teachers agree that cooperative learning is one method that can turn on an attractive atmosphere in the classroom as well as to build a more positive attitude in the learning process. Cooperative learning can also forma student-centered teaching and learning compared to existing methods that are more teacher-centered. However, the study also found an efficient implementation of cooperative learning requires a strong commitment from teachers. Teachers need to spend more time preparing for a lesson designing their teaching plan especially when they need to use teaching aids such as audio and video equipment. Mimi H et al. , also believes that the implementation of cooperative learning methods require much more time compared to traditional teaching methods, especially for teachers who are inexperienced.

Although respondents expressed the constraints in the implementation of cooperative learning, this study also proves that these constraints do not prevent teachers to implement it. Items in the teacher needs element, most of the respondents are willing to implement cooperative learning even require more control and commitment. Therefore, even though cooperative learning is not easy to implement but the teacher is still willing to do it for the positive impact on the students gained from this method.

At the same time, as a whole, more respondents agreed with the positive effects from the social and cognitive benefits derived from cooperative learning. These findings are consistent with studiesby Mohaffyza M et al. , which concluded that cooperative learning makes students more confident to provide ideas and be actively involved in learning. In addition, cooperative learning also improves communication and increase student interaction as defined by Effendi et al. , in 2006, Ibrahim et al. , in 2011, Zahara et al. and Mimi H et al. . Each item in the element of cognitive benefit got a positive response from respondents. This proves that the respondents agreed with the cooperative learning positive impact on the cognitive development of students which can be judged from their understanding, presentation ideas, problem solving skills and academic achievement.

Overalls, teachers have a positive view towards cooperative learning. Even though it requires a higher commitment than traditional teaching methods but all the teachers are confidence to practice cooperative learning in order to improve student achievement and make students to become a better person. Cooperative learning is positively viewed as effective learning practice. However, some improvement in terms of equipment availability and school management should be reviewed to make cooperative learning to be more effective.

10. 8   Summary

The impetus for this study comes out of a personal desire of improving the learning environment of Chinese College English Teaching classroom for non-English majors. So this thesis is focused on the research of implementation of CL for English-majors' courses. Holding this belief, the main research questions are solved as follows:

(1) Prove the effectiveness of carrying out CL approach in teaching of English-majors' courses. Students in the experimental group do outperform those in the control group in language learning.

(a) Pretest and Posttest.

With the help of Independent Sample Test of SPSS 10. 0, both the experimental class and control class behaved much similar in the pretest.

On this basis, the posttest mean scores of the experimental class were higher than the means scores of the control class according to Independent Sample Test of SPSS 10. 0; the CL method did play a significant and effective role in teaching of English-majors' courses.

(b) Questionnaire 1 and 2.

Contrast between theexperimental class and control class clearly showed students' learning situation. Most of them admitted they were educated under the teacher-centered boring class for such a long time and were not quite interested in English. With the purpose of passing English exams, the students learning habits behaved traditional for only listening to the teacher, taking notes, and seldom obtaining opportunities of answering questions because of worries of making errors. Most of the students in the experimental class thought that CL had broken the traditional, boring, teacher-centered classroom atmosphere and had created a relaxed and harmonious new classroom environment. Meanwhile, CL stimulated the students to learn actively with the increasing chances of communication. Most of them felt the concern and love from the group mates and they could learn knowledge not only from the book, but also from others, under the teacher's supervision and help when necessary. A majority of students agreed that they had gained self-confidence during the process of group learning in English-majors' classes. Also, the students' psychology had changed in the experimental class. CL strengthened their collective responsibility and collective honor. Meanwhile it brought them pressure and motivation.

(2) Summarize a series of meaningful CL achievements in teaching of English-

majors' courses.

CL made a complete reform on the teaching model from the traditional teacher-centered model to student-centered model. Frequent interactions and communications made the teaching of English-majors' courses more attractive to students than before. Without the worries of being humiliated, the students were willing to have more chances to communicate with each other. Simultaneously, their self-confidence, senses of collective responsibility and collective honor were strengthened. Also, the students' learning habits were changed: (a) Students learned actively through various forms of group work, while teacher was no longer the lecture-center, but was supposed to supervise group activity and give help when necessary. (b) Students could learn not only from the textbooks, but also from group mates and classmates. (c) The teaching of English-majors' courses is full of love for each other's communication and help in the group, even in the class.

(3) Find out the obstacles affecting the implementation of collaborative learning inteaching of English-majors' courses.

First of all, the fixed chairs anddesks brought embarrassment for face-to-face communication and group work. The implementation of CL arouses chaos in teaching of English-majors' courses at the very beginning. For the individual differences, i. e. knowledge ability, also brought difficulties of communication. In the experiment, a phenomenon is found that expressions in Chinese often shift faster and easier than in English, especially meeting with some difficulties or facing greater complexity of expression which is hard to explain clearly to partners. An additional obstacle is that, most of the students, as we know, speak not good English with poor pronunciation and limited vocabulary.

From the analysis of the tests, questionnaires and the interviews, the author reaches a conclusion that the experiment proves the feasibility and effectiveness of CL in college English reading class.

Firstly, CL emphasizes the practical results of activities in classroom. The atmosphere is greatly changed. Students enjoy completing tasks by discussing with others.

Secondly, the author employ heterogeneous group to promote students to have interest in learning from partners. The facts proved that CL builds a dynamic and interesting model to students. All of the students in EC can learn and think actively which do good to learners' academic improvement. Thirdly, students in cooperative classroom do tasks jointly and assist each other. The interactive learning process strengthened their friendship. The implementation of cooperative learning in experimental class is a success. However, there is no denying that some obstacles exist in this experiment. Some students in interviews stated that they cannot present in English fluently, as a consequence, sometimes they don't dare to stand up to express their ideas. Apart from that, some difficult and complicated questions dampen their interest in participation.

Lastly, time allotment and role assignment is the hard nut for the author to arrange them in a perfect form. The possible solutions for the problems above should be as follows: teaching material and methods should be adjusted constantly. The author should take all these factors into consideration by means of thinking it over and making deep research in the research field of college English reading.

Chapter Eleven Conclusion

11. 1   Answers to the Research Questions

In this experiment of the research, the author has explored the effectiveness CL theory in extensive reading teaching for English-majors. The two research questions proposed before the experiments are:

(1) Can the implementation of CL theory improve students' reading ability?

(2) Can the implementation of CL theory improve students' reading interest?

11. 1. 1   The Implementation of CL Theory Can Improve Students' Reading Ability

In CL class, students are able to develop their reading ability, including ability of guessing words' meaning, ability of reading comprehension, ability of fast reading and ability of summarizing the main ideas. CL develops students' ability to construct their knowledge system mostly by themselves with the help of teacher and classmates. The students begin to read independently and they feel confident in reading activities, at the same time, they are active to use proper reading strategies to deal with problems and finish the tasks.

According to the analysis of test scores of the pretest and posttest, it can be concluded that before the experiment, the students in the CC and in the EC don't have significant differences in their reading ability. After the experiment, the EC has outperformed the CC in reading ability. CL theory does have positive influence on students' English learning and it confirms that theimplementation of it can improve students' reading ability.

11.1.2 The Implementation of CL Theory Can Increase Students' Reading Interest

Theimplementation of CL theory increases students' active participation and language performances. When the students have a clear communicative need for the target language, they are more likely to take an active part in the activities. The carefully designed CL activities help to meet students' communicative need so that the students are willing to cooperate. Certainly, the active participation leads to the positive classroom atmosphere. Besides, each student is able make his or her own contribution to the group, and win respect from other students, which leads to his or her increasing confidence and self-esteem in interactions. CL also helps to build students' teamwork spirit. Compared with the traditional language classroom, students have much more opportunities to work with different classmates in activities. In this way, they learn how to communicate with different people appropriately, how to take different opinions from others modestly and how to express their own opinions.

According to the analysis of students' answers to the questionnaires as well as the interviews, classroom atmosphere in CL became more harmonious, students' anxiety level decreased, their reading interest increased, student-student and teacher-student relationships became closer and positive influence of CL on students' English learning could be easily found in the EC.

11.2 Limitations of the Research

There still remain some limitations which may affect the validity of this research.

(1) The experiment is a small-scaled and short-term project. One semester is not long enough to completely prove the effectiveness of a pedagogical approach, although consistent positive outcomes have been achieved in this study. CL needs long-term preparation and strict arrangement. Both teachers and students need long time to adjust to it. Besides, the number of the subjects was not large enough since it's only a classroom research which involved only one teacher and eighty students.

(2) All the English learning skills should be closed related to each other and can't separated from others. This research didn't sufficiently combine reading with

listening, speaking and writing. As a result, to some degree the efficiency of the experiment was affected.

(3) Due to teaching condition limitation, there's not an effective combination of CL with modern teaching techniques.

(4) The experiment of the implementation of CL theory in extensive reading teaching was properly implemented but some practical problems did exist in the implementation of this research. (a) Sometimes the tasks of each member were not clearly assigned. Some members had too much to do while some members have much less even nothing to do. This leads to the result that some students got more training chances than others. (b) Sometimes the teacher didn't play her role very properly. The teacher sometimes couldn't help explaining some information to students especially when they met some problems instead of giving them chances to find out the correct understanding by themselves. (c) When evaluating the students' performances, the result was paid more attention to than the process. To some degree this will decrease students' motivation. (d) Sometimes there were still a few students taking a free ride in the activities, or they couldn't help speaking in Chinese to conduct the task, especially when they found their teacher was communicating with other teams. These problems decreased the fruitfulness of the implementation to some degree.

There are some other unavoidable limitations in this research though we have benefited a lot from it. Firstly, a 1 6-week semester is a relatively short time for all of the participants, which leads to ignorance of many other aspects that possibly affect the results. Students are not having enough time in directing their study but it costs too much time in familiarizing the concept and procedures of this new learning method. Therefore, the results of the thesis are far from conclusive. Secondly, the sample and scope of the research are limited to one class and the subjects are limited to 34 students. So the result would be much more persuasive if more college teachers are involved. And the techniques would be much feasible if more experimental student and activities were involved in the experiment. Thirdly, from where I stand, variate in cooperative learning model is another important factor such as participants' English level and their emotion change during the experiment which leads to a technical problem. A more reasonable and effective grouping is to be constructed. Finally, it is a little subjective in the whole process for it was done by one researcher. Will it be more reasonable if a network is built within school?

Finally, it would be possible for people to argue whether cooperative grouping is beneficial to students at all levels. Since the cooperative learning is a variety of internal processes, will it be affected by students' temperament and other individual factors? All these problems entail plentiful experience to solve.

11.3　Differences between CL and Traditional Group Learning

According to Johnson, there are many differences between CL groups and traditional learning groups. Many Chinese researches have also noticed this. Firstly, CL groups are based on the active cooperation of the members. During the learning process, all the members must concentrate on their own performance as well as that of others. The learning aim is reached through cooperation. Secondly, in the model of CL, each member has definite responsibilities, while in traditional group learning, the responsibilities are often not taken on definitely enough to ensure the learning efficiency. Thirdly, in the CL groups, the members are not at the same level in their abilities and their character is different from each other. As a result, the members can help each other and benefit from others' strong points. The members in traditional learning groups are similar to each other in their abilities and character. Fourthly, all the members in CL groups should act as leaders while the leaders in the traditional learning groups are assigned to be responsible for the activities. Fifthly, each member in CL groups should share the learning tasks. They will help and encourage each other to ensure that everyone can fulfill the assigned tasks, while few people will be responsible for others' learning tasks in traditional learning groups. Sixthly, in CL groups, the students lay emphasis on how to maximize everyone's learning ability and keep good relationship of cooperation between members. While in traditional learning groups, the students lay more emphasis on whether they can fulfill their own assigned tasks on time. Seventhly, in CL groups, the teachers will directly teach the students some necessary social communication and cooperation techniques. In traditional groups learning, however, the teachers always ignore this kind of guidance and help. Eighthly, in CL groups, the teachers pay more attention to whether the members really learn by cooperation and whether each member takes on his own responsibility and plays his role. In traditional groups learning, however, the teachers pay more attention to the learning result and ignore the learning process.

As Panitz in 1999 mentioned that well-developed instructional strategies offer many potential benefits to learners. Much difference exists between cooperative learning and traditional methods in various aspects. In other words, cooperative learning is considered as the complement and breakthrough against traditional reading instruction. The cooperative learning method lays its emphasis on the students themselves, which is the main force of the novel approach. The teacher is the center of the class in the traditional method, which constrains students' improvement in academic achievement. In the traditional class, what the teacher always does is to present and give an order to students. Students have to listen and respond to the teacher only when called on. Students stand alone and have no chance to practice the language and other non-intelligence qualities which influence their interest and learning motivation in English.

However, cooperative class is such a kind of multi-functional class in which students Can exchange information, actively gather information by themselves. Students take on different roles in activities. Such complex social system enlarges their involvement skills. Each student get the sense of self-esteem in a positive atmosphere than in competitive and individualistic classroom, students' autonomy will be raised gradually. In effective cooperative learning groups, every student plays their role in the same task, they talk about a same topic, express their own opinions, listen to partner's ideas and debate, then they reach a consensus from which they gain a deeper understanding of the new knowledge and form the critical thinking.

In cooperative learning groups, heterogeneous group mixed students with distinct sex, personality, academic achievements, and social skills and SO on. Grouping is the key element to carry out cooperative model successfully especially in the beginning of the research. In the present research, the author divided students into 8 heterogeneous groups of four based on their pre-test results and observations. Each group consists of a high-performing student, two average students and a student of low-level. The author shows great expectation for the results of this study.

11.4　The Advantages of CL Against Traditional Models in English-majors' Courses

CL differs in several aspects from traditional models of teaching. A comparison of traditional and CL models of teaching was made by Kohonen.

As shown in Table 11.1, the traditional model of teaching assumes that the teacher is the person in authority in the class whose job is to import knowledge and skills to the learners. Knowledge is seen as definable in terms of right and wrong answers. Students tend to see their roles as relatively passive recipients of the knowledge, expecting the teacher to be in charge of their learning.

Table 11.1　A Comparison between Traditional and CL Models of Teaching

Dimension	Traditional Model	CL Model
1. View of learning	Transformation of knowledge	Transmission of knowledge
2. Power relation	Emphasis on teacher's authority	Teacher as 'a learner among learners'
3. Teacher's role	Providing mainly fontal-instruction; professionalism as individual autonomy	Facilitating learning (largely in small groups); collaborative professionalism
4. Learner's role	Relatively passive recipient of subject matter; mainly individual work	Active participation, largely in cooperative small groups
5. View of knowledge	Presented as "certain"; implementation, problem solving	Construction of personal knowledge; identification of problems
6. View of curriculum	Static, hierarchical grading of subject matter, predefined contents	Dynamic; looser organization of subject matter, including open parts and integration
7. Learning experiences	Knowledge of facts, concepts and skills; focus on content and product	Emphasis on process: learning skills, self-inquiry, social and communication skills
8. Control of process	Mainly teacher-structured learning	Emphasis on learner: self-directed learning
9. Motivation	Mainly extrinsic	Mainly intrinsic
10. Evaluation	Product-oriented: achievement testing; criterion-referencing (and norm-referencing)	Process-oriented: reflection on process, self-assessment; criterion-referencing

The CL, on the other hand, would seem to offer potential for a learning atmosphere of shared partnership, a common purpose and a joint management of learning. Class behavior is owned by the whole group, of which the teacher is one member. As the rules of conduct are agreed upon jointly, and are based on mutual trust and respect, they are there to remind the participants of their joint responsibilities. Knowledge is seen as open to negotiation and redefining by challenging existing constructions of meaning. Learning can become a discovery of new understandings. As there are fewer underlying tensions, energy can be channeled into more creative pursuits.

11. 5   Suggestions for Future Research

The researcher puts forward some suggestions for future researches.

(1) To increase the validity of the experiment, the research time should be extended to two semesters or four semesters. The result of the experiment can be more conniving and effective.

(2) Cooperation between teachers should be encouraged. CL can be better carried out if it is applied by different teachers in teaching of different subjects.

(3) CL theory should be combined with modern teaching techniques. Modern techniques can make teaching more interesting and save time.

(4) CL theory should be combined with other advanced teaching method. For example, before this research, the researcher did another experiment using interaction teaching mode in extensive reading teaching in another class. The former experiment left much experience in organizing class activities, collecting data and analyzing data. It was the foundation of this research and ensured the successful fulfillment of this research. The effect may be greater if two teaching methods were combined properly.

The research is still in its infancy. A future study is badly needed. Some more suggestions are as follows: (a) The author intended to expand the research to a larger scope of students and last for a longer period of time, for the whole experiment is conducted in two classes within sixteen weeks, which is restricted for fully proving the effectiveness of a new teaching method. (b) The author planed to assess oral English in the future study. Due to the limitation of tapes and other facilities, the author has given up the original thought of testing oral English. The author will compensate for this pity in future study. Therefore, further research to a larger scope of students, a longer period of time, and the extension of research item will be the aim of the second stage, which is both necessary and fruitful. It's indicated in this research that CL does have positive influence on extensive reading teaching for English-majors. In spite of the limitations, the author still hopes that the study can contribute to the language teaching reform and provide language teachers some experience for reference.

11. 6 Reflections on the Research

Now, we can refer to the question of this research study: What is the impact of cooperative learning projects on undergraduate students reading skills in a public university?

It was demonstrated through the data collection procedures (surveys, group interviews and teacher's journal) that collaborative learning activities and the implementation of reading strategies actually helped students to understand an article deeper and engaged students in group discussions that fostered communication with others. One of the projects that clearly illustrated this was the implementation of the second project Cooperative Integrated Reading and Composition (CIRC), students integrated the reading strategies used in the first project, Students Teams-Achievement Division (STAD), and they started to be more aware of how their learning process was and how they selected what they read as an important component of their process to become professionals. Hence, it can be appreciated how making learners more aware of their own learning process and "teaching students to become constructively responsive readers can promote skillful academic reading, which, in turn, can enhance academic achievement" as Sheorey et al. stated in 2001. That is consistent with some assertions found in students' comments in the survey and the teacher's journal: "Developing reading strategies during the class has helped me to understand the texts that I have to read in robotics (now I can participate because the teachers speaks English too); I liked analyzing titles because it helped my brain to start thinking in English". "Today students' attitudes were much better. At jigsaw, they laughed, worked together without yelling at anybody. Their faces were happy, they didn't show any stressed when reading the magazines as in previous classes. It was evident that communication among the participants of each group has improved a lot" Teacher's Journal.

These results highlight another benefit of group cooperation, that is, interaction became more active because students had to infer, summarize and present a whole report about the article they read. Though these projects were intended to help students implement a set of different strategies to comprehend a text it also helped to build a positive attitude to the reading activities. Student F affirmed during the third group interview that now he loved English classes because he noticed he was good at inferring and proposing questions related to the article; this allows us to see that the more motivated students are, best results can be seen during the student's performance in class. A motivated student interacts easily with the reading texts and influences positively on their group development.

At the end of this research study the same initial survey was implemented. Results showed that 25 out of 45 students started to read in English especially magazines or articles related to their programs. 10 students started to read in English other topics of interest such as literature and sociopolitical issues after being involved in the research and the last 10 students were not interested in reading in English.

In the last interview 25 students agreed that their reading proficiency improved, they said that the way they used to read changed throughout the project implementation. 10 students affirmed that after the English course skills such as planning, organizing their academic activities improved. The other 10 students explained that they do not read in English during their free time, but enjoy reading in class because they learnt new vocabulary related to their majors and they have the teacher right away to clear up doubts. Mistar, et al. stated "The students who are taught reading by using reading strategies training technique have significantly higher scores of literal and inferential comprehension than those who are taught using more traditional one" in 2016. From this perspective, it can be inferred that students became more aware of what strategies or techniques can be implemented to understand a whole text as identifying its organization, different types of texts, understanding main ideas, and the use of new vocabulary. These aspects are important to improve reading comprehension skills.

To summarize, it can be said that thanks to the implementation of the projects, the use of reading strategies increased and improved students' reading comprehension skills. 57% of the participants strongly agreed that they were able to make associations when they did not understand a word; 43% agreed that their ability to contextualize the reading with their real context improved. Students were also able to make decisions in the way they want to improve their reading comprehension skills; student H said in the last group interview "I am able to decide if I have to foster comprehension by making questions or by selecting main ideas which are the strategies that I now employ the most". Motivation and confidence were also important factors because they let students have a more active participation and a positive attitude regarding the reading activities. 57% of the participants strongly agreed that after the English course they enjoyed reading technical engineering online magazines because it helps their career development so they were more confident to participate in other subjects. The other 43% established that they now enjoy reading literature and other topics.

As a final remark, it can be inferred that students enhanced their reading comprehension skills by using different reading strategies and texts they were interested in.

Students also felt that activities helped them to improve their attitude and ability to read in English and the projects were suitable to promote interaction in the class instead of the traditional use of English textbooks.

"I did not attend English classes of English before because they were boring, the activities were the same every semester, and all teachers used the same book so I asked my friends to lend their books. This course was different; dynamic I was always doing things and shared with different people too" "I liked to have the feeling that the teacher was a classmate too, she was always sitting with us instead of writing verbs or grammar on the board as in previous courses".

Along the implementation of the projects, students expressed their insights about cooperative learning, they showed a positive attitude toward working in teams because they received support, feedback of their learning performance and they had an active participation during the English classes as it was evidenced in the third and fourth students` interviews "This is the first time I understand how to work in groups; everyone did what had to do. it was fun to correct my classmates without being annoyed".

Similarly, it is possible to say that motivation, interpersonal, group work skills, goal achievement, communication among students and teachers, and a safe learning environment provide students with security and confidence to work and learn. Those aspects led to evidence of the improvement of social skills in the group work which would result in an excellent student's performance in class. Additionally, students were able to foster their problem solving skills.

Even though results were significant to see changes during the English course, it is necessary to continue examining the effectiveness of cooperative learning and how its implementation can foster not only the reading skills but also all English language skills. Further research should look for other alternatives of cooperative learning projects to be implemented at the university level to have an important impact on the bilingualism policies of the current government.

This research study has examined the impact of cooperative learning projects by mainly fostering reading skills. The study revealed that students changed the way they perceived the English subject by working in a cooperative environment that promotes confidence, communication, motivation and problem solving skills. It was evidenced that no matter what the student's English level is, the amount of vocabulary they know or their content knowledge based they have because if the students are highly motivated and the interaction in the class is active, their reading performance unquestionably rise.

Cooperative learning projects used in this research study, they fostered group work and social skills since they had the opportunity to manage the roles and activities they had to report. They took advantage of having the language teacher as a language facilitator when they did not understand or did not know how to share an idea. Moreover, students displayed confidence levels when interacting in groups and working in a safe environment.

Opportunities to improve their reading skills were also evident when they were exposed to authentic material related to their majors. Motivation here was crucial to have an active reading participation along the project, in this way the most motivated students got the most significant academic results.

Cooperative learning implementation has positive effects on students' English language performance in class and it was evidenced with the results of the final tests students took and also with the activities done in class. They shared their ideas without feeling ashamed about making mistakes. Student's perceptions and confidence to interact in the English language were enhanced. Results emerged from this research study have a great significance in the teaching context and the value of implementing cooperative learning into all the English language levels that offer the university because students can transform their passive role to an active and responsible role of their own learning process and improve goal achievement and autonomy.

11.7 Benefits from the Implementing CL in English-majors' Courses

The outcomes of cooperative learning techniques fall mainly into two categories: academic achievement and group cohesiveness. The effects of the techniques on the group cohesiveness variables, such as mutual concern and race relations, are unquestionably positive. The achievement results, though usually positive, seem to depend on the particular techniques, settings, measures, experimental designs, or other characteristics. This section considers possible explanations for these different effects in different studies.

11.7.1 Achievement

Why have some of the cooperative learning techniques and some of the individual studies shown more positive effects on academic achievement than others? One obvious possible explanation for different findings in a program of research is differences in methods. More rigorous studies might be less likely to find significantly positive effects than less rigorous ones. Experimental rigor does explain some of the differences between studies (and between techniques). The TGT studies have the largest number of positive effects on achievement of all the cooperative techniques. Many of the studies used control groups in which the teachers were given the experimental groups' objectives and curriculum materials, but were not held to the same schedule of instruction as the experimental groups. STAD, which is similar to TGT, had somewhat less strong effects on achievement, and all of the STAD studies used the parallel schedule of activities in the control group. This might indicate that the special, focused schedule of activities explains part of the effect of TGT (as well as STAD when it is compared to untreated classrooms), and in fact such an argument is made by

Slavinin 1978. It is of further interest that in the studies on Jigsaw and the Johnson techniques (but not Small-group Teaching, which gave the teachers the same materials but did not standardize the schedule of instruction) the curriculum was similarly standardized between the experimental and control groups. In the research done to date, Jigsaw and the Johnson techniques have been less successful than TGT and STAD in increasing academic achievement.

Other methodological differences between studies do not seem to be related to the outcomes. Studies that did not use random assignment or that conducted random assignment at the class level rather than the student level were not particularly more or less successful than those that were able to randomly assign students to treatments. One feature that may discriminate studies with positive achievement effects from those without is subject matter. Within the TGT studies, effects were much less likely to be found in social studies than in mathematics, language arts, or reading vocabulary. The combined study found effects on language arts and reading vocabulary, but not social studies. The fact that the Jigsaw studies and one of the Johnson studies were in social studies might contribute to the weak effects of these techniques, although one of the Wheeler studies found greater social studies achievement in the cooperative groups than in control groups. The Small-Group Teaching Study, also in social studies, might shed some light on why the effects of cooperative techniques on social studies achievement might be so spotty. Sharan et al. divided their dependent measures into "high cognitive level" and "low level" sets of items. They found positive effects on high level items in three of the five grade levels in which they conducted their study, but found positive effects on the low level items only in the second grade. The dependent measures in the TGT, Jigsaw, and the Johnson studies, as well as the social studies measures in the combined program, were undifferentiated by conceptual level and were apparently weighted toward the low level skills. If these studies had broken their measures into high and low level items, the achievement effects on the high level items might have been positive. The successful Wheeler study also assessed understanding of a process, not simply factual knowledge. One problem that is particularly serious in social studies is that unless the teaching content is very explicitly structured, it is difficult to make certain that what is taught corresponds to what is measured. Students in cooperative social studies classes may be learning effective ways to approach high level material that will show up on a posttest, but their learning of the facts may not correspond enough to the content of the posttest to show a difference.

One relatively consistent difference between the techniques, which is not completely explained by differences in methodology or subject matter, is the stronger effects on achievement for TGT and STAD than for the other techniques, particularly when low level skills are assessed. This is probably due to the use in these techniques of a highly structured system of instruction, team tasks, and team rewards. Students in TGT and STAD are given worksheets to study in their teams. They also receive answers to the worksheet items, so that each team has all the resources it needs to make sure that every team member knows the academic material. Also, each student is individually responsible for his or her learning; teammates cannot help each other during the games (TGT) or the quizzes (STAD). In contrast, studies in the Johnsons' classrooms handed in a single worksheet each day that represented the team product, and the steps that lead to that product were left up to the students, so that this technique is low in individual responsibility for learning and low in structure. Small-Group Teaching is somewhat more structured, and, by encouraging students to establish a division of labor, still has an element of individual accountability for learning (but not nearly as much as in TGT and STAD). Jigsaw is very tightly structured in terms of learning activities, but the original Jigsaw model forces students to rely on one another totally to learn each other's sections. If a student does a poor job of presenting his or her section to the group, the section just does not get learned.

The difference between TGT, STAD, and the Hamblin techniques on the one hand, and the other techniques on the other, is a conceptually interesting one. TGT, STAD, and the Hamblin techniques explicitly use the team structure as a motivational device—a reward system that motivates students in their teams to go over academic material again and again until they and their teammates know it. They do not use the team structure as a way to pool individual skills and ideas. The other techniques use the team structure primarily as a. facilitative device, to encourage students to share ideas, to brainstorm, to decide how to structure its own activity, and so forth. TGT, STAD, and the Hamblin techniques have much in common with group contingencies used in behavior modification, while the other techniques, particularly the Johnson techniques and Small-Group Teaching, have more in common with the open school or other humanistic educational programs. Much of the successful laboratory research on cooperation, including that by Deutschin 1949, has involved high level skills, such as problem solving and brainstorming. For these tasks, group membership clearly has a facilitative effect, as the number and quality of ideas produced may be increased by group interaction. For learning how to multiply fractions or punctuate sentences, however, the group might have only a minimal facilitative effect; the important issue is how to get individuals to practice these skills until they master them. The group that is organized as a discussion group might be a poor structure for learning basic mathematics, as Johnson et al. discovered. On the other hand, it may be an excellent structure for learning high level cognitive skills, as found by Sharan et al. High level skills have not been specifically measured in the TGT and STAD studies, but it is unlikely that such effects would be found; these techniques focus heavily on the basic skills, such as computation, punctuation, and vocabulary.

Another factor that may be systematically related to study outcomes, even within techniques, is the population. In general, studies in middle class white schools have been somewhat less successful in showing achievement gains than those in integrated and/or working class schools. This is further borne out by the findings of Lucker et al. and Slavin et al. of an interaction between ethnicity and treatment favoring gains in cooperative classes by minority students. Wheeler's finding of a strong interaction between cooperative predisposition and achievement gains emphasizes the importance of the particular population involved in a study, particularly as many studies have shown that white, middle class Americans are less cooperatively predisposed than other groups, including American blacks and Mexican-Americans. Only one study reviewed here showed greater achievement in a control group than in a cooperatively taught group, and several studies in white middle class settings showed positive achievement effects, so it is unlikely that these techniques would hurt the achievement of white middle class students. If the ethnicity x treatment interaction holds up, cooperative classroom techniques may be a means of reducing the achievement gap between white and minority students while still increasing the achievement of the whites more than in traditional classrooms. However, the contrary evidence is not inconsiderable; study No. 14, one of the largest and best-controlled of the STAD studies, took place in working class, integrated (40 percent black) junior high schools, and no achievement effects or race x treatment interactions were found.

The use of group competition appears to have some positive effect on achievement, although it is confounded with other factors. What may be important is less whether the groups are in competition or not, but whether or not there is an explicit group reward. The Hamblin techniques did not use competition but did use tangible rewards based on the group score, and found positive effects on achievement, while the Johnson techniques did not use any concrete group rewards and did not find positive effects. On the other hand, Small-Group Teaching did not use group competition or explicit group rewards, but did find positive effects on achievement.

One additional factor that differentiates the various techniques is the use or nonuse of training of teachers and students in group processing skills. The Jigsaw, Small-Group Teaching, and Johnson studies in particular place a heavy emphasis on this training, while TGT, STAD, and the Hamblin techniques do no group process training at all. From the pattern of results in these studies, it does not appear that group process training is a useful addition to a cooperative learning model, but this needs further study.

11.7.2   Race Relations

The effects of student teams on interracial friendship and related variables may be the most important of the outcomes of cooperative techniques. They are relatively consistent and often quite striking. Further, while there may be many ways of increasing student achievement other than the use of student teams, there is some evidence that fostering interracial cooperation is by far the most effective means of improving racial attitudes and behaviors in schools. In 1979, Slavin and Madden conducted a secondary analysis of data collected in a national sample of high schools by the Educational Testing Service, and found that teacher workshops, multiethnic texts, minority history, heterogeneous groups, and classroom discussions of race relations had very few effects on students' racial attitudes and behaviors. On the other hand, assignment of students of different races to work with each other and participation of students on multiracial sports teams had strong and consistent effects on race relations.

There is not yet enough evidence to differentiate among the different techniques or studies for effects on race relations. Only two studies have failed to find positive effects. Weigel et al. found increased positive evaluations of Mexican-Americans by whites in a study using a general cooperative technique, but did not find changes in perceptions of or by blacks or in perceptions of whites by Mexican-Americans. The authors ascribe the failure to find these effects to possible ceiling effects, but it is also possible that their intervention was not structured enough to make the group system salient to the students. One of the four TGT studies failed to find an effect on cross-racial friendship, even though significant effects were found on cross-racial helping. These effects did not appear to be due to a ceiling effect, and are surprising given that three of the successful studies took place in the same school (but with different students and teachers). Weigel et al. also suggest that the use of group competition may have a deleterious effect on race relations, but the positive findings in the TGT and STAD studies do not support this theory.

While none of the cooperative learning techniques are demonstrably more effective than others in improving race relations, the TGT and STAD effects are by far the best established. Of the 11 studies that measured race relations, seven evaluated TGT and STAD; of the four remaining studies, one did not use an adequate measure of race relations, and two found effects for white attitudes toward Mexican-Americans only. On the other hand, positive effects were found in six of the seven TGT-STAD studies. The general applicability of the findings is enhanced by the wide variations in types of schools and percent minority in the schools, as well as the repeated positive findings.

11.7.3 Mutual Concern

As with race relations, the effects of cooperative learning techniques on mutual concern have been generally quite positive, and there are no obvious methodological or technique differences in the effects. The two TGT studies that fail to find effects on mutual concern both took place in third-grade classrooms, where students were initially high on the measure, suggesting a possible ceiling effect, but this was not true in studies, which also found no effects on this variable.

11.7.4 Implications

Presently, the research on cooperative learning in classrooms justifies the following conclusions:

(1) For academic achievement, cooperative learning techniques are no worse than traditional techniques, and in most cases they are significantly better.

(2) For low level learning outcomes, such as knowledge, calculation, and implementation of principles, cooperative learning techniques appear to be more effective than traditional techniques to the degree that they use:

(a) A structured, focused, schedule of instruction;

(b) Individual accountability for performance among team members;

(c) A well-defined group reward system, including rewards or recognition for successful groups.

(3) For high level cognitive learning outcomes, such as identifying concepts, analysis of problems, judgment, and evaluation, less structured cooperative techniques that involve high student autonomy and participation in decision-making may be more effective than traditional individualistic techniques.

(4) Cooperative learning techniques have strong and consistent effects on relationships between black, white, and Mexican-American students.

(5) Cooperative learning techniques have fairly consistent positive effects on mutual concern among students regardless of the specific structure used.

(6) There is some indication that cooperative learning techniques can improve students' self-esteem.

(7) Students in classes using cooperative learning generally report greater liking of school than do traditionally taught students.

What these results indicate is that cooperative learning techniques can achieve both cognitive and affective goals, but that there is still much to be discovered about when they do so-for which kinds of students, under what conditions, in which subjects, and for which techniques or components of techniques are positive effects likely to be observed?

There is already enough evidence from field research to support the use of cooperative learning techniques in schools, particularly desegregated schools. Many of the techniques are not difficult to learn, for example, teacher training for the STAD studies has taken no more than 3 hours, and often less. All of the techniques can be used by individual teachers in traditionally structured classes without outside help, additional expense, or radical changes in schedules or other external features of school organization. The combined program, as well as work by Johnson and by Sharan outside of research studies, has indicated that cooperative learning techniques can be used in classrooms as the dominant instructional mode. That is, cooperation need not be a supplement to the traditional competitive classroom, but can be used to largely supplant it.

11.7.5 Next Steps

The next steps in research on cooperative learning should be directed at explicating the conditions under which these techniques can maximally influence student outcomes. The comparison of techniques presented in this paper is no substitute for a program of research in which important factors are systematically varied in the same design. Some of the factors that might lead to improved understanding of cooperative learning are listed below:

(1) What are the effects of group competition as opposed to non-competition especially on race relations and mutual concern?

(2) What are the effects of teacher and student training in group processing skills?

(3) How important are explicit group rewards in improving performance and cohesiveness outcomes?

(4) How important are racial and ethnic differences in determining the effectiveness of cooperative learning techniques?

(5) For which kinds of learning are cooperative techniques most likely to represent an improvement over traditional techniques, and which techniques are most appropriate for which kinds of learning?

(6) How important is individual accountability in increasing the effects of cooperative learning on achievement?

(7) What are the effects of high student autonomy on outcomes of cooperative learning?

(8) What are the long-term effects of cooperative learning on achievement and positive race relations?

(9) What are the important components of cooperative learning for increasing students' self-esteem?

(10) What are the effects of cooperative learning on teachers' role perceptions, attitudes toward children, and other attitudes?

(11) How can cooperative learning be adapted for such specialized uses as:

(a) Mainstreaming;

(b) Individualization of instruction;

(c) Bilingual education;

(d) Remedial education.

Of course, there are many other issues, both theoretical and applied, that should be addressed. Cooperative learning represents a substantial change in the technology of classroom instruction. It usually involves simultaneous changes in the reward, task, and authority structures of the classroom. Explicating the consequences of these changes, as well as interactions of the changes with participant and setting characteristics, will be an enormous job, but the results that have been obtained to indicate that it is a job worth doing. Research on cooperative learning techniques represents an unusual event in the history of educational research. The techniques arose out of social psychological theory; they have been evaluated in numerous field experiments that were generally high in both internal and external validity; and they are in use in hundreds of classrooms across the country and inIsrael. As in any program of research there is a need for further investigations of interactions, limitations, and extensions of findings, but the basic model has been validated in classroom settings.

11.8   Summary

Teachers who wish to use cooperative learning should ideally base their classroom practices on theory validated by research. The closer classroom practices are to validated theory, the more likely they will be effective. When more directly practice is connected to theory, furthermore, the more likely practice will be refined, upgraded, and improved over the years. There are, however, few classroom practices that are directly based on validatedtheory. The close relationship between theory, research, and practice makes cooperative learning somewhat unique. It also creates a set of issues for teachers using cooperative learning.

The first issue is to understand the nature of social interdependence. Social interdependence is created when goals are structured so that the accomplishment of a person's goal is affected by others' actions. The interdependence may be positive (which results in individuals working cooperatively to achieve their mutual goals) or negative (which results in individuals competing to see who will achieve the goal). The absence of interdependence indicates no connection between people's attempts to achieve their goals. In cooperative situations, students' actions substitute for each other, students are inducible, and a positive cathexis is created toward other's actions. In competitive situations, the opposite psychological processes may be found. The fundamental premise of social interdependence theory is that the way in which goals are structured determines how individuals interact, and those interaction patterns create outcomes. Positive goal interdependence tends to result in promotive interaction, negative goal interdependence tends to result in oppositional interaction, and no interdependence tends to result in no interaction.

The second issue is to understand the research validating social interdependence theory. There are hundreds of studies indicating that cooperation, compared to competitive and individualistic efforts, tends to result in greater effort to achieve, more positive relationships, and greater psychological health. The diversity of this research provides considerable recognition to the findings.

The third issue is to understand the five basic elements that make cooperation work. There is nothing magical about putting students in groups. Students can compete with group-mates, students can work individualistically while ignoring group-mates, or students can work cooperatively with group-mates. In order to structure cooperative learning effectively, teachers need to understand how to structure positive interdependence, individual accountability, promotive interaction, appropriate use of social skills, and group processing into learning situations.

The fourth issue is to understand the flexibility and manyfaces of cooperative learning. When the five basic elements may be effectively implemented in formal cooperative learning situations (formal cooperative learning may be used to structure most learning situations), informal cooperative learning situations (informal cooperative learning may be used to make didactic lessons cooperative), and cooperative base groups (which are used to personalize a class and the school). Together they provide an integrated system for instructional organization and design (as well as classroom management). When utilizing these three types of cooperative learning, any learning situations in any subject area with any age students and with any curriculum can be structured cooperatively.

This study compared the effectiveness of cooperative learning with that of individualistic learning with time on task carefully monitored. The relative effectiveness of the two learning methods was evaluated and compared by conducting a series of experiments in the spring semester using 42 students following a core engineering course in the mechanical engineering department of a national university of science and technology. The major conclusions and contributions of this study can be summarized as follows:

(1) Out-of-class homework sessions were arranged to minimize the risk of confounding the cooperative learning and individualistic learning conditions during out-of-class studies. These sessions made it possible to carefully monitor the learning method and time on task both in and out of the class, which in turn enabled a proper comparison of the relative effectiveness of the two learning methods.

(2) Homework and unit tests were scheduled during the semester to measure students' learning performance at the end of the corresponding homework session or teaching unit. The results of both the homework and unit tests showed that cooperative learning is less effective than individualistic learning in the early stages of the team's development. However, after sufficient time for the team to mature (e. g., 18 weeks in this present study), cooperative learning becomes more effective than individualistic learning.

(3) The students in the cooperative learning condition experienced attention conflict. These results help explain why the consequent improvement in performance occurred gradually, and more importantly, may indicate that students in the cooperative learning condition endured additional pressure due to cooperation. Studies on how to measure and quickly relieve this pressure, and other social-psychology

aspects of the cooperation learning, may increase our understanding of cooperative learning. This in turn may lead to innovative interventions that complement existing cooperative learning methods and enhance the benefits of cooperative learning.

(4) The methodology presented in this study can be adopted by engineering professors, educational practitioners and students to achieve a successful implementation of cooperative learning. The findings presented in this study also remind those first starting out with the cooperative learning methodology, or disappointed with its initial results, that patience and persistence are required if the full benefits of cooperative learning are to be realized.

Bibliography

[1] Aronsen E. The Jigsaw Classroom[M]. California: Sage Publications, 1978.

[2] Allen W H, R L Van Sickle. Learning Teams and Low Achievers[J]. Social Education, 1984(1): 60-64.

[3] Archer-Kath J, Johnson D W, Johnson R T. Individual versus group feedback in cooperative groups[J]. The Journal of Social Psychology, 1994, 134 (5): 681-694.

[4] Baloche L, Brody C M. Cooperative learning: Exploring challenges, crafting innovations[J]. Journal of Education for Teaching, 2017, 43(3), 274-283. doi: 10. 1080/02607476. 2017. 1319513.

[5] Barkley E F, Cross K P, Major C H. Collaborative learning techniques. A handbook for college faculty[M]. San Francisco, CA: Jossey-Bass, 2005.

[6] Bejarano Y A. Cooperative Small-group Methodology in the Language Classroom [J]. TESOL Quarterly, 1987(3): 483-504.

[7] Biggs J. What the student does: Teaching for enhanced learning[J]. Higher Education Researchand Development, 1999, 18 (1): 57 - 75. doi: 10. 1080/0729436990180105.

[8] Biggs J, Tang C. Teaching for quality learning at university (4th ed.)[M]. Berkshire: McGraw Hill, Open University Press, 2011.

[9] Biggs J, Watkins D. The Chinese learner in retrospect. In D. A. Watkins and J. B. Biggs (Eds.), The Chinese learner: Cultural, psychological and contextual influences[J]. CERC and ACER, HongKong: The Central Printing Press 1996, 269-285.

[10] Biggs J B, Kember D, Leung D Y P. The revised two factor study process questionnaire: R-SPQ-2F[J]. British Journal of Educational Psychology, 2001, 71: 133-149. doi: 10. 1348/000709901158433.

[11] Bray M, Adamson B, Mason M. Comparative education research: Approaches

and methods (2nd ed.)[J]. Cham: Springer, 2004.

[12] Brown H, Ciuffetelli D C. 'Foundational Methods: Understanding Teaching and Learning[M]. Toronto: Pearson Education, 2009: 165.

[13] Buchs C, Gilles I, Dutrévis M, et al. Pressure to cooperate: Is positive reward interdependence really needed in cooperative learning [J]? British Journal of Education Psychology, 2011, 81: 135-146. doi: 10. 1348/000709910X504799.

[14] Bulut S. A cross-cultural study on the usage of cooperative learning techniques in graduate level education in five different countries[J]. Revista Lnoamericana de Psicología, 2009, 42: 111-118.

[15] Carcolini P J. Curricula for Sustainability in Higher Education [Book Review]. Journal of Ethnic and Cultural Studies, 2017, 4(2): 102-104.

[16] Cavanagh M. Students' experiences of active engagement through cooperative learning activities in lectures[J]. Active Learning in Higher Education, 2011, 12(1): 23-33. doi: 10. 1177/1469787410387724.

[17] Chalmers D, Gardiner D. The measurement and impact of university teacher development programs[J]. Educar, 2015, 51(1): 53-80.

[18] Cheryl Moen, Bob Adamson. A Course in English Language Teaching [M]. Beijing: Beijing High Educational Press, 2004: 118.

[19] Chong W H, Kong C A. Teacher collaborative learning and teacher self-efficacy: The case of lesson study[J]. The Journal of Experimental Education, 2012, 80 (3): 263-283. doi: 10. 1080/00220973. 2011. 596854 .

[20] Clarke A, Collins S. Complexity science and student teacher supervision[J]. Teaching and Teacher Education, 2007, 23(2): 160-172. doi: 10. 1016/j. tate. 2006. 10. 006.

[21] Coffey M, Gibbs G. Measuring teachers' repertoire of teaching methods [J]. Assessment and Evaluation in Higher Education, 2002, 27(4): 383-390. soi: 10. 1080/0260293022000001382.

[22] Cohen J. Statistical power analysis for the behavioral sciences[M]. New York, NY: Academic Press, 1988.

[23] Cohen J. A power primer[J]. Psychological Bulletin, 1992, 112(1): 155-159.

[24] Çolak E. The effect of cooperative learning on the learning approaches of students with different learning styles [J]. Eurasian Journal of Educational

Research, 2015, 15(59): 17-34.

[25] Felder R M. A longitudinal study of engineering student performance and retention. IV. Instructional methods and student responses to them[J]. Journal of Engineering Education, 1995, 84(4): 361-367.

[26] Du C. The effect of cooperative learning on students' attitude in first-year principles of accounting course [J]. Business Education Innovation Journal, 2015, 7(2): 107-116.

[27] Economides A. Culture-aware collaborative learning[J]. Multicultural Educationand Technology Journal, 2008, 2(4): 243-267. doi: 10.1108/17504970810911052.

[28] Ellisand Rod. The Study of Second Language Acquisition[M]. Oxford: Oxford University Press, 1998: 74.

[29] Felder R M, Brent R. Cooperative learning in technical courses: Procedures, pitfalls, and payoffs. ERIC Document Reproduction Service Report ED 377038, 1994.

[30] Felder R M, Brent R. Effective strategies for cooperative learning[J]. Journal of Cooperative and Collaboration in College Teaching, 2001, 10(2): 69-75.

[31] Felder R M, Brent R. Designing and teaching courses to satisfy the ABET engineering criteria[J]. Journal of Engineering Education, 2003, 92(1): 7-25.

[32] Felder R M, Felder G N, Dietz E J. A longitudinal study of engineering student performance and retention. V. Comparisons with traditionally-taught students [J]. Journal of Engineering Education, 1998, 87(4): 469-480.

[33] Fraenkel J R, Wallen N E. How to design and evaluate research in education [M]. New York, NY: McGraw Hill, 2006.

[34] Garet M S, Porter A C, Desimone L, et al. What makes professional development effective? Results from a national sample of teachers [J]. American Educational Research Journal, 2001, 38(4), 915-945. d10.3102/00028312038004915.

[35] Gay L R, Mills G E, Airasian P. Educational research: Competencies for analysis and implementations [M]. Upper Saddle River, NJ: Pearson Education, Inc, 2006.

[36] Gerstner S, Bogner F X. Concept map structure, gender and teaching methods: An investigation of students' science learning[J]. Educational Research, 2009, 51(4): 425-438.

[37] Gilles R M, Adrian F. Cooperative Learning: The Social and Intellectual Outcomes of Learning in Groups[M]. London: Farmer Press, 2003:79.

[38] Gillies R M. Cooperative learning: Review of research and practice [J]. Australian Journal of Teacher Education, 2016, 41 (3): 39 – 54. doi: 10. 14221/ajte. 2016v41n3. 3.

[39] Gillies R M, Boyle M. Teachers' reflections on cooperative learning: Issues of implementation[J]. Teaching and Teacher Education, 2010, 26(4):933–940. doi: 10. 1016/j. tate. 2009. 10. 034.

[40] Gokhale A A. Collaborative learning enhances critical thinking[J]. Journal of Technology Education, 1995, 7:22–30.

[41] Haller C R, Gallagher V J, Weldon T L, et al. Dynamics of peer education in cooperative learning workgroups[J]. Journal of Engineering Education, 2000, 89(3):285–293.

[42] Hammond J A, Bithell C P, Jones L, et al. A first year experience of student-directed peer-assisted learning[J]. Active Learning in Higher Education, 2010, 11(3):201–212. doi: 10. 1177/1469787410379683.

[43] Herrmann K. The impact of cooperative learning on student engagement: Results from intervention[J]. Active Learning in Higher Education, 2014, 14 (3): 175–187. doi: 10. 1177/1469787413498035.

[44] Haynes N M, Gebreyseus S. Cooperative learning: A case for African American students[J]. School Psychology Review, 1992, 21: 577–585.

[45] Heywood J. Engineering education. Hoboken, NJ: John Wileyand Sons, Inc, 2005. Hibbeler R C. Engineering mechanics dynamics. Jurong, Singapore: Prentice-Hall, Inc, 2004.

[46] Hicks C R. Fundamental concepts in the design of experiments[M]. New York, NY: CBS College Publishing, 1982.

[47] Hinkle D E, Wiersma W, Jurs S G. Applied statistics for the behavioral sciences [J]. Boston, MA: Houghton Mifflin, 2003.

[48] Ho A, Watkins D, Kelly M. The conceptual change approach to improving teaching and learning: An evaluation of a Hong Kong staff development programme[J]. Higher Education, 2001, 42 (2): 143 – 169. doi: 10. 1023/ A: 1017546216800.

[49] Hofstede G H, Hofstede G J. Cultures and organizations: Software of the mind (2nd ed.)[M]. New York: McGraw-Hill, 2005.

[50] Hoon T, Chong T, Binti Ngah N. Effect of an interactive courseware in the learning of matrices[J]. Journal of Educational Technology and Society, 2010, 13(1): 121-132.

[51] Hsiung C M. Identification of dysfunctional cooperative learning teams based on students' academic achievement[J]. Journal of Engineering Education, 2010, 99(1): 45-54.

[52] Hwang G J, Yin P Y, Hwang C W, et al. An enhanced genetic approach to composing cooperative learning groups for multiple grouping criteria[J]. Journal of Educational Technology and Society, 2008, 11(1): 148-167.

[53] Hwong N C, Caswell A, Johnson D W, et al. Effects of cooperative and individualistic learning on prospective elementary teachers' music achievement and attitudes[J]. The Journal of Social Psychology, 1993, 133(1): 53-64.

[54] Ifeoma O E, Ngozi O V, Nkem E D. Insights on implementation of Johnson and Johnson's five elements of cooperative learning to health education curriculum delivery[J]. International Journal of Innovative Research and Development, 2015, 4(8): 356-361.

[55] Jacobs G M, McCafferty S G, Iddings C. Roots of cooperative learning in general education[M]. In S. G. McCafferty, G. M. Jacobs, and C. Iddings (Eds.), Cooperative learning and second language teaching. New York: Cambridge University Press, 2006: 9-17.

[56] James G. A narrative inquiry perspective into coping mechanisms of international postgraduate students' transition experiences[J]. American Journal of Qualitative Research, 2018, 2(1): 41-56.

[57] Johnson D W, Johnson F P. Joining together: Group theory and group skills [M]. Boston, MA: Allyn and Bacon, 2002.

[58] Johnson D W, Johnson R T. Cooperative, competitive, and individualistic learning[J]. Journal of Research and Development in Education, 1978, 12(1): 3-15.

[59] Johnson D W, Johnson R T. Learning together and alone: Cooperative, competitive, and individualistic learning[M]. Englewood Cliffs, NJ: Prentice-

Hall, 1987.

[60] Johnson D W, Johnson R T. Cooperation and competition: Theory and research [M]. Edina, MN: Interaction Book Co, 1989.

[61] Johnson D W, Johnson R T. Learning together and alone: Cooperative, competitive, and individualistic learning [M]. Boston, MA: Allyn and Bacon, 1999.

[62] Johnson D W, Johnson R T, Ortiz A E, et al. The impact of positive goal and resource interdependence on achievement, interaction, and attitudes [J]. The Journal of General Psychology, 1991, 118(4): 341–347.

[63] Johnson D W, Johnson R T, Roy P, et al. Oral interaction in cooperative learning groups: speaking, listening, and the nature of statements made by high-, medium-, and low-achieving students [J]. The Journal of Psychology, 1986, 119(4): 303–321.

[64] Johnson D W, Johnson R T, Smith K A. Cooperative learning: Increasing college faculty instructional productivity [M]. ASHE-ERIC Higher Education Report No. 4 George Washington University, 1991.

[65] Johnson D W, Johnson R T, Smith K A. Cooperative learning returns to college: What evidence is there that it works [J]? Change, 1998, 30 (4): 26–35.

[66] Johnson D W, Johnson R, Ortiz A, et al. Impact of Positive Goal and Resource Interdependence on Achievement, Interaction, and Attitudes [J]. Journal of General Psychology, 1991(4): 341.

[67] Johnson D W, Johnson R, Holubec E. Cooperation in the Classroom [M]. Edina, MN: Interaction Book Company, 1998.

[68] Johnson D W, Johnson R T, Holubec E J. The Nuts and Bolts of Cooperative Learning [M]. Minnesota: Interaction Book Company, 1994: 23.

[69] Johnson D, Johnson R. Learning Together and Alone, Cooperative, Competitive, and Individualistic Learning [M]. Needham Heights, MA: Prentice-Hall, 1995a: 67.

[70] Johnson D, Johnson R, Holubec E. Advanced Cooperative Learning [M]. Edina, MN: Interaction Book Company, 1988.

[71] Johnson D W, Maruyama C, Johnson R, et al. Effects of Cooperative,

Competitive, and Individualistic Goal Structures on Achievement: A Meta-analysis[J]. Psychological Bulletin, 1981(1): 47-62.

[72] John F. Teaching Reading Using Literature[M]. Boston: Boston College Press, 1994: 145.

[73] Kember D. To control or not to control: The question of whether experimental designs are appropriate for evaluating teaching innovations in higher education [J]. Assessmentand Evaluation in Higher Education, 2003, 28: 89-101. doi: 10. 1080/02602930301684.

[74] Kember D, Kwan K P. Lecturers' approaches to teaching and their relationship to conceptions of good teaching[J]. Instructional Science, 2000, 28(5): 469-490. doi: 10. 1023/A: 1026569608656.

[75] Krashen S D. Second Language Acquisition and Second Language Learning [M]. Oxford: Pergamon Press, 1981: 68.

[76] Kagan S. Cooperative Learning: Resources for Teachers[J]. Laguna Niguel, 1989: 45-48.

[77] Kaufman D B, Felder R M, Fuller H. Accounting for individual effort in cooperative learning teams[J]. Journal of Engineering Education, 2000, 89 (2): 133-140.

[78] Lafer S, Tarman B. Editorial 2019: (2)1, Special Issue[M]. Journal of Culture and Values in Education, 2019, 2 (1), i-v. Retrieved from http://cultureandvalues. org/index. php/JCV/article/view/34.

[79] Ledolter J, Hogg R V. Applied Statistics for Engineers and Physical Scientists [M]. Upper Saddler River, NJ: Pearson Education, Inc, 2010.

[80] Lim D H. Cross cultural differences in online learning motivation [J]. Educational Media International, 2004, 41 (2): 163 - 175. doi: 10. 1080/09523980410001685784.

[81] Little Soldier L. Cooperative learning and the Native American student[J]. Phi Delta Kappan, 1989, 71: 161-163.

[82] Littlewood W T. Communicative Language Teaching: An Instruction [M]. Cambridge: Cambridge University Press, 1981: 87.

[83] Loh C Y R, Teo T C. Understanding Asian students learning styles, cultural influence and learning strategies[J]. Journal of Education and Social Policy,

2017, 7(1): 194−210.

[84] Lou Y, Abrami P C, d'Apollonia S. Small group and individual learning with technology: A meta-analysis[J]. Review of Educational Research, 2001, 71 (3): 449−521. doi: 10. 3102/00346543071003449.

[85] Malatji K S. Moving away from rote learning in the university classroom: The use of cooperative learning to maximise students' critical thinking in a ruraluniversity of South Africa[J]. Journal of Communication, 2016, 7(1): 34−42.

[86] Manning M L, Lucking R. Cooperative learning and multicultural classrooms [J]. Clearing House, 1993, 67(1): 12−16.

[87] Márque J, Peña C, Jones L, et al. Academic success and resiliency factors: A case study of unaccompanied immigrant children [J]. American Journal of Qualitative Research, 2018, 2(1): 162−181.

[88] Marin-Garcia J A, Lloret J. Improving teamwork with university engineering students: The effect of an assessment method to prevent shirking[J]. WSEAS Transactions on Advances in Engineering Education, 2008, 5(1): 1−11.

[89] Mertler C A, Charles C M. Introduction to educational research[M]. Boston, MA: Omegatype Typography, Inc, 2008.

[90] Millis B J, Cottell P G. Cooperative Learning for higher education faculty[M]. Phoenix, AZ: Oryx Press, 1998.

[91] Montgomery D C, Runger G C. Applied statistics and probability for engineers [M]. Hoboken, NJ: John Wiley and Sons, Inc, 2007.

[92] Mourtos N J. The nuts and bolts of cooperative learning in engineering[J]. Journal of Engineering Education, 1997, 86(1): 35−37.

[93] Neo M. Engaging students in group-based co-operative learning: A Malaysian perspective[J]. Journal of Educational Technologyand Society, 2005, 8(4): 220−232.

[94] Nguyen J, Paschal C. Development of online ultrasound instructional module and comparison to traditional teaching methods [J]. Journal of Engineering Education, 2002, 91(3): 278−283.

[95] Oakley B, Felder R M, Brent R, et al. Turing student groups into effective teams[J]. Journal of Student Centered Learning, 2004, 2(1): 9−34.

[96] Drew C J, Hardman M L, Hart A W. Designing and conducting vesearch[M]. Boston, MA: Allyn and Bacon, 1996.

[97] Olds B M, Moskal B M, Miller R L. Assessment in engineering education: Evolution, approaches, and future collaborations [J]. Journal of Engineering Education, 2005, 94(1): 13-25.

[98] Opfer V D, Pedder D. Conceptualizing teacher professional learning [J]. Review of Educational Research, 2011, 81 (3): 376 - 407. doi: 10. 3102/0034654311413609.

[99] Ortiz A E, Johnson D W, Johnson R T. The effect of positive goal and resource interdependence on individual performance [J]. The Journal of Social Psychology, 1996, 136(2): 243-249.

[100] Patesan M, Balagiu A, Zechia D. The benefits of cooperative learning [J]. International Conference Knowledge-Based Organization, 2016, 22(2): 478-483.

[101] Piaget J. The Psychology of Intelligence[M]. New York: Harcourt, 1950: 107.

[102] Pimmel R. Cooperative learning instructional activities in a capstone design course[J]. Journal of Engineering Education, 2001, 90(3): 413-422.

[103] Porter S R. Institutional structures and student engagement[J]. Research in Higher Education, 2006, 47(5): 521-558. doi: 10. 1007/s11162-005-9006-z

[104] Postholm M B. Teachers' professional development: A theoretical review[J]. Educational Research, 2012, 54 (4): 405 - 429. doi: 10. 1080/00131881. 2012. 734725.

[105] Prince M J. Does active learning work? A review of the research[J]. Journal of Engineering Education, 2004, 93(3): 223-231.

[106] Prosser M, Trigwell K. Qualitative variation in approaches to university teaching and learning in large first-year classes[J]. Higher Education, 2014, 67(6): 783-795. doi: 10. 1007/s10734-013-9690-0.

[107] Ramsden P. Learning to teach in higher education [M]. Madison, NY: Routledge, 2003.

[108] Reynolds. Reading for Understanding[M]. California: Wadaworth Publishing Company, 1997: 128.

[109] Rogoff B. Cognition as a collaborative process[M]. In W. Damon (Ed.), Handbook of Child Psychology. New York, NY: Wiley, 1998: 679-744.

[110] Roseth C J, Johnson D W, Johnson R T. Promoting early adolescents' achievement and peer relationships: The effects of cooperative, competitive, and individualistic goal structures[J]. Psychological Bulletin, 2008, 134(2): 223−246. doi: 10.1037/0033−2909.134.2.223.

[111] Ross J, Smythe E. Differentiating Cooperative Learning to Meet the Needs of Gifted Learners: A Case for Transformational Leadership[J]. Journal for the Education of the Gifted, 1995(1): 63−82.

[112] Saavedra A R, Opfer V D. Teaching and learning 21st century skills: Lessons from the learning sciences[M]. Asia Society, Partnership for Global Learning: RAND Corporation, 2012.

[113] Seng E L K. Investigating teachers' views of student-centred learning approach [J]. International Education Studies, 2014, 7(7): 143−148.

[114] Shagrir L. Collaborating with colleagues for the sake of academic and professional development in higher education [J]. International Journal for Academic Development, 2017, 22(4): 331−342. doi: 10.1080/1360144X. 2017.1359180.

[115] Sharan S. Cooperative learning and helping behaviour in the multi-ethnic classroom. In H. C. Foot, M. J. Morgan, and R. H. Shute (Eds.), Children helping children[M]. New York, NY: Wiley, 1990: 151−176.

[116] Shimazoe J, Aldrich H. Group work can be gratifying: Understanding and overcoming resistance to cooperative learning[J]. College Teaching, 2010, 58 (2): 52−57. doi: 10.1080/87567550903418594.

[117] Singer E R. Espoused teaching paradigms of college faculty[J]. Research in Higher Education, 1996, 37(6): 659−679. doi: 10.1007/BF01792951.

[118] Singh J R. Co-operative learning—an alternative approach to large group lectures with postgraduate students: A case study[J]. Journal of Co-operative Studies, 2013, 46(2): 46−52.

[119] Slavin R E. Research on cooperative learning: Consensus and controversy[J]. Journal of the Educational Leadership, 1989, 47(4): 52−54.

[120] Smith K A, Sheppard S D, Johnson D W, et al. Pedagogies of engagement: Classroom-based practices [J]. Journal of Engineering Education, 2005, 94 (1): 87−101.

[121] Springer L, Stanne M E, Donovan S S. Effects of small-group learning on undergraduates in science, mathematics, engineering, and technology: A meta-analysis[J]. Review of Educational Research, 1999, 69(1): 21–51.

[122] Sharan S. Cooperative Learning in Teams: Recent Methods and Effects on Achievement, Attitudes, and Ethnic Relations [J]. Review of Educational Research, 1980: 54–57.

[123] Slavin R. Cooperative learning[M]. New York: Longman, 1988: 33.

[124] Slavin R. Student Teams and Achievement Divisions[J]. Journal of Research and Development in Education, 1978(1): 39–49.

[125] Slavin R. Educational Psychology: Theory and Practice [M]. Massachusetts: Allyn and Bacon, 1994 a: 112.

[126] Slavin R. Cooperative Learning: Theory, Research and Practice [M]. Massachusetts: Allyn and Bacon, 1994 b.

[127] Taber K S. Constructivism as educational theory: Contingency in learning, and optimally guided instruction. In J. Hassaskhah (Ed.), Educational theory. Hauppauge, NY: Nova Science Publishers, 2011: 39–61.

[128] Tadesse T, Gillies R M. Nurturing cooperative learning pedagogies in higher education classrooms: Evidence of instructional reform and potential challenges [J]. Current Issues in Education, 2015, 18(2): 1–18.

[129] Terenzini P T. Collaborative learning vs. lecture/discussion: Students' reported learning gains[J]. Journal of Engineering Education, 2001, 90(1): 123–130.

[130] Tan C. Teaching critical thinking: Cultural challenges and strategies in Singapore[J]. British Educational Research Journal, 2017, 43(5): 988–1002. doi: 10.1002/berj.3295.

[131] Thanh P T H, Gillies R, Renshaw P. Cooperative learning (CL) and academic achievement of Asian students: A true story [J]. International Education Studies, 2008, 1(3): 82–88.

[132] Tharp R G, Gallimore R. Rousing minds to life: Teaching, learning, and schooling in social context[J]. Cambridge, England: Cambridge University Press, 1988.

[133] Tombak B, Altun S. The effect of cooperative learning: University example

[J]. Eurasian Journal of Educational Research, 2016, 64: 173-196.

[134] Tran V D. The effects of cooperative learning on the academic achievement and knowledge retention[J]. International Journal of Higher Education, 2014, 3 (2): 131-140.

[135] Valiente C. Are students using the 'wrong' style of learning? A multicultural scrutiny for helping teachers to appreciate differences [J]. Active Learning in Higher Education, 2008, 9(1): 73-91. doi: 10.1177/1469787407086746.

[136] Vygotsky L S. Mind in society: The development of higher psychological processes[J]. Cambridge, MA: Harvard University Press, 1978.

[137] Webb N M. The teacher's role in promoting collaborative dialogue in the classroom[J]. British Journal of Educational Psychology, 2009, 79(1): 1-28. doi: 10.1348/000709908X380772.

[138] Wong J K K. Are the learning styles of Asian international students culturally or contextually based[J]? International Education Journal, 2004, 4(4): 154-166.

[139] Wyk M M V. The effects of the STAD-cooperative learning method on student achievement, attitude and motivation on economics education [J]. Journal of Social Science, 2012, 33 (2): 261 - 270. doi: 10.1080/09718923. 2012.11893104.

[140] Yager S, Johnson D W, Johnson R T. Oral discussion, group-to-individual transfer, and achievement in cooperative learning groups [J]. Journal of Educational Psychology, 1985, 77(1): 60-66.

[141] Yager R E. The constructivist learning model[J]. The Science Teacher, 2000, 67(1): 44-45.

[142] Yost D S. Reflection and self-efficacy: Enhancing the retention of qualified teachers from a teacher education perspective [J]. Teacher Education Quarterly, 2006, 33(4): 59-76.

[143] 蔡慧萍, 蔡明德, 罗毅. 合作学习在英语教学中的应用[M]. 北京:首都师范大学出版, 2005: 23-24.

[144] 迟志娟. 浅谈如何提高学生英语阅读能力[J]. 山东省农业管理干部学院学报, 2004(6): 153-154.

[145] 董宏乐, 邱东林. 也谈大学英语阅读教学的地位和方法[J]. 西安外国语学院学报, 2004(2): 69-71.

[146]高翔,杨远萍.互助性督促与评价:合作学习的有力保障[J].现代校长,2007(6).

[147]高向斌.合作学习教学的几个基本问题[J].教育理论与实践,2000(11):3-6.

[148]庚鲜海,王月会.合作学习原则在英语教学中的应用[J].外语教学,2003(5):63-64.

[149]郭世明.论共同学习的原理与技巧对大学外语教学改革的意义[J].北京联合大学学报,1999(1):89-93.

[150]郭砚冰.英语课堂中合作学习的实施与评价[J].厦门教育学院学报,2002(3):53-61.

[151]金艳红,中学英语阅读理解中合作学习新模式探讨[J].外语教学与研究,2001,(7).

[152]靳玉乐.合作学习[M].成都:四川教育出版社,2005.

[153]韩永丽.合作学习在我国教学运用中的问题及对策研究[J].内蒙古师范大学学报,2012(4):79-81.

[154]郝英丽.提高英语阅读能力策略分析[J].辽宁师专学报,2007(5):80-82.

[155]花晓艳.浅议英语阅读能力的提高策略[J].海外英语,2011(1):25-26.

[156]李丽,陈志安,蒋玉红.策略、类型和属性:学会如何学英语[M].上海:上海外语教育出版社,2006:252.

[157]李萌萌.合作学习在初中英语写作教学中的应用研究[D].中央民族大学,2020.

[158]李俏.合作学习的研究及其在英语教学中的应用[J].课程教材教法,2003(6):38-42.

[159]林立,王之江.合作学习在英语教学中的应用[M].北京:首都师范大学出版社,2005.

[160]罗少丽.合作学习在实施过程中存在的问题及改进意见[J].河北广播电视大学学报,2010(1):63-66.

[161]刘润清.外语教学中的科研方法[M].北京:外语教学与研究出版社,1999.

[162]刘巍.大学英语教学中任务型课堂活动设计的研究[D].河北:燕山大学,2008.

[163]卢建筑.高中新课程教学策略[M].广东:广东教育出版社,2004.

[164]马红亮. 合作学习的内涵, 要素和意义[J]. 外语教学研究, 2003(5): 16-19.

[165]马兰. 合作学习[M]. 北京: 高等教育出版社, 2005: 4.

[166]马骁骁. 合作学习研究及其对大学英语教学的启迪[D]. 长春: 吉林大学, 2006.

[167]裴娣娜. 合作学习的教学策略[J]. 学科教育, 2000(2): 1-6.

[168]全辉霞. 合作学习在英语教学中的应用[J]. 衡阳师范学院学报, 2009(4): 133-136.

[169]盛群力, 郑淑贞. 合作学习设计[M]. 杭州: 浙江教育出版社, 2006.

[170]舒白梅. 现代英语教学[M], 北京: 中国环境科学出版社. 1997.

[171]汪航. 合作学习认知研究综述[J]. 心理科学, 2004 (2): 438-440.

[172]王谧. 合作学习在职业高中英语听力教学中的应用研究[D]. 渤海大学, 2015.

[173]王穗平, 杨洁. 洋为中用——合作学习法的移植应用[J]. 外语与外语教学, 1997(5): 34-36.

[174]王坦. 合作学习——原理与策略[M]. 北京: 学苑出版社, 2001.

[175]王坦. 合作学习的理念与实施[M]. 北京: 中国人事出版社, 2002.

[176]王文君, 浅析任务型教学法 [J]. 浙江师范大学学报(社会科学版), 2003 (S1).

[177]吴荣辉, 何高大. 合作学习在大学英语写作教学中的应用效应研究[J]. 外语教学, 2014(3): 44-47.

[178]邢琳慧. 基于合作学习理论的大学英语写作教学实证研究[D]. 西安工程大学, 2017.

[179]徐路. 浅议提高英语阅读教学的方式方法[J]. 读写算(教育教学研究), 2012(34): 220-221.

[180]姚喜明, 潘攀. 英语阅读理论研究的发展 [J]. 外语教学, 2004 (1): 72-75.

[181]叶植嫦. 基于合作学习的形成性评价在英语听力教学中的应用研究[D]. 广东技术师范大学, 2017.

[182]张法科, 赵婷. 合作学习理论在大学英语阅读教学中的应用[J], 外语界, 2004(6): 46, 51.

[183]尹丽娜. 合作学习在大学英语教学中的有效实验研究[D]. 华北电力大学(北京), 2006.

Appendix

Appendix 1

Pretest Scores of the CC and EC

Number	Control Class	Experimental Class
1	50	68
2	63	43
3	62	68
4	71	44
5	43	64
6	42	62
7	62	46
8	71	67
9	64	71
10	82	74
11	65	49
12	72	72
13	85	65
14	46	71
15	69	51
16	67	72
17	82	82
18	72	63
19	47	64
20	66	71
21	72	81
22	79	63
23	53	66
24	64	52

Continued

Number	Control Class	Experimental Class
25	76	72
26	54	91
27	64	62
28	60	73
29	73	64
30	74	61
31	52	83
32	63	56
33	74	65
34	61	74
35	63	61
36	74	77
37	47	60
38	73	47
39	81	74
40	60	84

Appendix 2

Posttest Scores of the CC and EC

Number	Control Class	Experimental Class
1	61	64
2	69	67
3	67	70
4	72	57
5	52	77
6	43	80
7	66	62
8	60	66
9	51	88
10	90	90
11	60	69
12	73	80
13	81	76
14	41	75
15	74	69
16	64	75
17	81	96
18	74	68
19	45	69
20	71	75
21	76	86
22	73	79
23	64	76
24	72	70
25	71	85

Continued

Number	Control Class	Experimental Class
26	60	90
27	61	78
28	64	85
29	73	75
30	71	78
31	62	92
32	73	68
33	71	78
34	63	70
35	71	70
36	75	87
37	55	77
38	84	55
39	78	87
40	62	94

Appendix 3

Questionnaire One

实验前学生对合作学习了解情况及学习态度调查问卷

亲爱的同学们：

大家好！

为了调查同学们对合作学习的了解情况以及以往英语学习经历和感受，以便进行合作学习课堂研究，我们特此进行调查。请同学们如实选择答案。问卷答案与考试无关，并对此保密。希望同学们认真如实地完成该卷，非常感谢你的合作！

一、基本信息

性别＿＿＿＿＿＿＿＿＿＿＿

年龄＿＿＿＿＿＿＿＿＿＿＿

二、具体问题。请仔细阅读下面每个问题，根据自身情况如实选择答案。

1. 你在以前的英语课堂上参加过合作学习吗

A. 经常参加

B. 有时参加

C. 从未参加过，不知道合作学习是什么

2. 你以往的英语课通常是以

A. 学生参与活动为主

B. 老师讲解为主

C. 有少量学生活动

3. 在以往的英语课堂上你

A. 总是主动发言

B. 老师点到名时才发言

C. 希望老师不要点到我

4. 你认为最使你紧张的情况是

A. 被老师单独叫起回答问题

B. 与同学讨论后再回答问题

C. 提前准备后回答问题

5. 你认为哪种学习气氛有助于英语学习

A. 紧张有压力

B. 严肃认真

C. 轻松活泼

6. 在学习中遇到难题时,你通常会

A. 问老师

B. 和同学讨论

C. 放弃

7. 如果同学问你问题,你认为

A. 想办法帮他解决,这同样也会促进自己的学习

B. 这是浪费我的时间

C. 会的话就告诉他,但这对我无益

8. 同学间会彼此分享学习的经验

A. 经常是这样

B. 偶尔这样

C. 从不这样

9. 你认为同学间应该经常分享各自的学习心得、经验吗

A. 应该　　　　B. 不应该　　　　C. 无所谓

10. 在英语课堂上,你认为对于老师来说,最重要的是

A. 激发学生的学习兴趣和主动性,培养学生自主学习能力

B. 想办法让同学们听讲

C. 传授知识

11. 在以后的英语学习中,你最想提高的是

A. 语法知识

B. 写作水平

C. 口语表达能力

12. 你希望在今后的英语泛读课堂上

A. 老师讲解,我听课为主

B. 学生活动与老师讲解相结合

C. 无所谓

Appendix 4

Questionnaire Two

实验后学生对合作学习相关问题的看法调查

亲爱的同学们：

大家好！

感谢大家一学期以来的认真学习,积极配合！为了了解目前同学们对英语泛读课程的学习情况及对合作学习中的一些问题的看法,检验合作学习的学习效果,以便将来有所改进,我们特此进行调查。请同学们如实选择答案。问卷答案与考试无关,并对此保密。希望同学们认真如实地完成该卷,非常感谢你的合作！

一、基本信息：

性别_____

年龄_____

二、具体问题。请仔细阅读下面每个问题,根据自身情况如实选择答案。

1.目前的英语泛读课堂气氛通常是

A.严肃紧张,令人觉得压抑

B.轻松融洽,令人觉得放松

C.枯燥乏味,令人觉得无聊

2.在目前的英语泛读课上,同学之间的关系是

A.互相帮助与支持,共同进步

B.比较紧张,存在激烈竞争

C.学自己的,互不关心

3.在目前的英语泛读课教学中,老师与同学的关系是

A.比较融洽

B.有些紧张

C.就是一般的师生关系

4.在英语泛读课堂上轮到你发言时,你的感受是

A. 紧张,生怕自己说不好

B. 放松,想要好好表现自己

C. 说得怎样无所谓

5. 你在合作学习活动中

A. 积极主动参与配合,把自己的任务做好

B. 被动地配合,勉强完成小组任务

C. 想办法推脱,把任务推给别人完成

6. 当小组合作学习活动中,有成员持不同意见时你会

A. 和同学共同讨论后尽量达成一致

B. 坚持己见

C. 懒得争论,听他的好了

7. 你觉得其他组员提供的观点或信息对你

A. 很有帮助,取人之长,补己之短

B. 稍有帮助

C. 没有帮助,浪费时间

8. 小组合作学习使你对所学的知识:

A. 有了更深、更好的理解

B. 比之前的理解稍有深入

C. 没什么帮助

9. 在与同学的合作交流中你

A. 总是对他人不满,很难与他们沟通

B. 能够理解他人情感,学会接受不同意见以及与人沟通交流的技巧

C. 总是一味附和别人观点

10. 老师要求完成的课堂内外作业你

A. 乐于完成   B. 完成一部分   C. 从来不做

11. 你对英语泛读课的学习兴趣比以前

A. 有很大提高   B. 稍有提高   C. 没有提高

12. 你认为在今后的英语学习中,合作学习

A. 很有必要,希望继续进行

B. 没有必要,浪费时间

C. 无所谓,听老师安排